AVID AGILITY

Working Faster and More Intuitively with Avid Media Composer

Steven Cohen

THIRD EDITION

D1359862

Avid Agility: Working Faster and More Intuitively with Avid Media Composer
Third Edition

ISBN-13: 978-1-477-65435-4
ISBN-10:   1-477-65435-6

Printed in the United States of America.
10 9 8 7 6 5 4 3

If I had eight hours to chop down a tree,
I'd spend six sharpening my axe.

— Abraham Lincoln

We shape our tools and afterwards
our tools shape us.

— Marshall McLuhan

Contents

6. Edit Functions   69

7. Trim Mode   85

Preface

Software development seems to come in waves. Technology creates opportunities, competition drives innovation, and developers and users come together in a complex dance that pushes each to create something new. I've been privileged to be involved in several such periods, editing some of the first films to employ digital technology, working closely with Montage and then with Avid helping them develop interfaces that would be appropriate for professional editors, and encouraging my friends to try the new tools. In the early days, that work led to a book, *Avid Media Composer Techniques and Tips*, which I self-published for several years, selling copies to editors all over the world. Many people told me that it changed the way they edit.

I also taught editing and helped create a magazine, all the while continuing to edit feature films and television. Then, in 2007, I cofounded the Avid Editors Advisory Committee, a group of prominent editors and post-production professionals hoping to help Avid modernize the system. As the group was finishing its early white papers, the company went through a major reorganization, and a new focus was placed on improvements to Media Composer. The result has been a series of upgrades, one following closely on the heels of another. Because so much had changed, it seemed to me that the time was right for a new book focused on the Media Composer of today.

That first edition, published in late 2010, was widely praised by both working professionals and relative beginners. Meanwhile, Avid continued to make major improvements to the software, and I have attempted to keep up with a series of revisions. This third edition focuses on Media Composer 6, but also includes material about Versions 5 and 5.5, as well. Avid redesigned the UI with Version 6 and the illustrations you'll see here reflect the new design. Many sections have been rewritten, and I've included a new chapter covering Script Integration and ScriptSync, as well. Principal new features are discussed on the following pages.

Introduced in Version 5: the Smart Tool, 28; the Track Control Panel, 34; changes to Trim Mode, 85; Real-Time AudioSuite Effects (RTAS), 164; Stereo Audio, 153; Advanced Keyframes, 174; Avid Media Access (AMA), 221; Mixed Frame Rates, 227; and the Reformat Attribute, 229.

In Version 5.5: the Transition Tool, 31; Find and PhraseFind, 63; compatibility features added to Segment Mode, 33; and to Trim Mode, 90.

In Version 6: Bins and Tabs, 4 & 121; changes to Marks and Markers (Locators), 8; changes to the Composer window, 56 & 66; Open I/O, 67; the Audio Mixer, 149; Surround Audio, 153 & 156; and AMA enhancements, 221 & 224.

I hope you'll find this volume helpful if you already know something about using Media Composer, but are looking for ways to move beyond the basic editing model and get at the underlying power of the system. Unlike other manuals, it's a book for editors. Instead of focusing on data management or I/O, it emphasizes techniques that will help creative people tell stories. It's not intended to be comprehensive; that would be impossible in a book of this size. But I believe it offers something other manuals don't: a concise, well-illustrated, and easy-to-read look at some of the best ways to use the system. Regardless of your skill level, whether you've been using the system for years or are just moving to it, I hope you'll find things here that will help you work faster and with more facility.

The paradox of the teaching process is that when it works, the teacher learns more than the student. I have certainly learned a great deal putting this volume together. I hope you get as much out of it as I have.

1 Interface Fundamentals

Windows

The Media Composer interface is focused on three primary windows: the Composer, the Timeline and the Project. The Composer window contains the source and record monitors and is the place where you'll play and mark clips or sequences. The Timeline displays the contents of the source or record monitor and allows you to manipulate sequences, transitions and effects.

The Project, Composer and Timeline Windows.

The Project window is divided into tabs that provide a list of all bins, settings and visual effects, as well as information about project format and memory usage. Double-click a bin or setting to open it. Double-click an effect to apply it to a selected clip.

The three primary tabs in the Project Window:

Bins   Settings   Visual Effects

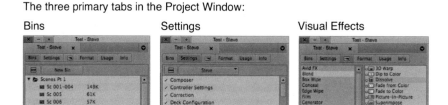

Projects

Your materials will normally be organized into projects. A project is essentially a group of bins and settings collected in a folder. Projects can be stored in several places on disk. With standalone systems they're typically in the Documents folder in your User Folder. With Unity or Isis systems, projects can be shared and will reside on the server. You'll normally create and access projects from the Select Project dialog box. This is the first thing you'll see when you initially start up the system, and you'll need to create a project and a user before you can do much of anything.

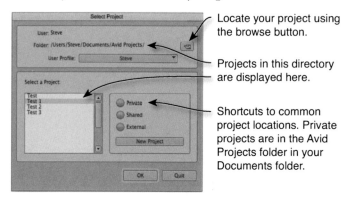

Locate your project using the browse button.

Projects in this directory are displayed here.

Shortcuts to common project locations. Private projects are in the Avid Projects folder in your Documents folder.

To switch projects, close the Project window. The dialog box above will reappear, allowing you to open another project or create a new one. For more about user settings see "Users and User Profiles" on page 257.

Modes and Tools

The user interface is structured around several modes, accessed via buttons in the timeline window. They alter the toolset in various ways, optimizing it for specific tasks. Source/Record Mode is the system's basic editing environment, organized around the source and record monitors. Segment Mode allows you to select clips and drag them in the timeline. Trim Mode allows you to adjust transitions, displaying outgoing and incoming video in separate windows. The Effect Editor lets you manipulate visual effects, the

Motion Effect Editor helps you create speed changes, and Color Correction Mode allows you to adjust color.

In the past, these functions were accessed via buttons at the bottom of the Timeline. They now appear along the Timeline's left edge, whenever a clip or sequence is loaded into a monitor. More important, Segment Mode and Trim Mode have been integrated into what Avid calls the Smart Tool. When turned on, it alters the behavior of the mouse cursor as you move it around in the timeline, allowing you to move clips, adjust transitions, and manipulate effects or audio keyframes, all in an integrated way. Each Smart Tool can be independently activated; if you leave them off, you'll be able to work traditionally, using only the tools you need for a specific task.

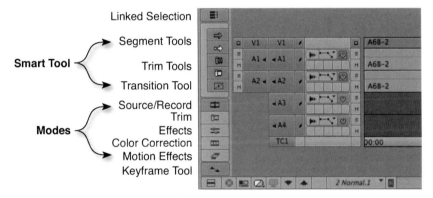

The Smart Tool will be covered in detail in the Timeline chapter. Trim Mode will be covered in the Trim chapter. Audio keyframes are covered in the Audio chapter, and effects and motion effects are covered in the Visual Effects chapter. Source/Record Mode is implicitly covered throughout the book.

Bins

Bins contain your clips. They can be displayed in several views, allowing you to organize material any way you like. Note that each bin is stored as a separate file on disk, making it easier to isolate a portion of your project and transfer it from one system to another.

Bins displayed in Frame View and Text View.

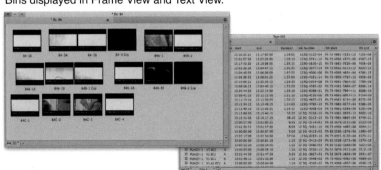

Use the Bin View menu, located at the bottom left of every bin, to change bin views. You can now drag Media Composer windows on all four edges to resize them. A double-arrow cursor appears to make this clear.

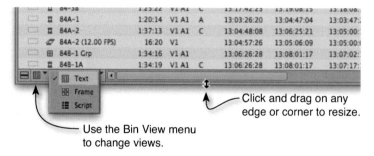

Use the Bin View menu to change views.

Click and drag on any edge or corner to resize.

Tabs

New in Version 6, bins and many windows contain tabs. They work much like tabs in a web browser, allowing you to dock multiple windows together inside a single frame, and then switch between them with a single click.

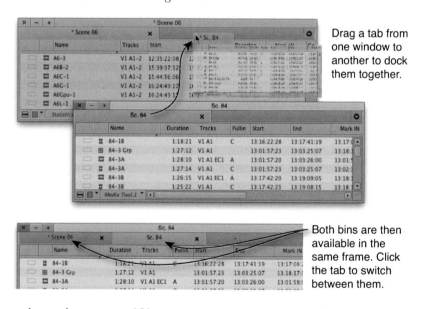

Drag a tab from one window to another to dock them together.

Both bins are then available in the same frame. Click the tab to switch between them.

For more about tabs, see page 121.

Clips and Media

The Media Composer architecture makes a fundamental distinction between clips and media. Media are video and audio files on disk; clips are the representations of that media, which you'll use for editing. They contain the metadata associated with the underlying media: timecodes, key numbers and the like. Common clip types include master clips, subclips, group clips and sequences.

Master clips typically match the duration of the underlying media: if you have a five-minute master clip, you'll find five minutes of media for it somewhere on disk. Subclips are sections of master clips, generally created to help you organize your material. For most editing purposes, subclips and master clips can be used interchangeably. Group clips are used for multi-camera editing and are created by aligning and merging multiple, synchronized clips into a single object. Sequences are constructed from edited source clips, and are the primary product of the editing process. Each type of clip is displayed with a unique icon.

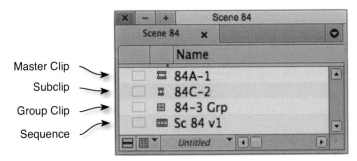

Unlike some editing applications, Media Composer employs an "inheritance" model. When you edit a clip into a sequence and later change certain kinds of data in the source clip, that data will propagate into the clip in the sequence. If you change a clip name after using it for editing, for example, the new name will appear on the sequence clips. Subclips and Group Clips also inherit certain kinds of source changes. For this to work, the bins containing the clips must be exposed to each other by being open in the same editing session. See "How Bin Data is Stored" on page 119 for details.

Managed and Unmanaged Media

Media Composer has long been known for its bulletproof media management, which is achieved by storing all media in a specific, tightly controlled folder, usually named Avid MediaFiles and located at the root level of a drive. As it starts up, the system checks every mounted drive for such a folder and then constantly monitors and indexes their contents. You should avoid manipulating Avid media at the Finder level, and instead use Avid's Media Tool for that purpose (see page 215).

The system also allows you to work with unmanaged media via what's known as Avid Media Access. AMA media can be located anywhere and manipulated via the Finder, but with that added flexibility comes a degree of risk. If you move or rename files, the associated clip will go offline.

You can also convert AMA media to managed media via the Consolidate/Transcode dialog box, and point sequences from one kind of media to the other. Modern workflows often entail an initial link to file-based, camera-original media via AMA and a subsequent transcode to Avid's preferred file types for editing. For more about media management see "Projects and Media" on page 213.

Users and Settings

Media Composer derives much of it's power from the way it can be configured for individual use. You'll customize the behavior of the application using a wide variety of settings panels, listed in alphabetical order in the Settings tab of the Project window. Double-click a setting to open it and make changes. Individual settings are covered, as needed, throughout the book. You can change the behavior of buttons on the keyboard (p. 12), assign menu items to the keyboard for quick access (p. 66), and adjust the data displayed in the Composer (p. 56) and the Timeline (p. 49). You can also create memorized Workspaces and Bin Layouts to place windows where you like them for specific tasks (p. 260).

Avid calls a complete group of settings a User Profile. You can create and switch between profiles from the Settings tab of the project window. This lets you move your settings from one machine to another and allows multiple editors to work on the same machine in a customized way. Note that Version 6 employs a new XML-based settings architecture, and editors are strongly advised to create a new User Profile when moving from previous versions. For more about the settings architecture, see page 255.

Media Composer stores projects, user profiles and media in specific places, which helps the system provide you with a relatively bullet-proof editing environment. Though some file locations can be changed, beginners are best advised to leave files where MC puts them.

Interface Brightness

Adjusting the overall brightness of the interface is probably the most basic setting choice you can make. Select the Settings tab in the Project window and double-click the Interface settings panel. Then drag the Brightness slider to the level you prefer. Text colors automatically invert at the darker settings. You can also change the color used to highlight selected items. Illustrations in this book mostly employ the brightest setting with blue highlighting, but other options are sometimes used for clarity.

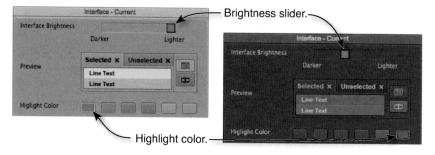

Starting Up the System

Media Composer normally presents you with the Select Project dialog box when it starts up, allowing you to choose the project you want to work on. If you'd rather have the system automatically open the project you used last, go to the Interface settings panel, and select Automatically Launch Last Project at Startup.

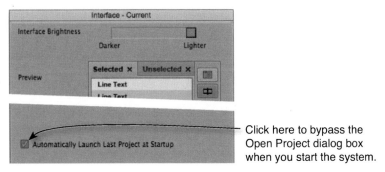

Click here to bypass the
Open Project dialog box
when you start the system.

Projects always open with all bins that were open last time. If you prefer that bins don't open, hold down the Option key while your project starts up. (You only need hold it down when you see the system begin to read in your settings.)

If you start up MC and change your mind you can cancel the startup. Hold down the Command key and tap a period when you see the Media Composer splash screen. (One hit should do it, but it may take a few seconds.)

The Position Indicator

Your current location in a source clip or sequence is displayed with Avid's venerable blue play cursor, known formally as the Position Indicator (and informally as the "blue bar"). Unlike in other editing applications, if all Smart Tools are deactivated you can click anywhere in your sequence to move there, which arguably makes the interface feel more open. If one or more tools are active, you'll need to click in a timecode track or in the Ruler at the top of the timeline window.

Position Bars under the Source and Record
Monitors, with their Position Indicators.

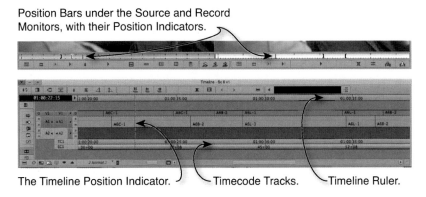

The Timeline Position Indicator.   Timecode Tracks.   Timeline Ruler.

Under the source and record monitors, you'll find Position Bars (not to be confused with the Position Indicator). The position bars represent your clip or sequence in condensed form. Like the Timeline, they display small position indicators, which allow you to move quickly through your material.

Marks and Markers

With Version 6, the icons for Mark In and Mark Out have changed, and Locators have been renamed Markers. Though their names are now similar, their functions are quite different. Marks are used for editing: to identify the beginning or end of a selected portion of material that you want to manipulate. Markers work like bookmarks, letting you add colored dots and text to frames, so you can easily locate them (see page 62).

Menus

In addition to the standard menu bar, the system features pop-up menus that conveniently bring various functions for a window together in one place. Avid calls them Fast Menus. You might hear them referred to as "hamburger menus," because that's what the icon looks like. You'll find them in most windows.

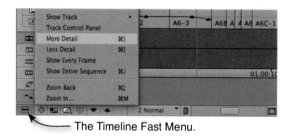

The Timeline Fast Menu.

This book uses angle brackets to indicate simple menu picks. For example, File > New Bin means "pull down the File menu and select New Bin."

Contextual

Contextual menus are enabled throughout the system. If you have a two-button mouse, simply right-click on an interface item to open its menu and make a selection. On the Mac, if you don't have such a mouse, use the standard Mac keyboard shortcut, Control-click. (Because the use of the Control key was changed in Version 5, some traditional keyboard shortcuts were modified. They'll be covered when appropriate in the text.)

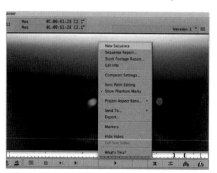

The contextual menu for the record monitor.

Keyboard

Mac and PC

Media Composer is designed to operate identically on the Mac and the PC. For simplicity, this book focuses on the Mac interface, but those of you who are using a PC will find that almost everything translates over. Macintosh keyboard shortcuts are used throughout the text. If you're working on a PC, substitute the Control key for the Command key (⌘) and the Alt key for the Option key.

Shift

In general, you'll use the Shift key to extend a selection. To select a group of sequential items, click on the first one and then Shift-click the last one, or simply click and drag to lasso them all. To select non-adjacent items, click the first one and Command-click each of the others. You can also deselect individual items in a group by Command-clicking them.

Command (Control on the PC)

In the Timeline, the Command key is used to snap the position indicator from cut to cut, or more specifically, from head frame to head frame. You can add the Command key either before or after you start to drag. To snap to tail frames, hold down both the Command and Option keys, instead.

Option (Alt on the PC)

The Option key is used in combination with other commands to modify them and add additional features.

Delete

As in most applications, the Delete key is context sensitive and will change its behavior depending on which window is active when you use it. In the timeline it will delete marks, markers (locators) and tracks. If a Segment tool is active it will delete effects and clips. If the Keyframe tool is active, it will delete audio keyframes. In Trim Mode it will delete match frame edits. And in bins it will remove clips and media files.

Escape

In most dialog boxes, Escape (esc) is a shortcut for the Cancel button.

Decimal Point

The decimal point key on the numeric keypad will insert a double zero (00) into time-code or footage fields.

Mice and Scroll Wheels

The mouse is a big part of your connection to the system, and it's worth spending some time finding the one that works best for you. I personally favor a multi-button mouse, where I can program a button as a double-click. You'll probably spend a lot of time double-clicking to load monitors, and doing it with a single click on a dedicated button is more positive and reduces wrist and forearm strain.

Using a mouse with a scroll wheel can make your work significantly easier. The Mouse settings panel lets you adjust scroll wheel sensitivity. The same setting also allows you to assign Media Composer functions to other mouse buttons.

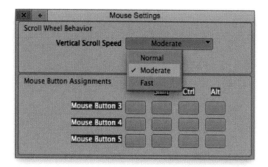

In most windows, you can use the scroll wheel or a trackpad as you would in a word processor, to move windows up and down. You can also scroll horizontally with a mouse that supports it. This can be especially handy in the timeline. With a trackpad, you can typically do this by dragging two fingers side-to-side. (You may need to enable horizontal scrolling in Apple's System Preferences.) But even if your mouse doesn't support horizontal scrolling, you can still scroll left-to-right. Just hold down the Shift key while scrolling up and down.

Undo and Redo

Media Composer uses a clip and sequence-based undo/redo system. You can undo just about anything you might want to do in the source or record monitor, but some of the things you might do in a bin (including the deletion of a sequence), can't be undone. That might seem like a limitation, but the simplicity of this approach has kept editors happy for years.

You can undo via the keyboard or the menu bar. Undo is Command-Z; Redo is Command-R. As you undo or redo, the timeline will change and the position indicator will move to show you what's happening at every step.

Undoing from the menu bar offers additional flexibility because it displays a list of labeled undos and redos. Using the menu, you can jump through a series of steps with a single menu pick. When you release the mouse button the timeline will step through the intervening events in rapid succession until it brings you backward or forward to the event you selected.

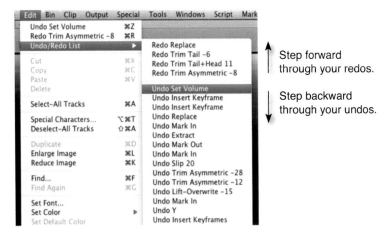

Step forward through your redos.

Step backward through your undos.

Because the undo system is sequence-based, loading a new sequence into the record monitor will clear the undo list. And the redo list is even more easily cleared. Doing just about anything new—making a mark, or even just loading a clip into the source monitor—will clear your redos.

But because some bin events aren't saved in the undo list, it's easy to work around this problem. Say you've made changes to a sequence that you're not sure about. You want to undo them, but you'd like to preserve the current version for comparison. Rather than rely on redo, make a subclip of the sequence (or a portion of it). Then undo as needed. The subclip won't change as you undo (see "Subclips" on page 124).

Another alternative is to have the system remember only record-side events in the undo list. To do this, select Undo Only Record Events in the Edit Tab of Composer Settings. This will make the redo list more resilient; making a source mark or loading a source clip won't clear it. But you won't be able to undo anything you did in the source monitor.

Select Undo Only Record Events to keep source-side actions out of the undo list.

The Command Palette

You'll accomplish much of your work by clicking on-screen or keyboard buttons. Button placement is defined by default, but it's easy to change the standard assignments. All functions are available in the Command Palette. Open it by selecting it from the Tools menu or hit Command-3.

The Command Palette's functions are organized into tabs.

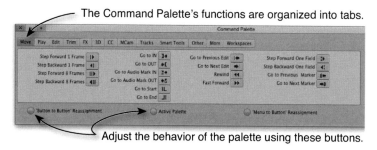

Adjust the behavior of the palette using these buttons.

The palette has three buttons along the bottom that determine its behavior. To reassign buttons, select Button to Button Reassignment and simply drag a button from the Command Palette to any button position in the interface.

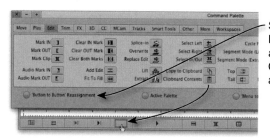

Select Button to Button Reassignment and drag from the Command Palette to a button position.

To customize the keyboard, open Keyboard settings and drag your buttons there.

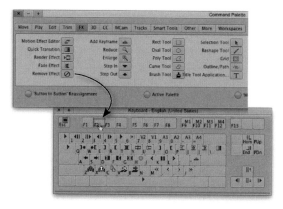

With the Command Palette open, you can also drag assigned buttons from one place to another. This will cause the two buttons to switch positions. If you want to remove a button, locate the Blank button in the Other tab and drag it to a button position.

You must close the Command Palette to begin using the new button assignments. But you can also leave the palette open and invoke functions simply by clicking buttons from there. To do this, select the Active Palette button.

Finally, you can assign any menu pick to a button. For details, see page 66.

Window Shortcuts

Moving Between Windows and Programs

Under OS X, if you're working in another application and you want to go back to Media Composer, you can simply click on an MC window. You'll activate the application, but only the window you clicked will come forward. You'll then have to click other windows in order to see the whole interface. To bring everything forward at once, click on the Media Composer icon in the dock or use Command-Tab.

Next Window

If you're short on screen real estate (on a laptop, for example) and you want to find a window that's currently hidden, use the OS X Next Window command. Hold down the Command key and tap the tilde/accent key (above the Tab key). In the same way that Command-Tab cycles through applications, Next Window cycles through windows within an application.

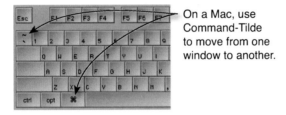

On a Mac, use Command-Tilde to move from one window to another.

Home

Command-' (the quote key) will put any active window back to its standard or "home" position.

Settings

You can get to the settings for most windows (Timeline, Composer, Bins, Audio Mix Panel, etc.) by simply clicking the window to activate it and then hitting Command-=. You can also right-click the window and open the setting from its contextual menu.

Project

In the Settings tab of the Project window, typing the first letter or letters of a setting will take you to it, highlighting it in the list.

Fonts

You can change the font and font size used in most windows by activating the window and then selecting Edit > Set Font. Make a note of the default font before you make a change so that you can restore it. You can't undo a font change.

The Console

Media Composer provides a command-line interface for troubleshooting the system and entering special commands called the Console. You'll find it in the Tools menu. Though you'll use it rarely (and should do so only with caution), it can be helpful in special situations. For a list of all available commands, enter "help commands" in the text entry field at the bottom of the window followed by the Return key.

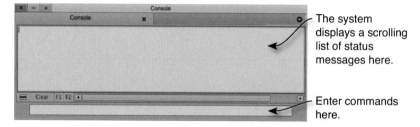

The system displays a scrolling list of status messages here.

Enter commands here.

Uninstalling and Installing

Before upgrading your Media Composer, you must uninstall the previous version and all Avid helper applications. Version 5 simplified this process with a unified Mac uninstaller and installer. The uninstaller is located on your install disk and in your Applications folder, under Avid_Uninstallers. It will automatically locate all relevant applications and remove them. (It's best to use the uninstaller that came with your currently installed version of Media Composer.) Then run the installer, making sure to review the helper apps you want. If you plan to use AMA media, you'll have to install plug-ins for most media types separately. You'll find links to them on Avid's website at www.avid.com/ama. For more on AMA, see page 221.

Uninstaller   Installer

Avid now uses a separate application called Avid License Control to register extra-cost features such as PhraseFind and ScriptSync. You can also use it to move a system license from one computer to another. You'll find it here:

> Mac: Applications/Utilities/Avid Utilities/LicenseControl
> Windows: Start/All Programs/Avid/Utilities/LicenseControl

Help

Avid's online help system covers most aspects of the interface and can be a important aid in learning about the application. It's available in the Media Composer Help menu and will display in your default browser.

To review a list of keyboard shortcuts organized by topic, select Shortcuts. To locate a list of pdf files covering various aspects of the system in detail, select Documentation (PDF). For a list of new features in your version of Media Composer, open the help system and click What's New in the Contents tab.

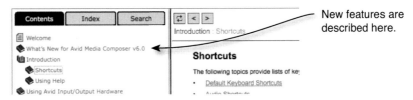

New features are described here.

Shutting Down

There's simply no reason to run a Media Composer, along with its many power-hungry accessories, when it's not doing anything. Save some energy and some atmospheric carbon and shut it down when it's idle.

2

Playing Clips

Loading Monitors

You'll normally view source material in the source monitor and sequences in the record monitor. But you can view either in pop-up monitors, as well. You can have as many pop-ups open as you like, and you can resize them and place them wherever you want on the screen. You can also play clip frames in bins. With the bin displayed in frame view, simply click on the clip and press play.

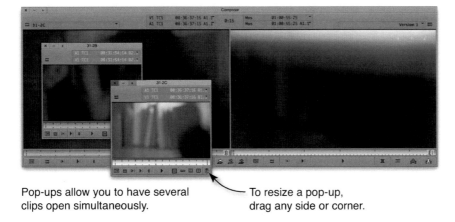

Pop-ups allow you to have several clips open simultaneously.

To resize a pop-up, drag any side or corner.

By default, double-clicking a source clip in a bin will load it into the source monitor; double-clicking a sequence will load it into the record monitor. But if you prefer, you can have double-click open all clips in pop-ups. The option is in Bin Settings. Whichever choice you make, you'll get the opposite effect by Option-double-clicking the clip. If you want to put a sequence into the source monitor, drag it there.

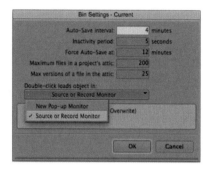

Single-clicking a clip and hitting the Return key produces the same effect as double-clicking, and it obeys the setting above. Adding the Option key works the same way, as well.

In a bin, you can navigate from one clip to another using the cursor arrow keys on your keyboard. In text view, use them to move up and down through your clips. In frame view, use them to move in all four directions. When you've selected the clip you want, hit Return to load it into a monitor.

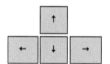
Use the cursor keys to move from one clip to another. Hit Return to load the clip.

In text view, you can also use your mouse's scroll wheel to select clips. Hold down the Control key and scroll up or down to move from shot to shot. Press Return to load the shot into a monitor.

Play

The standard Play button is located in several places on the default keyboard: the Tilde key, the 5 key, Tab and the Space Bar. It works as you might expect: hit it once to play forward at sound speed. Hit it a again to stop. But Play serves another function, as well. When you're in Trim Mode, it loops around the current transition. Thus it tends to do the right thing, regardless of the mode you're in.

Play Loop

Avid also offers a button that's designed solely for looping around the position indicator: Play Loop. In Trim Mode, it does the same thing as Play. But in Source/Record Mode it moves the position indicator to the head of the last Insert or Overwrite you made, puts you into Trim Mode and starts looping the cut. It's useful if you normally make an edit and immediately like to trim it up. Play Loop isn't included on the default keyboard. To access it, assign it to a custom key. The length of the loop is adjustable via the Play Loop tab in Trim settings or in the second row of buttons in Trim Mode. This affects both Play (in Trim Mode) and Play Loop.

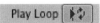

Mark on the Fly

One of the best ways to mark in and out is via the keyboard. Unlike marking with the mouse, using the keyboard won't stop video playback. By default, the mark buttons are in two places: E and R for the left hand, and I and O for the right.

Three-Button Play

Avid's Three-Button Player, also known as "JKL," consists of three buttons that together allow you to play media at a variety of different speeds. Designed to feel like film controls (a KEM Universal, actually), the speeds and options have been reworked several times to make them more organic and responsive, and today it represents a critical part of the way many people use the system. The default keyboard has the three keys on the home row for the right hand, but you can move them anywhere you like.

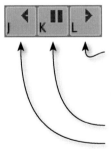

Play Forward
Hit it once to move at sound speed. Hit it again to go faster. Each additional key press will increase the speed up to a maximum of 8x. The Play button under the source or record monitor displays the current speed.

Pause

Play Reverse
Hit it to go backwards at sound speed. Hit it repeatedly to speed up reverse play, to a maximum of 8x. You can switch from forward to reverse directly. No need to hit Pause.

Pause + Play
Hold down the Pause key and press Play Forward or Reverse to move at 1/4 speed with slow audio.

Hold down Pause and *tap* Play Forward or Reverse to move one frame at a time with analog-style scrub audio.

Slowing Down Play Speeds

When you're playing forward and hit the Reverse key you'll immediately start playing backwards, regardless of the speed at which you were moving. But sometimes if you're playing at high speed, you simply want to slow down without reversing direction. To do that, hold down the Option key and hit Play Reverse. Instead of reversing direction, you'll slow down, one speed value with each button press. The same thing works if you're moving in reverse—hit Option with Play Forward to incrementally slow down reverse play.

Bumps on the F & J Keys

On most keyboards there's a little bump on the F and J keys. This lets you know where your hand is and avoids the need to look at the keyboard. It's one reason why JKL works well for the three-button player—you can find those keys by feel. But some Avid key caps don't have those bumps. One way around this is to put a small piece of tape on those keys, so you can feel them.

Three-Button Play for Your Left Hand

When trimming, you'll tend to go back and forth between the three-button player and Play, adjusting your cut and then looping it to check your work. One way to bring all this together is to assign the three-button player to keys that are appropriate for your left hand. Try putting it on S, D, and F. Then you'll be able to play and mark video with your left hand while keeping your right hand on the mouse. Here's a simplified arrangement for the left side of the keyboard, based on the use of the three-button player (see "Keyboard" on page 264).

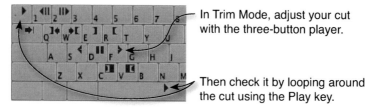

In Trim Mode, adjust your cut with the three-button player.

Then check it by looping around the cut using the Play key.

Step Forward/Backward

Avid offers dedicated buttons to move one frame left and right, as well as buttons that move one third of a second left or right (eight frames in 24-fps projects, ten frames in 30-fps projects).

Holding down the Option key while hitting a one-frame button will move the position indicator eight or ten frames instead.

Single-Frame Audio

There are two ways to hear single-frame scrub audio: with the three-button player or with Step Forward/Back. With three-button play, hold down Pause and tap Play Forward or Play Reverse to hear each frame with analog-style audio. With Step Forward/Back, hold down the Shift key to hear digital-style audio. This has a different sound than analog-style audio and is more precise. Experiment with both and see which you prefer.

Both kinds of scrub are available in Trim Mode—so you'll be able to make precise audio cuts while trimming (see "Single-Frame Trim Audio" on page 93).

In Source/Record Mode, the left and right cursor arrows work like the single-frame Step Forward/Back buttons, and they also work with the Shift key. They're arguably a bit more intuitive because they're easier to locate by feel.

The Destination Frame

With the default settings, digital scrub always plays the "destination frame." If you move forward from frame 1 to frame 2 with digital scrub, you'll hear frame 2, the frame you land on. If you move backwards from frame 2 to frame 1, you'll hear frame 1—again, the frame you land on. With a little practice you'll be able to find sounds quickly and precisely.

Caps Lock

You can use Caps Lock to leave digital scrub on all the time, but it can slow down the system. In particular, dragging through your sequence will be much less smooth. And, of course, you'll be listening to single-frame audio whenever you move the position indicator. For many people, it's easier to simply hold down the Shift key when needed.

Fast Scrub

To make scrubbing more responsive Avid has added the Fast Scrub option in Timeline settings. Once available only with Avid hardware, it's now enabled by default on software-only systems, too. When it's turned on and you use the Step Forward or Reverse buttons with Shift or Caps Lock, playback is more responsive. In fact, with Step Forward held down, playback can be so quick that it's almost like pressing the Play key. Fast Scrub makes dragging through the timeline a bit more responsive, as well.

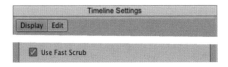

Play In to Out & Play to Out

The Play In to Out button plays your marked material, precisely starting and stopping at your marks. (Note that it's inclusive: the marked frames are played, as well as the material between them.) Play to Out plays from the current cursor position through your out point. You can do the same thing by holding down the Option key and hitting one of the Play buttons.

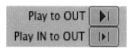

Mark In/Out

You can turn the Mark buttons into the Go to Mark buttons by holding down the Option key when clicking them. The same thing works in reverse: add the Option key and Go to Mark In or Out becomes Mark In or Out.

3   Basic Editing

Splice-In & Overwrite, Extract & Lift

Media Composer offers so many ways to construct a sequence that it may help to start with a brief overview of basic concepts. You'll typically begin by playing raw material in the source monitor and marking it to identify the section you want to use. You'll then edit the marked material into a sequence in the record monitor, using one of two primary edit functions: Splice-In or Overwrite. Splice-In (Insert) takes your marked material and copies it into the currently loaded sequence, pushing (or rippling) material following the new shot downstream. Overwrite replaces material that is already in the timeline and thus doesn't change length. You can edit by dragging from the source monitor to the timeline, but you'll probably find it easier to use the edit buttons (see page 76).

Avid also provides two analogous functions that let you remove material from your timeline: Extract and Lift. Extract is the inverse of Splice-In, rippling downstream clips toward the head of the sequence. Lift removes material without changing length and replaces it with filler (see page 72).

Much of the following will be covered in more detail later, but for now we'll look at two issues: making a straight cut before overlapping it, and three-point editing. One cut will serve as an example.

Make a Straight Cut First, Then Overlap It

With a blank sequence in the record monitor, double-click your source clips, view them, decide what you want to use as a first shot, mark in and out, and edit with either Splice-In or Overwrite. Since this is the first shot in the sequence, either will work.

Note that you don't necessarily need to make an exact source tail mark. It's often helpful to cut the shot in a little longer than you think you'll need. When you make your next cut it will be easier to compare the outgoing material in the record monitor with the incoming material in the source monitor.

Now add your second shot. If you're going to create an overlap (a split edit), the simplest approach is to do it in two steps, making a straight cut first and then trimming it to create the overlap. Think about which element, picture or sound, is most critical, and make the cut based on this element. For example, if you're making a match cut, picture will be dominant; if you are making a tricky dialog cut, sound will be more important.

Find your cut point in the record monitor and mark in there. Play your sources until you find your next cut and mark in and out in the source monitor. If necessary, select tracks using the buttons on the left side of the timeline.

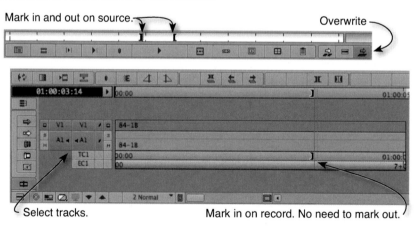

Edit using Overwrite (the red edit button). This will wipe out the long tail you included in the previous cut and replace it with your new material. Here's the timeline after the cut.

Now enter Trim Mode on the cut you've made and adjust it. You can do this by lassoing the cut, clicking above and to the left of the video edit and dragging down and to the right, surrounding both the video and audio edits. Or you can park near the cut and hit the Trim Mode button in the timeline, or you can click the video cut using the Ripple Trim tool and, if necessary, shift-click the audio cut to add it to your selection.

Video and audio selected for trimming.

Note that some editors don't like to refine their cuts right away. They'd rather throw a lot of material together quickly and come back after the sequence is assembled and trim everything up in a separate pass. If you prefer to work that way, you'll do the next couple of steps later, but the approach will be roughly the same.

Use any of the various trim techniques to adjust the cut (see page 85). Try using the three-button player. Select the side of the cut you want to work on by clicking the appropriate video image. Then press J, K, or L to play and trim it at the same time. Cut picture and sound together—don't try to overlap the cut yet. Remember that you are perfecting it for one element only.

When you've got your straight cut the way you want it, select the other element for trimming, either by deselecting the track you're finished with or by lassoing the other track (there's no need to exit Trim Mode). In this example, sound was cut first. The next step is to work on picture.

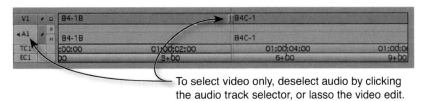

To select video only, deselect audio by clicking the audio track selector, or lasso the video edit.

You can use the three-button player to adjust the cut, or you can make the overlap on the fly. Press Play to loop the cut. As it plays, tap a mark button—either Mark In or Mark Out. Your transition will immediately be recut to the mark and it will play again, so you can see what you did. Keep doing this until you like the cut, or press stop and refine it using the three-button player and the trim buttons. The finished overlap is shown below.

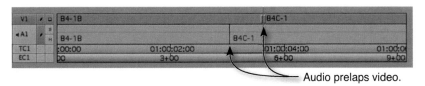

Audio prelaps video.

Three Marks Make an Edit

Every edit you make with Insert or Overwrite requires three marks, either two on the source side and one on the record, or two on the record and one on the source. (Replace, the blue edit button, is the exception. See page 69.) The following chart explains the four ways this can work. Create some examples for yourself and experiment with the options until their logic becomes clear. Pay particular attention to the Overwrite alternatives; they're much more commonly used. Inserts are typically made with the first option only. Note that the system allows for some exceptions to the three-mark rule. They're explained on page 77. Once you understand the rule, you may want to make use of the exceptions, but even the most experienced editors generally work with three marks.

Source Marks	Record Marks	Overwrite	Splice-In (Insert)
In & Out	In	Standard Overwrite. New material is overwritten, starting at the record mark in.	Standard Insert. Marked material is inserted at the record mark in.
In & Out	Out	New material is backed in from the record mark out.	Meaningless: you'll get an error message.
In	In & Out	New material replaces the marked section in your sequence, starting with the source mark in.	Source material is inserted at the record mark in. The length of the new material is determined by the distance between the record marks.
Out	In & Out	New material replaces the marked section in your sequence, backed in from the source mark out.	Source material is inserted at the record mark in. The tail of the new material is determined by the source mark out. The length is determined by the distance between the record marks.

Here are two examples: the first and second Overwrite alternatives above.

Standard Overwrite with two marks on
the source side and a record mark in.

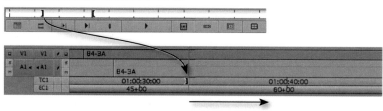

The same marks in the source, but with a record
mark out, will produce a different result.

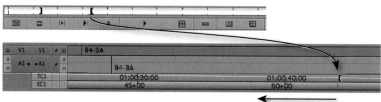

4   **Timeline**

Basic Navigation

You'll typically scale the timeline (zoom in or out) using the Scale Bar and scroll it (move left or right) using the Scroll Bar. But you may find it quicker to navigate with the keyboard, using commands from the timeline pop-up. Command-] (More Detail) will zoom in; Command-[(Less Detail) will zoom out. To see all clips in your sequence, use Command-/ (Show Entire Sequence). You can also use Command-M to display a magnification cursor, and then drag to create a rectangle, indicating the area you want to magnify. When you're done, hit Command-J to revert to the prior view.

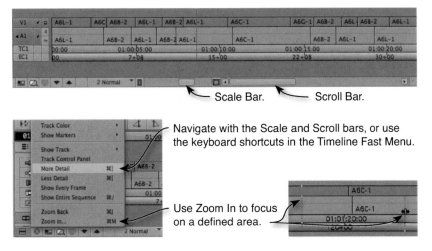

Scale Bar.   Scroll Bar.

Navigate with the Scale and Scroll bars, or use the keyboard shortcuts in the Timeline Fast Menu.

Use Zoom In to focus on a defined area.

As you zoom in, the position indicator expands to show you the beginning and the end of the frame you're parked on. This helps to clarify which frame you're looking at, and it gives you another visual indication of how far you're zoomed in.

Drag From Cut to Cut

Holding down the Command key and dragging the position indicator will jump or snap from cut to cut. This is a great way to quickly move around the timeline and land in a precise spot. Command-drag will take you to the first frame of every cut. Adding the Option key (Command-Option-drag) will take you to the last frame, instead. (The modifiers can be added either before or after you start to drag.)

The Smart Tool

Introduced in Version 5, the Smart Tool is a palette at the left edge of the timeline that unifies Trim Mode and Segment Mode, merging them into a non-modal, always-on interaction model that should appeal to those who prefer a more segment-based, grab-and-drag editing approach. Click a tool to turn it on and your mouse cursor is live for that tool, allowing you to manipulate clips (segments), cuts or audio keyframes. Version 5.5 added a tool for manipulating transition effects, as well.

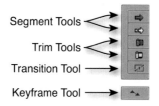

Turn on all the tools, and your cursor adjusts dynamically as you move around the timeline. When you're over a clip, it turns into a segment icon, allowing you to move the clip; when you're over a cut, it turns into a trim icon, allowing you to adjust clip length; when you're over a transition effect, it turns into a hand or double-headed arrow, allowing you to move the center or ends of the effect; and when you're over an audio keyframe, it turns into a pointing hand, allowing you to move the keyframe or change its level.

The Smart Tool changes as you move around the timeline.

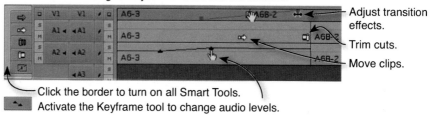

In fact, there are two segment tools and two trim tools—yellow and red in each case. Avid's color metaphor has always been yellow for things that change or ripple length (Insert and Extract), and red for things that don't (Lift and Overwrite). The Smart Tools work the same way, but there's a twist. If you have both tools on, the red one appears when you hover over the top of an object; the yellow one appears when you hover over the bottom. Thus all tools are available without a trip to the palette.

Overwrite Trim at the top of a cut.
Ripple Trim at the bottom.

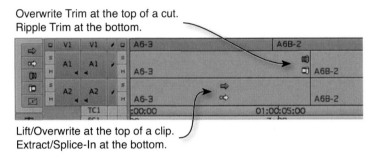

Lift/Overwrite at the top of a clip.
Extract/Splice-In at the bottom.

The traditional mode buttons have been moved to the left side of the timeline, and a button for the Motion Effect Editor has been added, as well (see page 3).

Moving Clips

The smart segment tools work just like Segment Mode did in earlier versions, allowing you to move clips around in the timeline. Red combines a Lift at the source of your drag with an Overwrite at the destination, and thus it doesn't change overall length. Yellow combines an Extract with an Insert, and thus it changes length in both places. As you drag, a clip outline in the timeline shows you what you're doing. The Composer window will change to display four frames, the A and B sides of the edits you're adjusting. The appropriate frames update as you drag, and the counter at the bottom of the Composer window displays the length of the move. If you prefer to use the three-button player and make your adjustment based on moving video, use Slip or Slide, instead (see page 96).

As you drag, the Composer window displays four
frames: the A and B sides of the cuts you're adjusting.

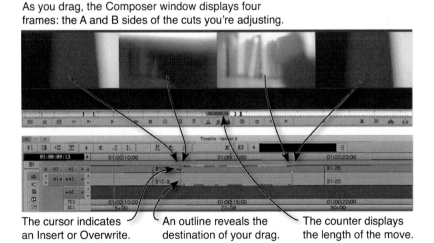

The cursor indicates   An outline reveals the   The counter displays
an Insert or Overwrite.   destination of your drag.   the length of the move.

Just as they do when dragging the position indicator, Command-drag and Command-Option-drag will constrain clip movement, allowing you to align segments to cut points. Align head frames with Command, tail frames with Command-Option. This also works in Trim Mode, allowing you to drag one cut and precisely line it up with another (see "Trim by Dragging" on page 91).

To quickly rearrange shots in the timeline, use Extract/Splice In (yellow). Select the clip you want to move. Hold down the Command key to turn on timeline snapping. Drag the clip until its head lines up with the cut where you want it inserted. Release the mouse button, and the sequence is recut.

To split tracks, use Lift/Overwrite (red). Select a clip that you want to move to another track. Hold down the Command and Shift keys, and drag the clip vertically. It will move straight up or down and can't move left-right.

If you'd rather not see the four-frame display when dragging, deselect Show Four-Frame Display in the Edit tab of Timeline Settings.

Trimming

When you click with a trim tool, you create Rollers or handles in the timeline, allowing you to play or grab clip edges and make adjustments. Because there are now two trim tools, Version 5 introduced colored trim rollers. If you've placed rollers on both sides of a cut, they'll display in purple, and function as they always have, adding to one shot and shortening the other by an equal amount. But single rollers are now colored either yellow or red. Yellow rollers, created with the yellow (Ripple) trim tool, behave like Avid's traditional single purple rollers, changing the length of the clip and the sequence.

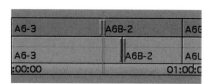

Red rollers, created with the red (Overwrite) trim tool, don't change length. They either overwrite or introduce black, instead.

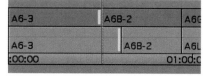

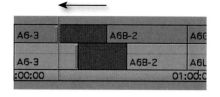

Note that you can still enter Trim Mode without the Smart Tool by clicking the traditional Trim Mode button at the left edge of the timeline window. (For more, see "Trim Mode" on page 85 and "Legacy Trim" on page 90.)

Lassoing

You can also select segments or transitions by lassoing them. This is often the quickest and most direct way to select a group of clips or cuts. Start by clicking in the blank space above or below the timeline track area and drag left-to-right around the clips or transitions you're interested in. Release the mouse button, and the clips or transitions will be selected. To make a selection in the middle of the timeline, hold down the Option key as you start to drag. This allows you to lasso anywhere. If you lasso a clip from right to left, you'll put rollers on it for slipping (see page 97).

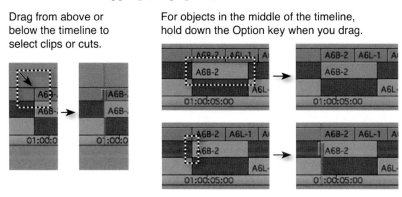

Drag from above or below the timeline to select clips or cuts.

For objects in the middle of the timeline, hold down the Option key when you drag.

Adjusting Transitions

The Transition Tool allows you to grab transition effects (those that connect two clips) and move them or change their lengths. Turn on the tool, and handles appear at effect end points. Then, click an effect icon to move the effect left or right, or an end point to adjust the effect's length. Either way, you will not be moving the underlying cut, so a centered effect may become uncentered. To change length equally at both ends (and keep a centered effect centered), hold down the Option key and drag either end.

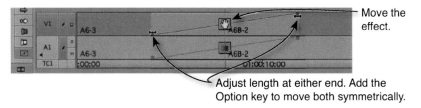

Move the effect.

Adjust length at either end. Add the Option key to move both symmetrically.

When you adjust an effect this way, MC shifts into Trim Mode, displaying effect counters and turning on the Transition Corner Display. For details see page 100. Note that you can't add new effects with the Transition Tool. See "Applying Effects" on page 169.

Linked Selection

In another break with past practice, you can now enable linked selection for the segment, trim and transition tools. This means that if you select a video clip, cut or effect, you'll simultaneously select the audio associated with it (and vice versa), as long as the clips overlap in the timeline.

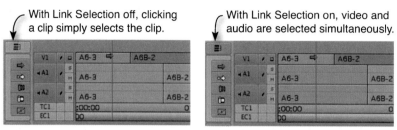

Link Selection works when choosing cuts and transition effects, as well.

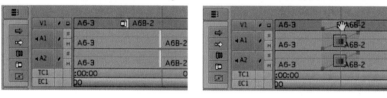

To toggle linked selection temporarily, hold down the Option key when selecting a clip or transition. If Link Selection is off, adding Option will turn it on and vice versa.

Smart Tool Toggle

The area surrounding the Smart Tool palette has a special function: it toggles the tools on or off. If no tools are selected, it will turn all tools on; if all are selected, it will turn them off. If you've manually chosen some tools and not others, it remembers your selection. When you hit the toggle, everything turns off. When you hit it again, your chosen tools are reactivated.

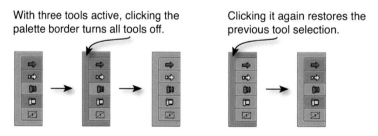

Note that when you first start Media Composer, it restores a snapshot of the last-used state of the tools. But it doesn't remember your previous selection. If you leave all tools off when you quit, you'll have to reselect the ones you prefer when you restart MC.

The Ruler

The new tools are designed to be persistent—you can leave them on all the time. This means that if you select a clip and then drag the position indicator elsewhere in the timeline the clip won't be deselected, making it a lot easier to rearrange clip order. To make this possible, Avid has added a Ruler along the top of the timeline, which you can use to move the position indicator. As in the past, you can use a timecode track for the same purpose. And with the Smart Tools turned off, you can still click anywhere in the timeline to move around, which arguably makes for a more fluid editing environment. At the left end of the Ruler, you'll find a convenient counter, displaying timecode at the position indicator (master timecode).

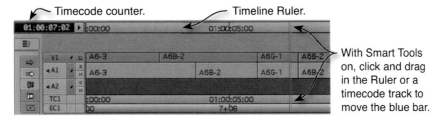

Timecode counter.   Timeline Ruler.

With Smart Tools on, click and drag in the Ruler or a timecode track to move the blue bar.

For most purposes, the Ruler and the timecode tracks are interchangeable. But there's a subtle difference. If you click in a timecode track, selected segments are deselected. If you click on the Ruler, selections are preserved.

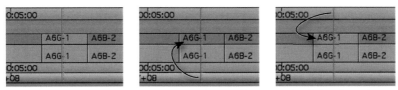

Clicking in a timecode track deselects all clips. Clicking in the Ruler doesn't.

From the Keyboard

By default, all the Smart Tools are assigned to the shifted keyboard, but you can move them wherever you like. You'll find them in a new tab in the Command Palette.

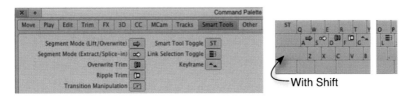

With Shift

The Smart Tool in Practice

Editors new to Media Composer should find a lot to like in the Smart Tool because it makes timeline manipulation more direct. You'll want to experiment with tool selection, activating only those appropriate to your working style or the material you're editing. Then, using the Smart Tool Toggle from the keyboard, you can turn them on or off with a quick tap. When they're off, you can move freely in the timeline, and then, just as quickly, turn them on and make adjustments.

Longtime Media Composer editors, on the other hand, may find the changing timeline cursor intrusive. But with Version 5.5 (and late releases of Version 5), most traditional timeline behavior can be restored. Two settings are important. In the past, clicking in a timecode track turned off both Segment Mode and Trim Mode. And in addition, only one Segment Mode could be active at once—if you turned on one, the other turned off. Both behaviors are now available via the Timeline settings panel.

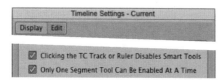

More important for some editors, Trim Mode now includes a hidden legacy feature. Entering Trim Mode by lassoing, or by hitting the Trim Mode button, produces traditional roller behavior, using the Smart Tool does not. For details, see page 90. Also note that with Version 5 Avid began using the Mac's Control key to access contextual menus, so some keyboard shortcuts changed. They're covered in the Trim chapter on page 85.

The Track Control Panel

Version 5 also introduced a new audio Track Control Panel to the right of the track selectors. Buttons and menus allow you to mute and solo, and display waveforms and audio keyframes, all on a track-by-track basis. In each case, if you add the Option key when you make a selection, you'll be applying that choice to all tracks simultaneously. You can also add up to five Real-time AudioSuite (RTAS) plug-ins to each track.

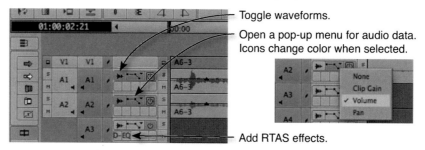

Toggle waveforms.

Open a pop-up menu for audio data. Icons change color when selected.

Add RTAS effects.

You can collapse the panel horizontally, and it will automatically shrink vertically if track heights are too short.

Click to hide or show the Track Control Panel.

When track height is too short, the RTAS buttons are hidden.

For more about audio keyframes and RTAS effects see "Automation Mode" on page 149 and "Real-Time AudioSuite Effects (RTAS)" on page 164.

Audio Monitoring

In the past, a single monitor button on each audio track served several purposes. Clicking it muted the track; Option-clicking prioritized it for scrubbing; Command-clicking soloed it. Now each track displays three separate buttons: Monitor, Solo, and Mute. Mute silences a track, Solo isolates it. The Monitor button, visible only when the Track Control Panel is displayed, has a new function. It allows you to *disable* a track. A disabled track uses no system resources, freeing them up for other purposes.

Two tracks are automatically assigned as "primary" and will be favored during high-speed play or when scrubbing many tracks. To make a track primary, Option-click its monitor button. Active tracks that are not primary will be scrubbed when possible, but will typically go silent during high speed play. Note that monitoring status sticks to clips. If you Mute a clip and then load another, the first clip remembers the way you left it. When you open it again it will still be muted.

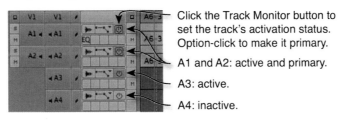

Click the Track Monitor button to set the track's activation status. Option-click to make it primary.

A1 and A2: active and primary.

A3: active.

A4: inactive.

To listen to a track in isolation, click it's Solo button. All other tracks will be automatically muted, and their Mute icons will turn pale orange. (You can solo as many tracks as you like.) To deliberately mute a track, click its Mute button. The button will turn bright orange. Click the Mute or Solo buttons again to turn them off. To affect all source or record tracks simultaneously, add the Option key.

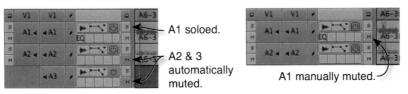

A1 soloed.

A2 & 3 automatically muted.

A1 manually muted.

Mute All

To mute all tracks, on both source and record sides simultaneously, use the Mute button. You'll find it in the Play tab of the Command Palette. Note that the button knows which tracks you've muted in the track panel. When you hit it a second time, their status is restored.

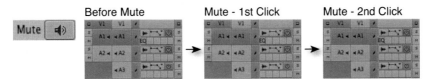

Before Mute   Mute - 1st Click   Mute - 2nd Click

Mute System Audio

With a software-only system, you can mute system audio using the Master Volume button on the timeline button bar. This silences the system, but doesn't affect the track
panel. On Windows systems, click and hold it to adjust overall output level.

Click the speaker icon
to mute system audio.

Video Monitoring

Video tracks include a single monitor button. Click it to monitor a track, Command-
click to solo it. (For details, see page 169.)

Waveforms

Waveform display in the timeline is quite detailed, making it a critical editorial tool.
There are now two ways to display waveforms. You can turn on all waveforms by select-
ing Audio Data > Waveform from the timeline Fast Menu, or you can turn waveforms
on for a specific track or tracks using the waveform icons in the Track Control Panel.
(To turn all waveforms on or off using the track panel, Option-click any waveform icon.)
Once you've set up per-track settings using the track panel, you can temporarily turn
waveforms off and then restore your view by selecting Allow Per Track Settings in the
Fast Menu.

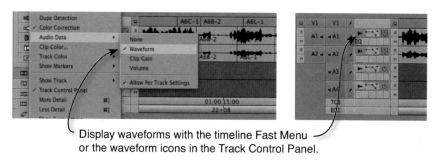

Display waveforms with the timeline Fast Menu
or the waveform icons in the Track Control Panel.

To enlarge waveforms, you can expand your audio tracks vertically using Command-L
(use Command-K to shrink them). But you can also enlarge the waveforms themselves,
without changing the height of the track, by hitting Command-Option-L.

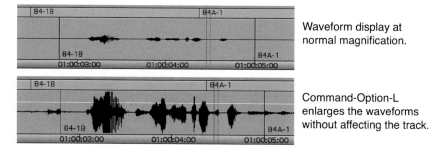

Waveform display at
normal magnification.

Command-Option-L
enlarges the waveforms
without affecting the track.

To shrink waveforms independent of track size, use Command-Option-K. To restore an enlarged waveform to standard size, hit Command-Option-K several times until the waveform no longer shrinks.

Waveforms From the Keyboard

Waveform display is much faster than it used to be, but it can still slow down timeline redraws. To make waveforms more usable, you may find it helpful to create a keyboard shortcut so you can turn them on and off quickly. To do this, assign a menu pick from the timeline Fast Menu to the keyboard. For all tracks, assign Audio Data > Waveform. For selected tracks, assign Audio Data > Allow Per Track settings. (See "Buttons from Menus" on page 66.)

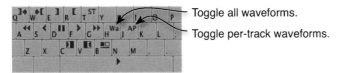
Toggle all waveforms.
Toggle per-track waveforms.

Note that these buttons sometimes won't interrupt a long waveform redraw while it's in progress, especially if you're working with Avid Unity storage. For that, there's another keyboard shortcut—Command-Period. This stops waveform redraw instantly, but it doesn't actually turn waveforms off. If you scale or scroll the timeline, they'll start drawing again. To stop the current redraw *and* turn off waveforms you may have to do both—hit Command-Period, followed by the custom button.

Video Quality

At the bottom of your timeline you'll see a small colored icon that indicates the video quality the system will display during timeline playback. Click it to cycle through the available choices, or right-click it to turn it into a contextual menu and make your selection from there. Depending on your hardware configuration, your options will change, but you'll typically see three choices: Full Quality (a green rectangle), Draft Quality (a yellow-over-green rectangle) and Best Performance (a yellow rectangle). Full Quality plays all the pixels you've got. Draft Quality plays at 1/4 resolution. Best Performance plays at 1/16th resolution.

Full Quality.   Draft Quality.   Best Performance.

If you're having trouble playing real-time visual effects, try adjusting the video quality setting. The lower your setting the more layers will play in real time. Note that the quality setting is not necessarily preserved when you restart Media Composer.

Playback Performance Indicators

By default, when you stop sequence playback, the system displays colored dots and lines at the top of the Ruler and the TC1 timecode track, indicating areas where it had trouble with playback. Three colors are used: red indicates areas where frames were dropped, yellow indicates areas where a lack of processing power created problems, and blue indicates areas where disk speed was an issue. Yellow and blue are warnings only and don't represent dropped frames. When you're seeing a lot of yellow or red lines, you should either render or switch to a lower video quality setting. To turn off performance indicators, go to the Display tab in Timeline Settings and deselect Highlight Suggested Render Areas After Playback.

Scrolling and Paging

When you press play, the position indicator normally moves across a stationary timeline. In the past, if it moved off the screen, you lost sight of it until playback stopped. But now the timeline will "page" as you play, jumping forward or backward so you can always see the position indicator. You can also have the timeline move under a stationary cursor. Make your selection in Timeline Settings. Paging is the default.

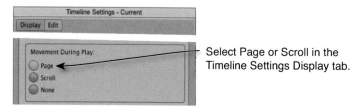

Select Page or Scroll in the Timeline Settings Display tab.

Page Up/Down

The Page Up and Page Down keys move the timeline to the right or left, one screenful at a time. The position indicator moves as well, centering itself on the new view. To quickly jump through your timeline, carrying your cursor with you, hit Page Down repeatedly.

On a full keyboard, Page Up and Down have their own dedicated keys. On a Mac laptop, hold down the Function key (fn) and tap the up or down cursor arrow, instead.

The Home and End keys are also useful, taking you to the beginning or end of the timeline, or a clip in the source monitor. On a laptop, use Function plus cursor left/right.

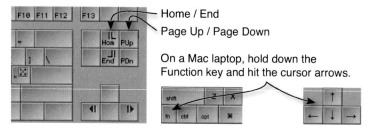

Home / End
Page Up / Page Down

On a Mac laptop, hold down the Function key and hit the cursor arrows.

Patching

Every time you make an edit, you are copying material from the source monitor to the record monitor. The Track Selector Panel, at the left side of the timeline, determines the tracks that will be edited and their destinations. Buttons on the left indicate tracks in the source monitor, those on the right, tracks in the record monitor. The metaphor refers to a patch bay where you plug one device into another with wires. By default, everything is patched straight across (V1 to V1, A1 to A1, etc.). Tracks that are selected on both sides of the panel will be affected when you make an edit. If tracks are selected on the right side but not the left, black will be edited instead of source material.

New sequences normally contain one track of video and two of audio (you can change this in the Edit tab of Timeline settings). To add tracks to your timeline, make a selection from the Clip menu. You can add video tracks, or mono, stereo or surround audio tracks. Video tracks are added at the top of the timeline, audio tracks at the bottom. To add tracks within the timeline use the Add Track dialog (see page 154). To delete a track, select it on the record side of the track panel and hit the Delete key.

To edit material from one track to another, simply click and drag on a source track selector (track button). A grey arrow will appear. Continue dragging to your desired destination track and release the mouse button. (Inappropriate destinations for the patch will be greyed out.) The track selectors rearrange to indicate the new patch condition.

Alternately, you can simply click and hold on a source or record track button. A pop-up menu will open, allowing you to select the other side of the patch.

Click and drag.   Or click and hold.

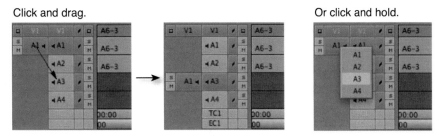

Restore Default Patch

When you're working in a sequence with many tracks, you sometimes need to make sure that everything is patched straight across. Avid offers a handy shortcut for this—Restore Default Patch in the Special menu.

You can do the same thing by simply selecting any memorized timeline view (see page 49).

Auto-Patching and Auto-Monitoring

Two settings can make patching simpler. Auto-Patching causes your patching to automatically follow your record-side track selection. When you select a track, your patching adjusts automatically.

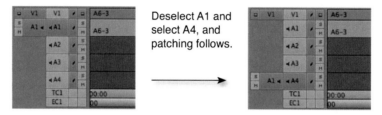

Deselect A1 and select A4, and patching follows.

Auto-Monitoring automatically selects tracks for monitoring. As you change patching, monitoring moves with you, so you're always monitoring the track you've just patched. It only functions when you've run out of available tracks, so it tends to be more useful for visual effects work. You'll find both options in Timeline Settings under the Edit tab.

Track Selection

Several shortcuts can make track selection easier. Some are a bit surprising, but you may find that they significantly speed up your work. With the timeline activated, Command-A selects all tracks for the active monitor, and Command-Shift-A deselects all.

You can also *shift-click and drag* through multiple track buttons to turn them on or off in a single step. The track you click on will change state: if it's on, it will turn off, if it's off, it will turn on. Then, as you drag through additional tracks, they will turn on or off to match the first track.

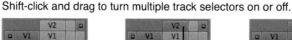

Shift-click and drag to turn multiple track selectors on or off.

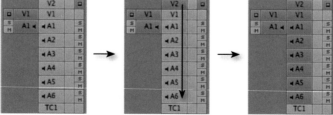

To invert track selection, drag a lasso through the track selector area (source side or record side or both). Any tracks that are on will turn off, any that are off will turn on.

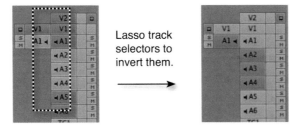

Lasso track selectors to invert them.

Use Shift-Lasso to turn all lassoed tracks on, and all un-lassoed tracks off.

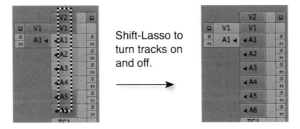

Shift-Lasso to turn tracks on and off.

You can also activate tracks from the keyboard. Some are available by on the default keyboard, and all are available in the Tracks tab of the Command Palette. Option-click a video track from the keyboard to monitor it, or an audio track to activate or deactivate it.

Remembering Source Track Selection

When a clip is loaded into the source monitor, Media Composer normally activates all of its tracks, making it ready for editing. But when you are working with clips containing many audio tracks it can be sometimes be helpful to have it reactivate your last-used tracks, instead. That behavior is available in the Composer settings panel. Simply turn off Auto-enable Source tracks. From then on, when you activate tracks on a clip and then come back to the same clip at another time, your previous track selection will be restored.

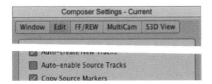

Track Height/Track Positions

To enlarge a track vertically, select it and hit Command-L; to shrink it, hit Command-K. Or hold down the Option key and position the cursor over the bottom of a track button. It will turn into a double-headed arrow. Click and drag to resize the track. Hold down the Option key over a track button to turn your cursor into a hand, then click and drag to rearrange the tracks. You can even move the timecode tracks. To preserve your custom track order, save it in a timeline view (page 49). You can also add a custom text identifier to your tracks (page 155).

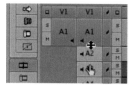

Option drag between tracks to resize. Option-drag on a track to change track order.

Viewing the Source Timeline

To display the contents of the source monitor in the timeline, simply click the Toggle Source/Record in Timeline button at the bottom of the timeline window. For quicker access, you may want to assign it to your keyboard. To make it clear that you are viewing the contents of the source monitor, the button and the position indicator both turn green. To view the record-side timeline, just hit the button again.

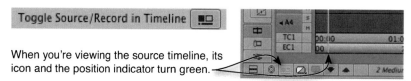

When you're viewing the source timeline, its icon and the position indicator turn green.

The source timeline feature makes it easy to edit material from one sequence to another. Load your source sequence into the source monitor by dragging it there. Take a look at it by clicking Toggle Source/Record in Timeline. Mark, patch tracks and edit as needed.

Match Frame

Park on any clip in a sequence and hit Match Frame to find the source clip for that shot and load it into the source monitor. Note that Match Frame obeys track buttons. If you want to match a sound clip, select the appropriate audio track; if you want to match picture, select video. When both are selected, you'll match video. If two video tracks are selected, you'll match the top one.

Match frame puts a mark in on your source clip at the frame you're matching and deletes any existing marks on the clip. If you'd rather not change the existing marks, hit Option-Match Frame. The clip will be loaded into the source monitor at the frame you selected, but existing marks will be preserved.

Match Frame also functions from the source monitor, where it serves to take you back through the hierarchy of a clip. For example, if you match frame on a group clip in the record monitor, MC will load the group into the source monitor. But if you then hit

Match Frame from the source side, you'll replace the group with the original source clip that was used to create it. If your group was composed of subclips, the subclip will be loaded. If you hit Match Frame once again, the source subclip will be replaced with the master clip it came from.

The same is true for motion effect clips. Match from the record side to find the effect; match again from the source side to replace it with the original unaffected clip.

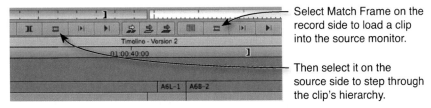

Select Match Frame on the record side to load a clip into the source monitor.

Then select it on the source side to step through the clip's hierarchy.

Reverse Match Frame

If you want to see whether you've used a specific frame from a source clip in a sequence, load the clip into the source monitor and park on the frame you're looking for. Load the sequence in the record monitor and park at the beginning of the section you're interested in. Select the source track you're looking for and the sequence tracks you want to search, and hit the Reverse Match Frame button. The cursor will jump forward in the sequence, to the first occurrence of the frame you're parked on in the source monitor. Hit the button again to find each subsequent occurrence.

If you select a track on the source side, and several tracks on the record side, reverse match frame will search through all the selected tracks, stopping on each occurrence in sequence order. (In Version 5, this worked correctly only for video.)

Reverse match frame also works when you have a sequence in the source monitor, and it works in either direction. Hit it on the source side to find material in the record monitor. Hit it on the record side to find material in the source monitor.

Match Frame Without Selecting a Track

You can quickly match frame on a specific track without first selecting it, using a contextual menu pick. Just right-click on the appropriate track button for the clip you're interested in and select Match Frame Track from the track's contextual menu. You'll match that track only, at the current timeline position.

Right-click on a track button and select Match Frame Track, to match the frame at the blue bar, in that track. This works even if the track is not selected.

Find Bin

The Find Bin button will open the bin that contains the clip you're parked on, with that clip selected. This can be very useful if you want to compare alternate takes. Try putting Match Frame under the record monitor and Find Bin under the source monitor. You can then hit Match Frame to find a clip from your sequence, and immediately hit Find Bin to look at alternate takes.

If you hit Find Bin from the *record* monitor you'll open the bin that contains your *sequence*. You can also hit Option-Find Bin from the record side. This produces a combination effect, opening the bin that contains the source clip you're parked on but without loading it into the source monitor.

Find Bin can be useful even if your source bin is already open. In this case, it will simply locate the clip in the bin and highlight it, scrolling the bin, as needed. This can be helpful if you're working with large bins. (Note that if you rename your bins after editing, Find Bin can sometimes have trouble locating them.)

Select Right/Left

Three buttons allow you to easily select groups of adjacent clips. Select Right highlights all clips at the position indicator and everything to the right of it, all the way to the end of your sequence, in all selected tracks. Select Left does the same thing to the left of the position indicator, all the way to the head of the sequence. Select In/Out highlights all clips between marks.

You'll find Select Left and Select Right in the default timeline toolbar and in the timeline contextual menu, as well.

These functions are particularly useful for opening up space in the middle of a complex, overlapped timeline. Here's an example. Let's say you want to insert space between scenes 84 and 86, below (ahead of the colored clips).

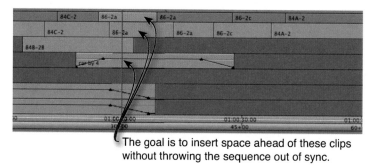

The goal is to insert space ahead of these clips without throwing the sequence out of sync.

In the past, you'd have to break up the clips using Add Edit, then insert filler at the cut, and finally, rejoin the broken clips. You can now do it much more easily with Select Right.

Place your cursor on the first clip or clips you want to move—to the right of the place where you want to insert space. Select all tracks and hit Select Right. Your entire time-line, starting at the cursor position, will be highlighted. If a segment tool is not selected, the default segment tool will activate (see page 47).

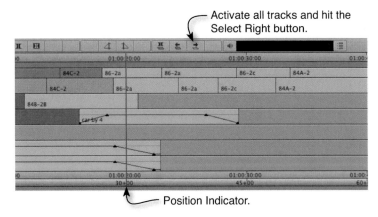

Activate all tracks and hit the
Select Right button.

Position Indicator.

Deselect the clips you don't want to move by Shift-clicking them.

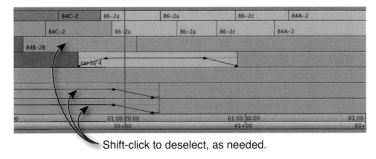

Shift-click to deselect, as needed.

Finally, click on any of the selected clips and simply drag to the right using the Lift/ Overwrite (red) segment tool. The farther you drag, the more space you'll create.

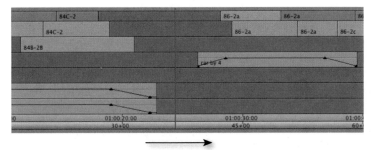

Click and drag to move all
selected clips to the right.

Moving Non-Adjacent Clips

Keep in mind that Media Composer won't allow you to move clips that aren't adjacent to each other. If you select a group of adjacent clips and then deselect a clip in the middle of the group, you won't be able to drag the group. Even if two clips are separated only by filler, you'll have to select the filler, as well, if you want to move them simultaneously.

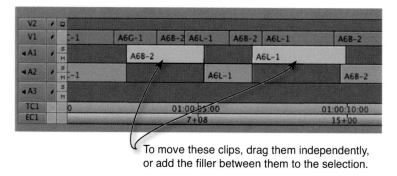

To move these clips, drag them independently, or add the filler between them to the selection.

Mark Clip

The Mark Clip button will mark the head and tail of the current clip, according to track selection. If one track is selected, the clip at the position indicator will be marked. If more than one is selected, marks will be placed at the nearest straight cuts to the left and right of the position indicator in those tracks. Option-Mark Clip will mark in at the nearest cut point to the left of the blue bar and mark out at the nearest cut point to the right of it, regardless of track selection.

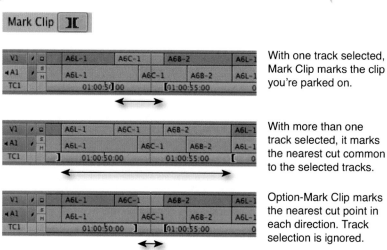

With one track selected, Mark Clip marks the clip you're parked on.

With more than one track selected, it marks the nearest cut common to the selected tracks.

Option-Mark Clip marks the nearest cut point in each direction. Track selection is ignored.

You can also select a clip with a segment tool and hit Mark Clip to mark it. If multiple clips are selected, you'll get a mark in at the beginning of the first one and a mark out at the end of the last one.

Cut, Copy and Paste

Using cut, copy and paste in the timeline has become more powerful and flexible over the years, and it's often the simplest way to move material around. Here are a few things to keep in mind. Cut and copy respect clip selection or, if nothing is selected, track selectors and marks. So either select a clip or clips with a segment tool, or mark a region and select tracks. Then hit Command-C or Command-X. (If you cut or copy non-adjacent clips in the same track, all the intervening clips will be cut or copied, as well.)

But paste (Command-V) *doesn't* obey marks or track selectors. When you paste, whatever was in your clipboard is edited at the position indicator, regardless of where your marks are, and it's always edited into the track or tracks from which it was copied.

If you copy overlapping clips, they'll be padded with filler. When you paste them, you won't lose sync.

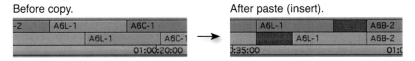

Default Segment Tool

Cut will extract or lift, and paste will insert or overwrite, depending on the segment tool selected in the Smart Tool. If one tool is selected, that's the kind of edit you'll get. If both or none are selected, the type of edit will be determined by a selection in the Edit tab of the Timeline settings pane: the Default Segment Tool. Insert is the default, but you may find Overwrite more useful.

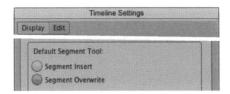

Clipboard Contents

If you prefer to paste your copied material into a different track, you'll need to load it into the source monitor and then patch, as needed. One way to do this is by selecting Clipboard Contents from the menu above the source monitor. This loads the monitor with the material you've most recently cut or copied. Another alternative is to put a Clipboard Contents button under your source monitor or on the keyboard. Click the button to load the source monitor with the material in the clipboard.

Even simpler, you can copy something from the timeline directly to your source monitor by hitting Command-Option-C. This creates a temporary subclip and puts it in the source monitor (but it bypasses the clipboard). Like a copy, this works with a range, or with clips selected using a segment tool.

Every time you Lift or Extract something, a copy of that material goes to the clipboard. You can then paste it elsewhere or select Clipboard Contents. Or you can send it to the source monitor in one step by holding down the Option key when you Lift or Extract.

Note that these techniques don't store a subclip of your copied material for future use. To do that, mark a range in the timeline and select tracks (you can't create a subclip from clips selected with a segment tool). Then Option-drag from the record monitor video image, or from the record monitor clip icon, to a bin (see "Subclips" on page 124). Then load the subclip into the source monitor and edit as needed. Or Option-drag from the record monitor to the source monitor. A dialog box opens asking you where you want the subclip to be stored.

Delete

With a segment selected, the Delete key will Extract or Lift, depending on the segment tool that's active. With red, it will Lift, with yellow, it will Extract. If both tools, or no tools, are selected, you'll lift or extract according to the default segment tool. Note that the shot will not go to the clipboard. If the clip carries an effect or audio keyframes, you'll delete the effect or keyframes first. To delete the clip itself, re-select it and hit delete again.

Delete removes segment effects and/or
audio keyframes if they are present.

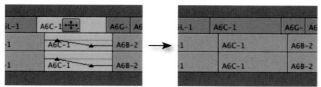

To delete a clip in one step, use the Cut command. Select the segment tool of your choice, click on the clip and hit Command-X. The clip is Lifted or Extracted, effects and all. You can also use this command to delete a range of clips without selecting them all. Click the first and last clips in a group and hit Command-X to delete the selected clips along with everything in between.

Cut deletes the clip(s).

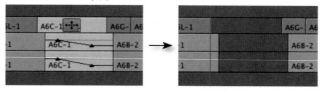

Timeline Views

Because you can customize the timeline in so many ways, the software allows you to create and save custom timeline configurations, or what Avid calls Timeline Views. You can then quickly switch between them and display only the data you're interested in. Start by selecting the timeline features you want from the timeline Fast Menu.

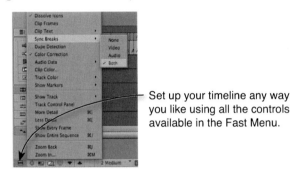

Set up your timeline any way you like using all the controls available in the Fast Menu.

Track height, waveform and keyframe display, dupe detection, clip color (page 51), the display of the track control panel, and many other options are available from this menu and will be stored in a saved view. When you've got your timeline set up the way you want, select Save As from the Timeline View Menu.

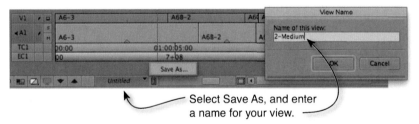

Select Save As, and enter a name for your view.

For example, you might find it helpful to create a view with waveforms and audio keyframes turned on and audio tracks enlarged.

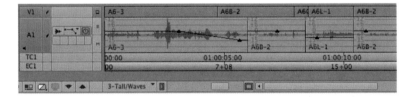

Once you've created several views, use the View Menu to switch between them.

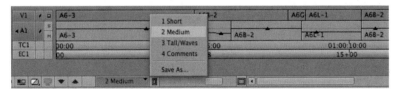

Note that options selected in the Track Control Panel are saved with each sequence, but not with a timeline view. Only the display of the panel, whether it's shown or hidden, is saved in a view.

Replace Timeline Views

To change an existing saved view, set the timeline up to your liking, hold down the Option key and open the Timeline View Menu. Every selection will be preceded with the word Replace. Select the view you want to change and it will be updated.

Timeline Views from the Keyboard

You can also switch timeline views from the keyboard. You'll find buttons for eight views in the More tab of the Command Palette. Timeline views are listed in the Project window alphabetically. Clicking the T1 button will bring up the first listed view, clicking T2 will bring up the second, etc. If you name your views with number prefixes, the names will sort properly and you can hit the button with that number to invoke it.

Timeline View buttons are assigned according to their order in the Project window.

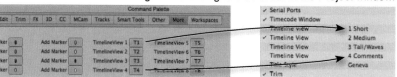

Dupe Detection

To see duplicated picture material in the timeline, select Dupe Detection in the timeline Fast Menu. Dupes will be displayed with colored bars along the tops of clips. Only the portion of the clip that is used more than once will display the bar. Multiple uses of the same material all display the same color, making them easy to find. Dupes are now detected across all video tracks. If you use the same shot in V1 and V2, for example, both instances will display a colored bar.

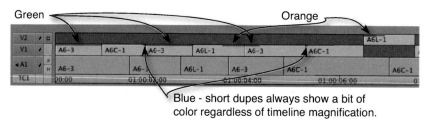

Green   Orange

Blue - short dupes always show a bit of color regardless of timeline magnification.

In film projects, dupe detection correctly accounts for negative cutting frames. Dupe detection settings can be found in the Edit tab of Timeline Settings. If you're planning to cut negative, select a handle length of half a frame.

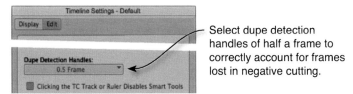

Select dupe detection handles of half a frame to correctly account for frames lost in negative cutting.

Clip Color

You can colorize clips in the timeline in several ways:

1. You can display all offline material in color (red, by default). This can be very helpful if you want to do a quick check before making an output.

2. You can change the color of an individual clip anywhere in a sequence. This is useful if you want to tag something so you can easily find it again (a visual effect, for example). Avid calls this Local color.

3. You can have MC color every instance of a particular source clip. This offers a quick answer to the question, "Where did I use this shot?" Or you might want to identify specific kinds of material, such as sound effects or music. Avid calls this Source color.

4. You can use color to distinguish between standard and high definition material.

5. If you're mixing frame rates in the same timeline, you can colorize clips whose speed doesn't match your project.

To adjust clip coloring, open the Clip Color dialog box from the timeline Fast Menu and choose the types of clips you want colored and the colors you prefer.

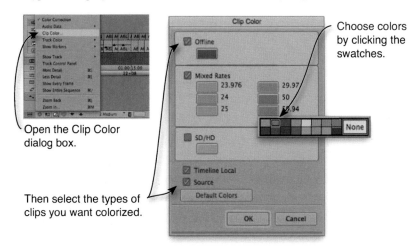

Open the Clip Color dialog box.

Then select the types of clips you want colorized.

Choose colors by clicking the swatches.

To change the color of a shot in a sequence, make sure Timeline Local is turned on in the Clip Color dialog box. Then, using a segment tool, select the clip you're interested in and change its color using the Edit menu, or by right-clicking it in the timeline. To remove local color, select Set Clip Color to Default, or choose None in the color picker.

Use the Edit menu or right-click the clip to change its local color.

To color every instance of a particular source clip, first turn on Source color in the Clip Color dialog. Then, open the bin containing the clip, display it in text view, right-click in the Color column and make a selection. The icon in the column changes to indicate the color you select. Every time you use the shot in a sequence it will be shown in that color. For more color choices, add the Option key when you right-click. (Prior to Version 6, use Edit > Set Clip Color instead of the Color column.).

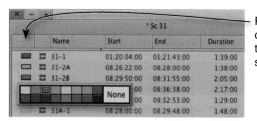

Right-click in the clip color column to open the color picker and select a source color.

To color offline, mixed frame rate or SD/HD clips, select those options in the Clip Color dialog. The SD/HD option reveals clips that don't match your project type. If you're in a high definition project, standard definition clips will be colored, and vice versa.

Note that if more than one coloring option applies to the same clip, the color you'll see is determined by the order in which the options are listed in the dialog box. Local color overrides source color, for example, because it's listed above it; offline color overrides everything. (Due to a bug, you may have to deselect Offline Color in order to see Local Color.)

Track Color

The system assigns a standard, default color to all clips in the timeline. This is fine for most purposes, but if you prefer a different color, you can override the default by making a selection in the Timeline Fast Menu. To restore the default, select an appropriate checkbox in the Interface settings panel or choose Default in the color picker. For more color choices, hold down the Option key when you select a color.

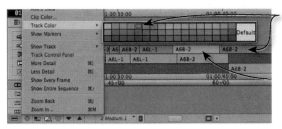

Use the Timeline Fast Menu to change the color of all clips in a selected track.

Clips that you've deliberately colored are not affected.

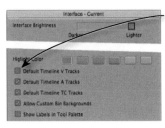

Restore the default color here. You have separate control of video, audio and timecode tracks.

Clip Text

In addition to clip names, you can choose to display all kinds of textual information on clips in the timeline, including durations, resolutions and media file names. Make your selection in the Timeline Fast Menu. If you work with source clips that contain many audio tracks, but only edit with some of them, you can now display source track names, allowing you to figure out which tracks are in use.

Source track names are shown next to clip names.

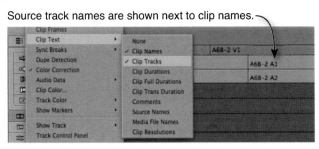

You can also add comments to clips and then display them in the timeline, or in EDLs and cut lists. Select a clip, pull down the Clip Name Menu above the record monitor and choose Add Comments. To add the same comment to several clips, select all of them before adding it.

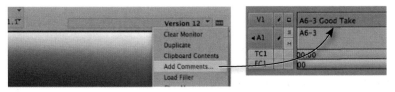

Toggle Client Monitor

You can now send black to your client monitor while continuing to play video in the Composer window. This makes it easy to operate semi-privately and only display your work when you're ready to do so. The function is called Toggle Client Monitor, and you'll find its button at the bottom of the Timeline window. (It's also in the Play tab of the Command Palette, so you can assign it to the keyboard.) Click it to turn the monitor on or off. The button will change color to let you know what's happening. It turns gray when no client monitor is present.

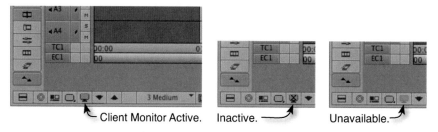

Client Monitor Active.   Inactive.   Unavailable.

5

Composer Window

The Composer Window contains the source and record monitors, and thus it's really two windows in one. You can independently activate either monitor, simply by clicking on the appropriate video image. This will turn the position bar under that monitor white. In addition, when the source monitor is active, the position bar under the record monitor indicates the part of your sequence you're currently seeing in the timeline. These distinctions can be subtle, so, when in doubt, click the monitor you're interested in to make sure it's active.

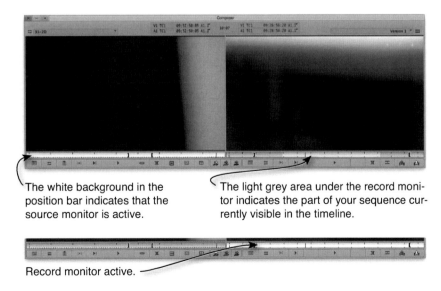

The white background in the position bar indicates that the source monitor is active.

The light grey area under the record monitor indicates the part of your sequence currently visible in the timeline.

Record monitor active.

Monitor Tracking Data

At the top of the Composer window, you can choose to display one or two rows of numerical data about the clips loaded into the source and record monitors. Avid calls this "tracking information" because it reveals data at the position indicator. You can display one or two rows of data, and, new in Version 6, you can have two numbers displayed side-by-side if there's room. Make your selection in Composer settings.

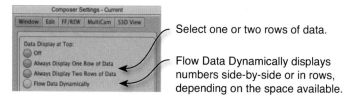

Select one or two rows of data.

Flow Data Dynamically displays numbers side-by-side or in rows, depending on the space available.

Then click on a row of data to open a cascading menu and select the data type you're interested in. You can display information in a wide variety of timecode and footage formats. Some of the choices are visible below. (To quickly see all the data logged for a clip—but not at the position indicator—use the Clip Info Window. See page 127.)

Tracking data is displayed above the source and record monitors.

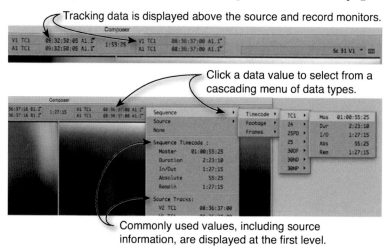

Click a data value to select from a cascading menu of data types.

Commonly used values, including source information, are displayed at the first level.

Starting Timecode and Footage

You can now set a sequence's starting timecode or footage by simply changing a value in the appropriate bin column. For timecode, use the Start column, for footage, the Master Start column. Or you can do the same thing in the Sequence Report window. Right-click a sequence in a bin, or load it into the record monitor, and right-click the monitor. Then select Sequence Report, make your change, and click Apply Changes.

Center Duration

The Center Duration display, located above the source and record monitors, makes it easy to measure things by continuously showing you the distance between your marks. It's context sensitive, displaying a measurement for either the source or record monitor, whichever is active. (It should be on by default. If you don't see it, select it in the Windows Tab of Composer Settings.)

If you make only one mark, the display will show you the distance from that mark to the blue bar. This makes it easy to set up an exact duration. Say you want to create a three-second clip starting on a particular frame. Mark in on that frame and clear your mark out. Then drag the blue bar until Center Duration shows 3:00. Mark out and edit as needed.

To switch to a different format, just click the number. The display will cycle through timecode, feet+frames and total frames.

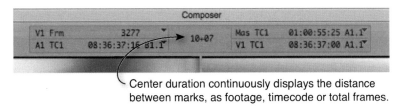

Center duration continuously displays the distance between marks, as footage, timecode or total frames.

The timecode format shown (drop frame, non-drop frame, 24p, etc.) will match the last-used format displayed in the top row of data above the active monitor. To measure a timeline distance in drop frame timecode, for example, click the top number above the record monitor, select Sequence, and choose any drop frame timecode value. Note that because the center duration display matches the selected monitor, it's possible to show record durations in one timecode format and source durations in another. Footages are always displayed in 35mm, 4-perf format.

Monitor Menus

The Clip Name Menus above the monitors contain a list of recently used clips. You can display the list in two ways. If you simply click on the menu, the list will be displayed in alphabetical order. But if you Option-click, it will be displayed in the order in which the clips were last used, with the most recently used clip at the top.

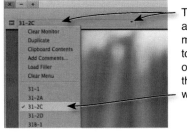

The clip name displayed above the source and record monitors is a menu. Click it to see clips in alphabetical order. Option-click to display the clips in the order they were loaded.

Moving by Footage or Time

To move forward or backward in the source or record monitor, click a monitor to activate it and then, using your numeric keypad, type a plus or minus sign, followed by a number and the Enter key. The position indicator jumps forward or backward by the duration entered.

Use the numeric keypad to move by footage or time.

If you're working on a laptop and don't have a numeric keypad, you have two choices. If your keyboard has Number Lock key, you can tap it and then use the embedded numeric keypad (be sure to tap it again when you're done). Or you can hit the Control key twice (on a PC, use the left Control key). A text entry window opens over the monitor and you can type your numbers using the keys in the number row.

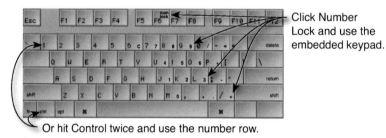

Click Number Lock and use the embedded keypad.

Or hit Control twice and use the number row.

You can enter numbers as either time (1:00:00:00) or footage (100+00). Don't type the punctuation. MC will add it for you based on the format of the tracking data displayed above the monitor. If you're displaying two rows of data, it will use the top row.

To move 23 feet and 8 frames, for example, make sure the top number above the monitor you're working in is set to a footage or keycode value. Then type "+2308" followed by the Enter key. As you type, you'll see MC interpret this as "+23+08".

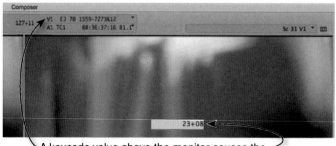

A keycode value above the monitor causes the system to interpret typed numbers as footage.

If you want to move 28 seconds and 8 frames instead, change the top number to time-code format, and again type "+2308" followed by the Enter key. MC will now interpret this as "+23:08".

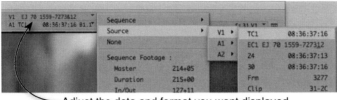

The same number, now interpreted as timecode.

Adjust the data and format you want displayed.

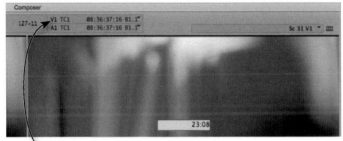

The same number, now interpreted as timecode.

To have your entry interpreted as total frames, follow it with the letter f ("+2308f"). The system will also remember the last move you made. To repeat it, simply hit the Enter key. (On a Mac laptop, hold down the Function key and hit Return.)

Go to Footage or Time

You can also search for and go to numeric values in clips or sequences. Load the clip you wish to search. Then pop open the upper tracking number above the monitor you're searching and display the track and data type you're interested in. If you're looking for timecode in V2, for example, display that value. Then type a number, but without a plus or minus sign or punctuation, and press Enter. The system looks at the top number above the monitor, formats the text accordingly, and searches that data for the value you entered. If it exists in the clip or sequence, the system will jump to it.

If you type only the last few digits, the system will go to the first occurrence of that value. For example, if you're parked on 01:04:18:00 and you enter 1902, you'll move forward to 01:04:19:02. You can go to a keycode value this way, as well. Ignore the prefix and just type the last four digits and the frame count.

Fast Forward & Rewind

The Fast Forward and Rewind buttons allow you to jump forward or backward to specific destinations. To configure them, use the FF/REW tab in Composer Settings. You can have them stop at head frames, tail frames or markers (locators). They normally take you to the next transition in selected tracks. If you'd rather they go to transitions in all tracks, choose Ignore Track Selectors. Or simply hold down the Option key when you hit them. To go to transitions and enter Trim Mode simultaneously, use the Go to Next/Previous Edit buttons (page 88).

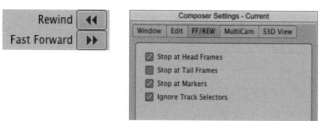

Fast Forward and Rewind also serve a special function in the Audio Mixer and the Effect Editor. When the mixer is in Automation mode and active (in front of other windows), they'll stop at audio keyframes and audio edits. When the Effect Editor is active, they'll stop at visual effect keyframes.

Timecode Window

If you need to see more than two rows of tracking data, or if you need to display data in large type, use the Timecode Window, available in the Tools menu. It floats over the interface and can display anything that can be shown above a monitor.

Click a displayed number to open a pop-up menu, where you can change the data type, add or remove lines, or adjust the font size.

Scaling the Composer Window

To adjust the size of the Composer window, just grab any corner of the window (or the left or right edge) and drag until the images are the size you prefer. Then resize other windows as needed. To memorize your new setup, click on the Project window and save. This saves everything, including your settings. If you're using a Workspace, open the Workspace menu and select Save Current. (See "Workspaces" on page 260.)

Hide the Source Monitor

You can even make the source monitor disappear and display only the record monitor. This can be handy when you're working with visual effects and don't have a lot of screen real estate. Source clips will automatically open in pop-up windows allowing you to edit with monitors of different sizes.

Hide the source monitor by Option-clicking the Source/Record Mode button at the left side of the timeline. (You can also drag the left edge of the window until the source monitor disappears, then drag it back to enlarge it alone.) To restore the source monitor, Option-click the Source/Record button again, or drag the monitor into a wide rectangle.

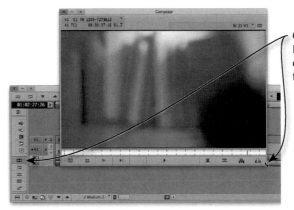

Option-click the Source/ Record button, and then drag the record monitor to the size you prefer.

Hide Video

It can also be useful to shrink the entire Composer window by hiding the video images completely and showing only buttons and controls. This gives you the maximum amount of screen real estate for the timeline and is especially helpful when working with lots of audio tracks, or when you want to see large waveforms. If you've got a client monitor, you can view your video there.

On the Mac, invoke this mode with the green "plus" button at the top left of the Composer Window. Hit it once to hide video, hit it again to restore video to normal. Or right-click on the source or record monitor and select Hide Video. In general, this smaller window (once called the "Mini-Composer") offers all the functionality of the full Composer, but it doesn't devote space to source and record video. You can even drag a clip from a bin to a monitor—by dropping it on the monitor's position bar, or on the shaded area above it.

Click to show or hide video.   To load a clip, double-click it in a bin, or drag and drop it here.

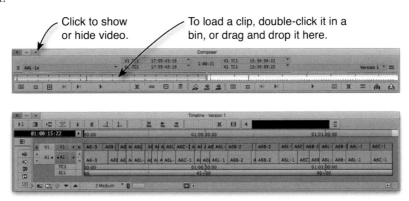

Trimming with Hidden Video

The Mini-Composer also works in Trim Mode. Select trim sides same way you would in normal Trim Mode.

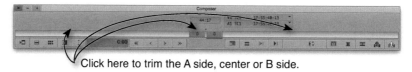

Click here to trim the A side, center or B side.

Markers

Markers (not to be confused with Mark In and Mark Out) allow you to identify frames in clips or sequences, using colored icons and text notes. Prior to Version 6 they were known as Locators, but the functionality hasn't changed. To add a marker, park on the frame you want to identify, select a track and click a marker button. The marker appears both in the timeline and the position bar and is superimposed over paused video in the source or record monitor.

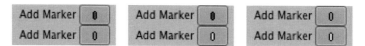

To move to an existing marker, simply click on it, or use the Go to Marker buttons. (You can also use the Fast Forward/Rewind buttons.) To remove a marker, click on it in a position bar or park on it in the timeline and hit Delete. To move a marker in time (left/right), Option-click it in a position bar and drag.

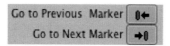

Two windows allow you to manage markers: the Markers Window, which provides a detailed list of all markers in a clip or sequence loaded into the currently active monitor, and the Marker Pop-up, which lets you set options for a specific marker. Click a marker icon superimposed over video to open the pop-up. (Depending on your settings, it may open automatically whenever you add a marker. See below.)

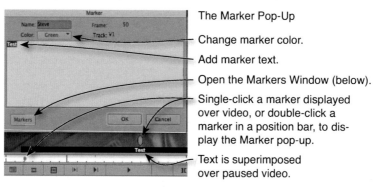

The Marker Pop-Up

Change marker color.

Add marker text.

Open the Markers Window (below).

Single-click a marker displayed over video, or double-click a marker in a position bar, to display the Marker pop-up.

Text is superimposed over paused video.

To open the Markers Window, select Tools > Markers, or click the Markers button in the Marker pop-up, above.

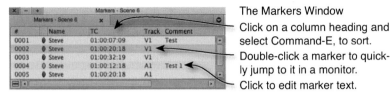

The Markers Window
Click on a column heading and select Command-E, to sort.
Double-click a marker to quickly jump to it in a monitor.
Click to edit marker text.

Click the Fast Menu at the lower left of the window (or right-click anywhere in the window) to print markers, export them to a text file, change colors, sort, etc. To suppress the Marker pop-up when adding a marker, choose Disable Marker Popup When Adding. To search for marker text, use the Find command, below.

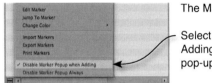

The Markers Window Fast Menu.

Select Disable Marker Popup when Adding if you'd rather not see the pop-up when you add a marker.

If you use the keyboard to add markers, you can do it while video is playing. Assign a marker button to a key; then tap it as many times as you'd like during clip play. When you stop, all the markers you created will appear. Try using this while reviewing a sequence, to flag areas you need to work on.

Find and PhraseFind

Media Composer has always allowed editors to search for text in Markers, Clip Names, or the timeline. But recent versions dramatically add to that capability, letting you search for text in any bin column in your entire project. If you install the PhraseFind add-on, it can also do a phonetic search for source dialog, scanning your audio and identifying words or phrases, again throughout the project. All these capabilities are managed with a single Find window. Select Edit > Find to open it (Command-F).

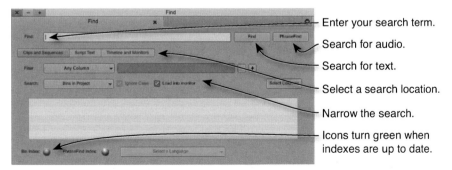

Enter your search term.
Search for audio.
Search for text.
Select a search location.
Narrow the search.
Icons turn green when indexes are up to date.

Icons at the bottom of the window change as MC automatically updates its indexes, turning half green when partially complete, fully green when complete. You can search either way, but you'll get more results when they are green. To search for text in the timeline, select the Timeline and Monitors tab, activate the monitor you want to search and choose Markers, Clip Names or Timeline Text. When you hit Find, the position indicator jumps forward to the first instance of the text. Hit Find again, or select Edit > Find Again (Command-G) to go to the next instance. Note that when searching in the timeline, the software only locates material displayed in the current timeline view. Track selection is ignored (see "Clip Text" on page 53).

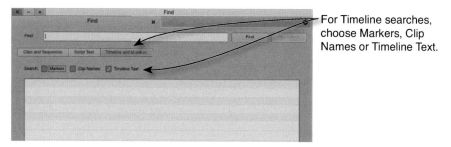

For Timeline searches, choose Markers, Clip Names or Timeline Text.

To search for text in the project, select the Clips and Sequences tab and choose a location from the Search pop-up: the current bin, all bins, scripts, or both.

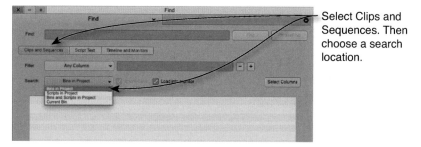

Select Clips and Sequences. Then choose a search location.

Enter the text you're looking for and click Find. If you choose to search in all bins or all scripts, Media Composer will display a list of clips that contain the text you entered, in any bin column. Double-click a clip to open the bin or script, with the clip highlighted. If Load Into Monitor is selected, the clip will also open in the source monitor.

Clips are sorted alphabetically by clip name. To sort on another column, click its heading; click again to sort in reverse order. Click Select Columns to choose the columns you want displayed.

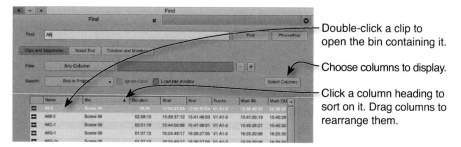

Double-click a clip to open the bin containing it.

Choose columns to display.

Click a column heading to sort on it. Drag columns to rearrange them.

To narrow your results, use the Filter pop-up, select a column and enter the text it should contain, adding or removing criteria using the plus and minus buttons.

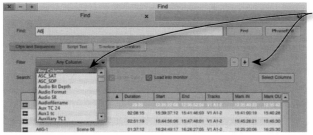

Filter search results by choosing a column and entering text. Add or remove additional criteria with the plus and minus buttons.

If you search the current bin, MC doesn't create a list of results; it takes you to the first clip containing the text (in a bin column) and highlights it. Hit Command-G to go to additional instances.

To search for script text, use the Script Text tab, select a location, enter your text and click Find. If you selected Scripts in Project, you'll see a list of results; with Current Script, you'll be taken to the first instance within the script. Note that the Script Text tab searches only script text, not clip names. To search for clip data within a script, use the Clips and Sequences tab.

If you make changes in a bin, MC indexes them automatically in the background, but you must save the bin before it will recognize them. In the Find window, the Return key repeats the type of search you last performed, either Find or Phrasefind.

PhraseFind

To search for phonetic audio, first let the software build the PhraseFind index, then select the Clips and Sequences tab, enter the dialog to look for and hit PhraseFind. The system will work for a while and then display a list of results, sorted on the Score column, an indication of how good the match is, on a scale of 0-100. Multiple instances within a clip are listed separately. Double-click an item to open the bin or script containing it. If Load into Monitor is selected, the clip opens with the position indicator cued to the found audio. AMA-linked clips are not searched.

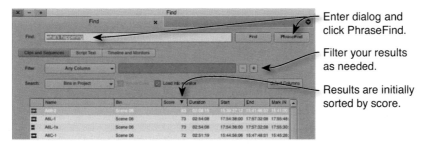

Enter dialog and click PhraseFind.

Filter your results as needed.

Results are initially sorted by score.

To search for words within a time span, use the ampersand character. Searching for John &5 Doe, for example, finds instances of John and Doe within five seconds of each other.

Gang

The Gang function allows you to interlock two monitors so that they move in lockstep with each other. If you drag one, the other moves with it. If you play one, the other pauses, but it will update its position as soon as you stop. You'll find a Gang button under the source and record monitors when you display two rows of buttons there, and you can assign it elsewhere using the command palette. (It no longer appears above the monitors.) Click either one and they both turn green to indicate that the two monitors are interlocked. In Version 6, green bars appear under the monitor images, as well. You can gang the source and record monitors, and you can gang one or more pop-ups to the record monitor. Note that if you gang two clips of unequal lengths and move them together, the shorter clip will stop when you reach its end, but the longer clip will continue to move.

Gang icons are available under the source and record monitors.

Green bars appear when gang is active.

The Tool Palette

The Composer window Fast Menu button lets you create a customizable tool palette. (It's also available in the Other tab of the Command Palette, so you can assign it wherever you like.) Click it to open the palette and select a function. Or click and drag to tear it off as a window. You can then move it, resize it, or customize it with buttons from the Command Palette.

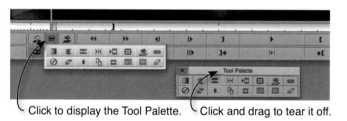

Click to display the Tool Palette.   Click and drag to tear it off.

Buttons from Menus

You can create a custom button to provide fast access to any menu item. First, open the Command Palette (Command-3), and select Menu to Button Reassignment.

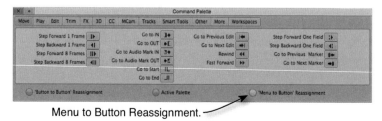

Menu to Button Reassignment.

Then open Keyboard Settings. Your cursor will turn into an icon that looks like a menu. In the keyboard template, click on the key you want to assign, and navigate to the menu item you want to assign to that key.

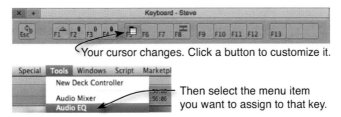

Your cursor changes. Click a button to customize it.

Then select the menu item
you want to assign to that key.

A new button will be created on the key you selected, identified with a couple of letters from the menu. For example, the Audio EQ tool will be abbreviated EQ. Hitting the new button will do the same thing as selecting that item from the menu.

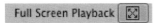

Your custom button is labeled
with a two-letter abbreviation.

Full Screen Playback & Open I/O

In the past, Media Composer only worked with Avid's own input/output hardware. But now, with the company's new Open I/O standard, it works effectively with devices from wide variety of third party manufacturers, allowing you to display your work on a client monitor and capture from or output to tape. Third party hardware will require a software plug-in. Be sure to install it after you install Media Composer. Hardware controls can be accessed from the Tools menu or via settings in the Project window.

If you're working with a software-only system (without I/O hardware), you can display the contents of the source or record monitor full screen via the Full Screen Playback button. The button doesn't appear on the default keyboard, so you'll need to assign it there from the Other tab in the Command Palette. Then click on either the source or record monitor and hit the button to have video fill the screen. Move through your material using the three-button player or any other keyboard commands you like.

Full Screen Playback

There's also a Full Screen Playback settings panel. Select Full Screen to scale the image to your display. For a more contrasty look, try Expand Luminance for Computer Displays. If you have two monitors, use this panel to designate one for full screen playback.

6 Edit Functions

While it's certainly possible to construct effective sequences using Avid's basic editing tools, much of the power and flexibility of the system lies beneath the surface: in hidden functions, and in the way the editing tools can be customized to suit your working style. I'll cover some of these techniques in the following pages.

Replace

Most editors are familiar with Insert and Overwrite edits. But there's a third kind of edit that's often overlooked. It's called Replace and is designed to quickly substitute shots in your sequence with new material. The system lines up the position indicator in both the source and record monitors and drops in the new shot, overlaps and all. Because the icon for this function is blue, it's sometimes called "blue edit."

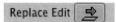

In the following example, we'll replace the middle shot, 84A-1, with 84A-2. Near the beginning of 84A-1, the actress turns her head. We want to replace it with 84A-2, so that the head turn in the new shot occurs at the same point in the cut.

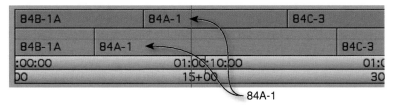

First, park the blue bar in the record monitor at the start of the head turn. Clear your record-side marks. Then put 84A-2 into the source monitor and park it at the start of the head turn there, as well. Select V1 and A1 and hit Replace. 84A-2 is substituted for 84A-1.

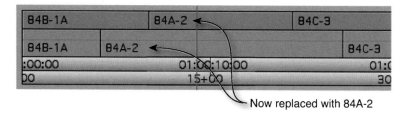

Now replaced with 84A-2

This works well unless you're parked in the middle of an overlap. In that case you have to show the system which clips you want to affect. In the following diagram, for example, there seems to be no way to replace the middle shot using the dialog in its pre-lap as a reference. If you hit Replace, you'll be editing the audio for 84A-1, but you'll be editing the video for 84B-1A.

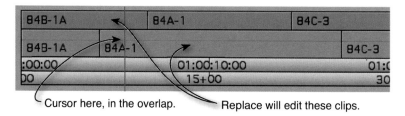

Cursor here, in the overlap.   Replace will edit these clips.

The solution is to first select the clips to be replaced. This tells MC what you want to do. Click the video clip with a segment tool and then shift-click on the audio clip to select it, as well. Then hit Replace to edit the selected clips.

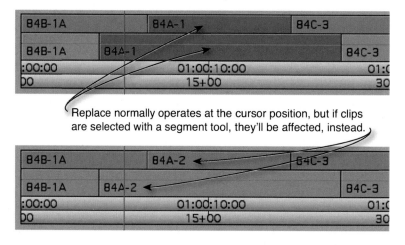

Replace normally operates at the cursor position, but if clips are selected with a segment tool, they'll be affected, instead.

It's usually best to clear your marks in the timeline before making a Replace edit. Replace ignores marks in the source monitor. But if you have both a Mark In and a Mark

Out on the record side, your edit won't stop at the nearest cut point, it'll stop at the marks, instead.

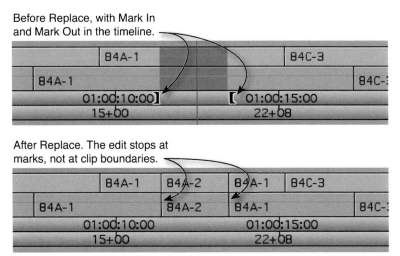

Before Replace, with Mark In and Mark Out in the timeline.

After Replace. The edit stops at marks, not at clip boundaries.

If you don't like having to clear marks before using Replace, simply turn off Show Marked Region in Timeline settings (see "Show Marked Region" on page 79). With edit highlighting turned off, Replace ignores both source and record marks.

Replace is missing on the default Composer window. A good place for it is between Insert and Overwrite, at the center of your screen.

Sync Point Editing

Sync point editing is much like Replace in that it edits by aligning the blue cursor in the source and record monitors. The difference is that a Sync Point Edit always stops at marks, not cut points, and it requires marks to work. You are allowed only two marks, and they can be on either the source or record side. The technique is useful when adding new material to an existing sequence and aligning the new material to a sync point in the body of the cut.

You can turn on Sync Point Editing via the Edit tab in Composer Settings or by selecting it in the Special menu. Either way, you'll use the Overwrite button to make these edits. It will change to indicate that Sync Point Editing is turned on.

1. Select the Composer Window by clicking anywhere in it. Then choose Sync Point Editing from the Special menu, or select it in Composer Settings. The Overwrite button changes.

2. Place the record-side position indicator on your sync point.

3. Put your new shot in the source monitor. Mark in and out (or mark in and out on the record side). Place the position indicator on the sync point (between your marks).

4. Hit Overwrite. The position indicators are lined up and the new material is overwritten.

Filler

Filler is negative space in the timeline, automatically present in all tracks wherever there are no clips. But it can also be edited in a limited way. You can trim it by adding rollers at the ends of filler segments, and you can add edits in it (see below). You can also insert filler anywhere in a sequence, which simply serves to push clips following the filler downstream. Filler appears as an unnamed source in cut lists and can be optionally included as black in an EDL.

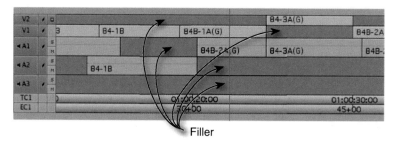

Filler

To load filler into the source monitor, pull down the Clip Name Menu and select Load Filler. Source filler typically contains one track of video and two tracks of mono audio. If your sequence contains stereo tracks, you'll also see a track of stereo filler. If it contains surround tracks, you'll see surround filler, as well. Select the tracks you need and edit normally. Marks you make in source filler are remembered even after you quit.

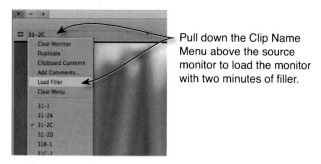

Pull down the Clip Name Menu above the source monitor to load the monitor with two minutes of filler.

Note that the system prevents you from inserting filler at the end of a sequence. If you need to put black there, you'll have to create a black source clip, either by digitizing black video or creating a simple title background without any text.

Add Edit

When you hit Add Edit, a cut is added in all selected tracks. If Sync Breaks are turned on (see "Sync Breaks" on page 103) the resulting cut will display an equal sign to indicate that the underlying material is continuous. The equal sign is used because it looks like a negative cutter's "run through" or "unintentional splice" mark, which has the same meaning. Avid calls a cut like this a Match Frame Edit. (Match Frame Edits in filler don't display the equal sign, since filler, by definition, is continuous.) Note that add edits are always applied at the beginning of the frame you're parked on.

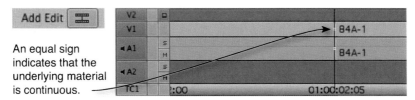

Removing a Match Frame Edit

Lasso a match frame edit, or select it with a trim tool, and hit Delete to remove it. To remove a series of such edits, mark in before the first one, mark out after the last one, select tracks and choose Remove Match Frame Edits from the Clip menu.

Note that these techniques won't remove match frame edits in visual effects or in audio clips with automation gain applied. In that case, your match frame edit mark will be colored red. You'll have to select it and drag it to the end of the clip to remove it, overwriting one end of the clip with the other.

Add Edit in Filler

In a complicated, multi-track sequence it's sometimes helpful to add edits in the middle of filler. This allows you to add rollers in the filler and trim it internally. Since filler is continuous, it doesn't matter where you extend it. (Note that EDLs will list each piece of filler separately, so if you intend to include black edits in an EDL, remove your match frame edits before making the list.)

To add an edit in all tracks that contain filler, regardless of which track selectors are active, hold down the Option key and hit Add Edit.

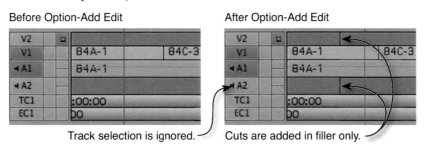

This also works effectively in Trim Mode. Select your transitions for trimming and hit Option-Add Edit. Cuts are created in filler and automatically selected for trimming.

Before Option-Add Edit in Trim   After Option-Add Edit in Trim

V2	□		
V1		84A-1	84C-3
◄A1		84A-1	84C-3
◄A2			
TC1		:00:00	
EC1		00	

V2	□		
V1		84A-1	84C-3
◄A1		84A-1	84C-3
◄A2			
TC1		:00:00	
EC1		00	

Cuts are added in filler and the new transitions are selected.

One-Step Pre-Lap

Media Composer includes an intuitive but hidden shortcut to help you quickly create a split edit at the end of your sequence. This is useful when you're part-way through a first assembly and want to overlap the next shot, the one you're attaching to the end of the sequence. Think of it as a one-step pre-lap of picture or sound.

1. Mark the next shot you want to use in the source monitor. Mark in where you want the pre-lap to begin. Mark out anywhere you like.

2. Mark the record monitor where you want the pre-lap to begin. Don't mark out on the record side.

3. Select the track you want to pre-lap on the record side of the track panel. Select all the tracks you want to edit on the source side.

4. Hold down Option and click the Overwrite (red) edit button. The selected tracks will be edited normally. But any track or tracks that were selected on the source side, *and not selected on the record side,* will fill in starting at the end of the sequence.

In the following example, we're ready to make a picture pre-lap. Head and tail marks have been added on the source side and V1 and A1 are activated. A head mark has been added on the record side, without a tail mark, and V1 only is activated.

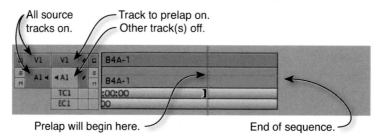

All source tracks on.   Track to prelap on. Other track(s) off.

Prelap will begin here.   End of sequence.

Now click Option-Overwrite. Video is edited at the record-side mark. Audio is laid in starting at the end of the sequence.

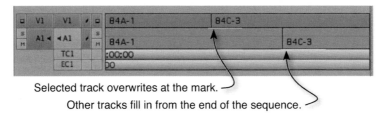

Selected track overwrites at the mark.
Other tracks fill in from the end of the sequence.

To make a sound pre-lap, select A1 on the record side instead.

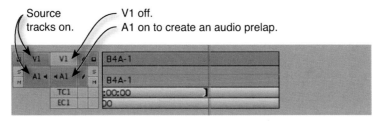

Source tracks on.   V1 off.
A1 on to create an audio prelap.

Then hit Option-Overwrite to produce the following:

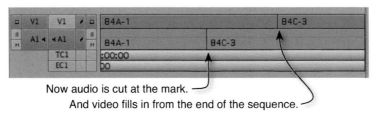

Now audio is cut at the mark.
And video fills in from the end of the sequence.

Audio Marks

You can also make overlap cuts using the Audio Mark In and Audio Mark Out buttons. Use them in combination with the normal Mark In and Mark Out buttons to create overlaps. The system will use your regular mark to edit picture and your audio mark to edit audio. This only works with Overwrite.

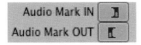

Here's an example. Mark your source clip using normal marks. Mark your timeline with both a Mark In and an Audio Mark In.

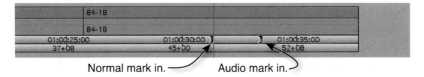

Normal mark in.   Audio mark in.

Now edit with Overwrite. The result is a video pre-lap. If the audio mark had preceded the video mark, you'd have an audio pre-lap.

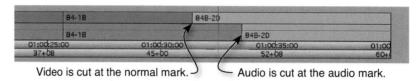

Video is cut at the normal mark. ⌐   ⌐ Audio is cut at the audio mark.

Audio marks also work from the source monitor. You could achieve the same result as above by making a normal mark and an audio mark in the source monitor, together with a normal mark in the timeline. Keep in mind that Media Composer only understands one audio mark per edit. If you create more, it will ignore them and you'll end up with a straight cut.

To clear audio marks, park on the mark, click the appropriate side of the composer window to activate it, and hit the Delete key. You can also use the appropriate Clear Mark button to clear normal marks and audio marks simultaneously.

To go to an audio mark, use a Go to Audio Mark button, or click on the mark in a position bar.

Edit by Dragging

Just as you can drag to move clips in the timeline, you can drag from a bin or the source monitor to the timeline, or from a bin to the record monitor.

To the Timeline

Start by marking your material, identifying the portion you want to edit, then drag, either from a bin or the source monitor. A clip outline will appear in the timeline, showing you where your material will go—record side marks will be ignored. You can create either an Insert or Overwrite this way, depending on which segment tool is active. The mouse cursor will display a yellow or red arrow as you drag, to make your choice clear. (If both tools are active, the type of edit will be determined by the Default Segment Tool selected in Timeline Settings. See page 47.)

The Composer window will change to display four frames, the A and B sides of the edits you are about to create (see page 29). Hold down the Command key to snap to head frames or Command-Option to snap to tails. Video- or audio-only clips can be dragged to any appropriate track. If you drag a clip containing both, you'll be able to drag video to any video track; but audio will go to the tracks used in the source. Note that tracks are not automatically created this way. If your source material contains A1 and A2, for example, and the sequence in the timeline contains A1, you'll edit only A1. Patching is ignored.

Dragging a *sequence* from a bin to the timeline behaves differently. You won't see a clip outline or the four-frame display and patching and track selection are respected. You'll edit according to the segment tool selected, but if no tool is active, you'll simply load the sequence into the timeline, replacing whatever is currently there. Thus, dragging a sequence to the timeline can be confusing and should probably be avoided.

To the Record Monitor

Dragging from a bin to the record monitor doesn't respect Smart Tool selection. To create an Overwrite, hold down the Shift key during the drag. For an insert, hold down Option. Either way, your cursor changes to indicate the type of edit you're making. Material will be edited according to your source and record marks.

If you Option-drag multiple clips simultaneously, the marked regions in all the clips, and the activated tracks in all the clips, will be edited together in the order in which they appear in the bin. In frame view this means left to right and top to bottom (reading order). In text view it means top to bottom. You'll effectively be making a series of edits, one clip or sequence at a time, and respecting all timeline selections: marks, tracks and patching. This can be handy when creating a first assembly or when building sequences into reels. To avoid editing clips from one track to another, select Special > Restore Default Patch before you drag (see page 39).

Exceptions to the Three-Mark Rule

As described earlier, it usually takes three marks to make an edit (see page 26). But you can edit with fewer or more. If there are too many, the system will ignore a mark. If there are too few, it substitutes the position indicator or the tail of the source clip for the missing mark or marks.

Substitutions are made like this:

Four Marks The system will ignore the source mark out and use the source mark in along with both record marks.

Two Marks If there's a mark in and mark out on the source and no mark on the record, the position indicator on the record side will be used as a mark in. The same is true for a mark in and out on the record side: the position indicator on the source side will be used as a mark in.

If there's a mark in on *both* sides but no mark out, the tail of the source clip will be used as a mark out.

If there's a mark out on both sides and no mark in, the position indicator on the *record* side will be used as a mark in.

One Mark   With a mark in on the source, the end of the source clip and the position indicator on the record side become the other marks.

With a single tail mark on either the source or record side, the source and record position indicators will be used as in marks.

No Marks   Source and record position indicators are used as in marks, and the source tail is used as an out mark.

The exception you'll probably use most is editing to the position indicator on the record side. Mark in and out on the source, clear your marks on the record, and edit your material to the place where you're parked.

Single Mark Editing

Single Mark Editing is a setting that allows you to work with only a single, source-side mark. Your position indicators, source and record, are used as implied marks. You'll find it in the Edit tab of Composer settings.

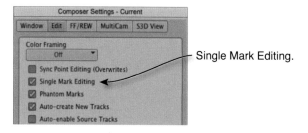

Single Mark Editing.

Normally, if you don't mark out on the source side, the tail of your source clip becomes your mark out. But with Single Mark Editing enabled, the position indicator becomes your second mark. If you mark in, it's used as your mark out. If you mark out, it becomes your mark in.

On the record side, whether Single Mark Editing is enabled or not, if you don't make a mark, the position indicator is used, instead. If you make a record-side mark or marks, they'll be used normally.

Hidden Marks and Marked Regions

Phantom Marks

Avid's Phantom Marks feature can make certain mark issues clearer. Like Single Mark Editing, it's available in the Edit tab of Composer Settings (above). With Phantom Marks on, the system displays implied marks so you can see clearly what's going to happen before you hit an edit button. To make sure you don't get confused, the phantom mark is shown in blue-green. You can click on a phantom mark or Go To it, just as you can with a normal mark. Play In to Out and Play to Out work with phantom marks, as well.

For example, if you mark in and out on the source side and mark in on the record side, the system will show you the record out—the tail of the edit you're about to make.

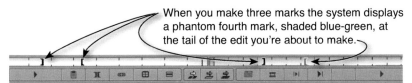

When you make three marks the system displays a phantom fourth mark, shaded blue-green, at the tail of the edit you're about to make.

With two marks, the system will display two phantom marks, showing the effect of the edit on both sides.

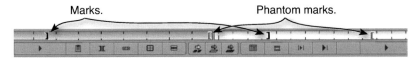

Marks.   Phantom marks.

When you make four marks, the system adds a fifth phantom mark. In the following example, the system will ignore the source out mark in favor of the record out. The phantom mark shows the actual source out.

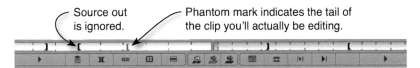

Source out   Phantom mark indicates the tail of
is ignored.   the clip you'll actually be editing.

Note that phantom marks don't respect the status of Single Mark Editing. If you don't mark out on the source side, your phantom mark will be shown at the end of your source clip, whether Single Mark Editing is on or not.

Implied Marks

Even with Phantom Marks turned off, you can go to an implied mark. And Play In to Out and Play to Out will work with an implied mark, as well. For example, mark in and out in the timeline and mark your in point in the source monitor. Press Go to Out on the source side. The system will jump to the tail of the material that will fit between the marks you made in your sequence.

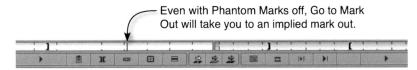

Even with Phantom Marks off, Go to Mark
Out will take you to an implied mark out.

Show Marked Region

By default, MC highlights the area you've marked in the timeline. This also helps clarify what's going to happen before you make an edit. However, timeline highlighting only displays record-side marks. When you have only one mark on the record side, nothing gets highlighted, even if you have made two source marks. Show Marked Region is an option in Timeline Settings. It's on by default.

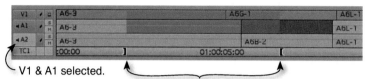

V1 & A1 selected.

Highlighting shows the marked region in selected tracks.

Top and Tail

The Top and Tail buttons can help you quickly trim up a sequence composed mainly of straight cuts. They perform an Extract, using the position indicator and either the beginning or the end of the current clip as marks.

Park the cursor where you want to make your cut and hit Top to extract from the position indicator to the head of the shot, or Tail to extract to the end. If more than one track is selected, Top and Tail will use the nearest straight cut common to all selected tracks as the second mark.

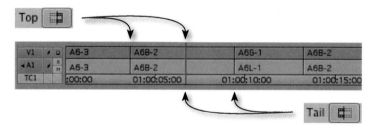

Combining Versions

One of the trickiest things editors have to do every day is manage versions. One approach that can help is to keep a single master or "hero" sequence clearly identified. Then, if you're not sure about a change, you can experiment using a shorter "alternate" sequence and compare it to the master. If you decide that the alternate is an improvement, you'll need to integrate it into the master. You can use match frame edit marks to make this easier.

First, put your master version in the record monitor and your alternate in the source monitor. Here's the master:

	B4-3A(G)	B4A-1		B4C-3	
B4-3A(G)			B4A-1	B4C-3	B4-1B
1:00:05:00		01:00:10:00		01:00:15:00	

And here's the alternate. The four colored shots have been added, replacing some of the original material.

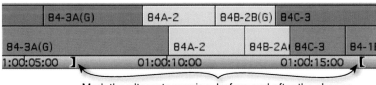

Identify two positions, one before and one after the change, where the alternate and the master match each other. Mark those frames in the source and the record monitors, two marks in each, for a total of four marks.

Reverse Match Frame can help you do this quickly. Locate your first frame in the source monitor and park on it. Select an appropriate track and hit Reverse Match Frame. This will cue the position indicator to the same frame on the record side. Hit Mark In. Then do the same thing for your out points.

Here's the source monitor:

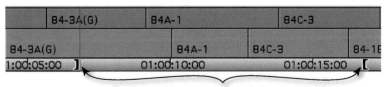

Mark the alternate version, before and after the change.

And the record monitor:

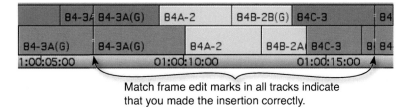

The same frames marked on the record side.

Check your patching—everything should go straight across. You don't want to be moving material from one track to another. Then simply hit Extract, followed by Insert (yellow edit). The old material is deleted and the new material is inserted. This is what the timeline looks like after the insertion:

Match frame edit marks in all tracks indicate
that you made the insertion correctly.

Note the match frame edit marks. They prove that you did the replacement correctly, that the new material dropped in at the right place and the cut points lined up. If you don't see those marks in every track, you've probably made a mistake. Undo twice, check your marks and try again.

You may want to play the beginning and end of the newly inserted section to make sure the cuts are working. To instantly locate and play the beginning of the new section, hit Play Loop (page 18).

All that remains is to remove the match frame edits. Lasso them or select them with a trim tool and hit the Delete key. Your master version is now up to date. (If your match frame edits are in clips that contain visual effects or volume adjustments they will be colored red and you'll have to lasso and drag to remove them.)

84-3A(G)	84A-2	84B-2B(G)	84C-3	
84-3A(G)		84A-2	84B-2A	84C-3	84-1E
1:00:05:00	01:00:10:00	01:00:15:00		

Remove the match frame edits and your versions are combined.

Transition Preservation

Transition Preservation is Avid's term for a set of changes in the way dissolves and other transition effects are handled when the clips they're attached to are moved or edited. In the past, when you did something like this, the transition either disappeared or you got an error message. With Transition Preservation, the dissolve is retained.

In the following illustrations, two audio clips are connected with a dissolve. When one is moved with a segment tool, the dissolve is preserved.

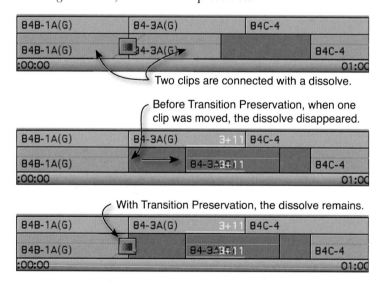

Two clips are connected with a dissolve.

Before Transition Preservation, when one clip was moved, the dissolve disappeared.

With Transition Preservation, the dissolve remains.

A similar thing happens when one clip is dragged against another that carries a dissolve. If we move the clip in the above example back where it was, the dissolve isn't lost—it reattaches itself to the moved clip.

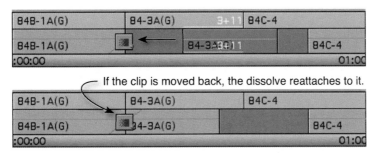

And if you lift or extract a clip connected with dissolves, the dissolves stay put.

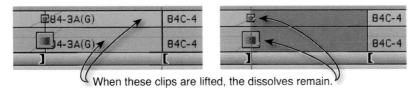

Transition Preservation also helps keep dissolves intact when cutting material from one sequence to another. With source marks at the center of a dissolve, the effect is simply reapplied after the edit.

Source timeline with marks at the beginning and end of the middle clip.

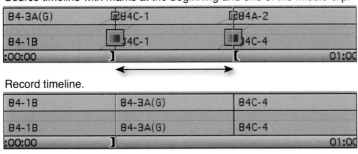

Record timeline.

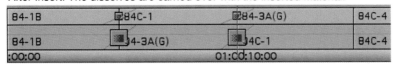

After Insert. The dissolves are carried over with the inserted material.

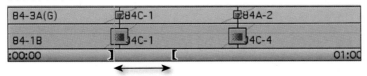

Here's what happens when the source marks aren't at the dissolve center. In the image below, the dissolve is included in the marked region.

Source timeline.

The dissolve is carried across but shortened.

After Insert.

84-1B	84C-1	84-3A(G)	84C-4
84-1B	84C-1	84-3A(G)	84C-4
:00:00		01:00:10:00	

But if the marked material doesn't include the dissolve center, it isn't carried over.

Source timeline with dissolve center outside the marked area.

84-3A(G)	84C-1	84A-2
84-1B	4-3A(G)	4C-4
:00:00		01:00

After Insert. The dissolve disappears.

84-1B	84C-1	84-3A(G)	84C-4
84-1B	84-3A(G)	84-3A(G)	84C-4
:00:00		01:00:10:00	

Transition Preservation also offers an improvement in Trim Mode. In the past, if you tried to drag through a cut to remove it, a dissolve would stop you. But now you can drag through the dissolve, removing the middle clip and connecting the other two.

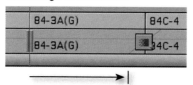

In the past, a drag would stop at the edge of a dissolve.

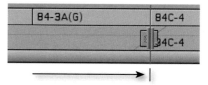

With Transition Preservation, you can drag to the dissolve center.

Keyboard Safeguards

The default keyboard assigns many keys in the bottom row to critical editing functions. This can be very useful, but it can also be dangerous. If you use the space bar to stop and start video, you're liable to hit a button by accident and recut your work. The default bottom row is shown below. To remove a function, drag a Blank button from the Other tab in the Command Palette to the appropriate key.

7

Trim Mode

Media Composer arguably offers the deepest and most intuitive trim controls in any editing application, permitting you to quickly do things that would be impossible elsewhere. But perhaps because its capabilities are so unusual, many editors are barely aware of them. The trim model is based on what Avid calls trim rollers: handles that you apply to the ends of clips. You can add rollers wherever needed, and when you trim, all rollers move together to preserve sync. They can be adjusted using a wide variety of techniques, and crucially, you can observe the changes you make from the position of any roller.

Three Ways to Trim

You can now trim in several ways. If you have rollers on both sides of a cut they'll display in purple and behave as they always have, lengthening one clip and simultaneously shortening the other. Avid calls this Dual-Roller Trimming.

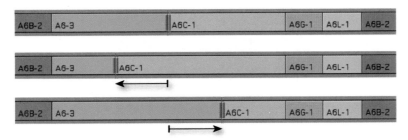

But with single rollers, you have a choice. Ripple Trim (yellow) works by lengthening or shortening the clip you're working on and simultaneously advancing or retarding downstream clips. This is the standard behavior that longtime Media Composer users have come to expect. The only difference is the color of the rollers.

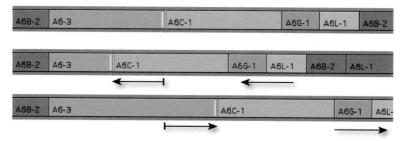

Overwrite Trim (red) is new and works like red Segment Mode, changing the length of the clip you're working on and either overwriting adjacent clips or adding black. Down-stream clips do not move.

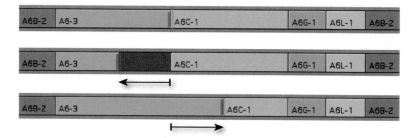

Getting In and Out of Trim Mode

Media Composer also gives you several ways to enter Trim Mode: with a Trim Smart Tool, with the traditional Trim Mode button, or by lassoing.

When clicking with the Smart Tool, your mouse cursor changes to tell you what kind of roller you'll create. As with the Segment Tools, if you turn both tools on, you'll see a red cursor when you're at the top of a cut and a yellow one when you're at the bottom. The cursor indicates which side of the cut you'll place rollers on. If your cursor is centered, you'll create rollers on both sides.

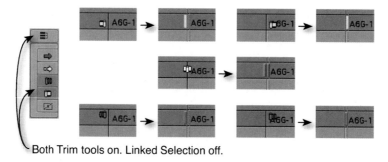

Both Trim tools on. Linked Selection off.

With Linked Selection turned on, you can select several transitions simultaneously. To turn it on temporarily, hold down the Option key when creating rollers.

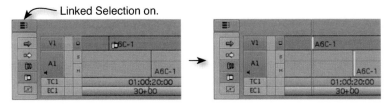

If you click the traditional Trim Mode button, you'll select the transition nearest to the position indicator, in any selected track. (See "Legacy Trim" on page 90.)

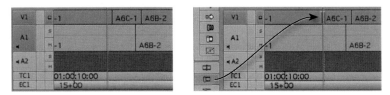

But lassoing is arguably the most direct way to select multiple transitions in a single step. Simply click in the gray area above or below the timeline and drag around the transition or transitions you're interested in. Release the mouse and you're trimming, with rollers on both sides of the cuts you surrounded. To select transitions near the bottom of the timeline, start dragging from the grey area below the timecode tracks.

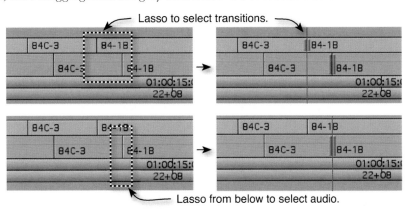

If you want to trim a clip that isn't available from the top or bottom of the timeline, hold down the Option key when lassoing.

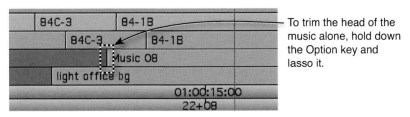

To get out of Trim Mode, click in the ruler or a timecode track. The position indicator will jump to the spot you clicked on, ready to play from there.

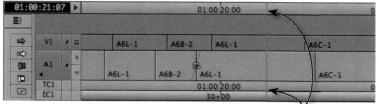

Exit Trim Mode by clicking in a timecode track or the Ruler.

You can also hit the Source/Record Mode button at the left end of the timeline, the Step Forward button, or the right cursor arrow key. Any of these techniques will take you out of Trim Mode and put you on the first frame of the clip following the transition.

Go to Next/Previous Edit

If you're working on a series of very short cuts, it can sometimes be difficult to lasso the transition you need. In that case, use the Go to Next Edit or Go to Previous Edit buttons. They'll take you to the next or previous cut and select it for trimming. Keep in mind that these buttons obey track selectors. If you have more than one track selected they'll take you to the next or previous edit that occurs in both tracks (ie. a straight cut).

Auto Focus

Auto Focus automatically zooms in the timeline when you enter Trim Mode. It's available in the Features tab of Trim Settings. Note that it won't work if the Trim Smart Tools are active. You must enter Trim Mode by lassoing or with the Trim Mode button.

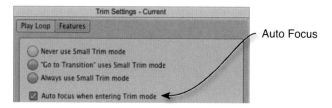

Adding and Deleting Rollers

In the Composer Window

You can trim the A side of a selected transition or transitions, the B side, or both simultaneously. (Avid calls the A side "outgoing," and the B side, "incoming.") To quickly move all rollers from one side to the other, single-click the video image you want to trim. To trim both sides simultaneously, click in the middle of the screen, between the two images.

The mouse cursor changes to show you which side of the trim you'll select. (To move video rollers only, leaving audio rollers where they are, Option-click, instead.)

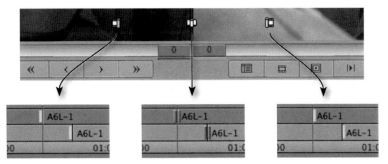

In the Timeline

Once you're in Trim Mode, you can add individual rollers by simply Shift-clicking on the ends of shots. Again, the mouse cursor changes to indicate the side of the cut you'll select. Shift-click on an existing roller to remove it.

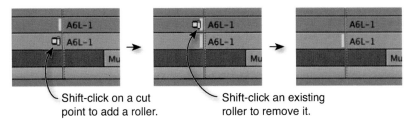

To add rollers to several cuts at once, Shift-lasso them. Be sure to completely surround the transitions. (If you surround a clip, you'll select it, instead.)

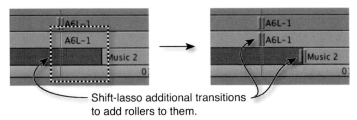

To simultaneously remove rollers and add new ones elsewhere, lasso without the Shift key.

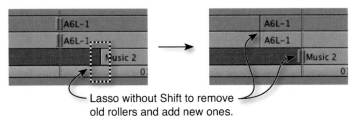

If rollers are on one side of a transition, Shift-lasso can be used to move them to the other side.

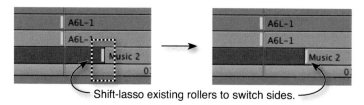

Shift-lasso existing rollers to switch sides.

Whenever you are lassoing, if you need to work on transitions that can't be accessed from the top or bottom of the timeline, add the Option key.

Note that you can have one or two rollers per track, but you must have the same number on each track. You can sometimes create different combinations, but you'll get a beep if you try to trim that way.

From the Keyboard

Instead of clicking on a video image, you can move rollers from the keyboard, using the Cycle Trim Sides button. Each time you click it, your rollers move from one side of the cut to the other, in this order: A side, Center, B side, Center, A side, Center, etc.

The button is unusual in that it does double duty. In Trim Mode it moves rollers, but in Source Record Mode it switches activation between the source and record monitors, and thus duplicates the function of the Toggle Source/Record button. By default, Toggle Source/Record is assigned to the Escape key. Try replacing it with Cycle Trim Sides.

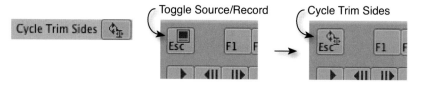

Legacy Trim

Some Media Composer users have found recent changes in Trim Mode problematic. One issue involves the behavior of the mouse cursor as you select rollers in the timeline. In the past, you saw only two cursors, left or right, allowing you to select A- or B-side rollers. But starting with Version 5, you see three. In some cases, that can make it harder to precisely select transitions—the center cursor gets in the way. (There have always been three cursors in the Composer window, and that hasn't changed.)

Legacy trim: two cursors.

With the Smart Tool: three.

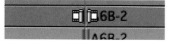
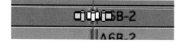

Version 5.5 restored traditional cursor behavior, making complex roller selection easier—but only when the Smart Tool trim icons are off. The easiest way to get into this mode is to lasso a transition or click the Trim Mode button.

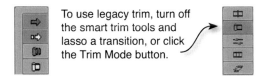

To use legacy trim, turn off the smart trim tools and lasso a transition, or click the Trim Mode button.

As long as you do that, Trim Mode will feel like it used to. (Some of these changes were first introduced in late releases of Version 5. Settings were also added to make the segment tools more familiar. See "The Smart Tool in Practice" on page 33.)

Adjusting the Cut

The Trim Buttons

The standard trim buttons are the most basic tools available for manipulating transitions. Enter Trim Mode, select rollers as needed, and hit a button to adjust your cut by either one or eight frames (ten in 30-fps projects). By default, the buttons are available on the left side of the Composer window when you're in Trim Mode. They're also on the M, comma, period and forward slash keys.

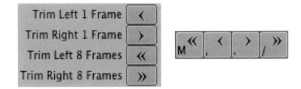

Trim by Dragging

You can also adjust a cut by simply dragging a roller. The video images will update to display the effect of your move. You can make precise adjustments this way or you can use the snap function to constrain the move.

To remove an overlap, for example, lasso the cut you want to move, hold down the Command key to turn on timeline snapping, click on a roller and simply drag the cut straight. It will jump to the nearest cut point, in this case, the other element of the overlap.

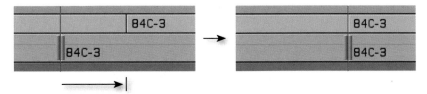

Command-drag to snap to the next cut.

Holding down the Command key not only snaps the position indicator to cut points, it snaps it to marks, as well. This makes it easy to move a cut point to a specific location. In Source/Record Mode, mark in or out at the point where you want your cut to be repositioned. Then simply lasso the cut or select it with a trim tool and Command-drag it to the mark.

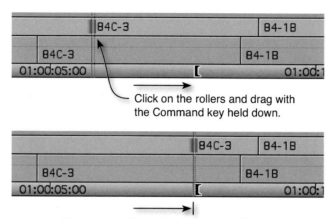

Click on the rollers and drag with
the Command key held down.

Your cursor will snap to marks as well as cut points.

The Three-Button Player

Media Composer allows you to use the three-button player (JKL) throughout the Trim interface, and it's just as valuable here as it is to play shots and sequences (see "Three-Button Play" on page 19). Get into Trim Mode any way you like. Select the side of the cut you want to trim. Then use the three-button player to play the selected side. You will be playing and trimming at the same time. Use all the speeds built into the player to adjust the cut. When you hit Pause, you're done. Tap the Play key to review the cut. This is one of the smoothest and most intuitive ways to use Trim Mode—by making your decisions based on moving video.

Don't forget that the standard Play key (on the space bar) performs two functions. In Source/Record Mode it plays at sound speed. In Trim Mode it loops the transition. (The Play icon under the record monitor changes to make this clear.)

The basic procedure looks like this:

1. Select a cut by lassoing, clicking the Trim Mode button or using the Smart Tool.
2. If necessary, select the side you want by clicking the appropriate video image.
3. Use the three-button player to adjust the cut.
4. Hit Play to review the transition.
5. Continue trimming with three-button play and checking with Play, as needed.
6. Click in a timecode track or the Ruler to exit.

This works particularly well if you arrange your keyboard so that the three-button player can be used with the left hand. You'll select transitions and rollers with the mouse in your right hand, and adjust and check the cut with your left hand on the keyboard. (If you're left-handed, you'll probably want to do the opposite.)

Single-Frame Trim Audio

Just as it does in Source/Record Mode, the three-button player offers responsive, analog-style scrub audio in Trim Mode. But for single-frame adjustments the trim buttons tend to be quicker and more precise. To hear digital-style scrub audio when using them, simply hold down the Shift key. Keep in mind that you are playing the *destination frame*—the frame you're arriving at—regardless of the direction in which you're trimming.

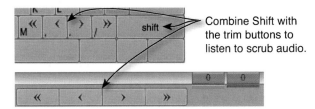

Combine Shift with the trim buttons to listen to scrub audio.

Cut on the Fly

If you tap a mark key while you're looping an edit in Trim Mode you'll recut the transition to the mark. The loop instantly restarts and plays the adjusted cut. For many people, this is one of the quickest and most intuitive ways to trim. Enter Trim Mode on the cut you want to adjust, and hit Play to loop it. Watch the edit until you have a feel for the new cut point, and hit a mark button when you see it go by (Mark In or Mark Out). Then let the transition play again, and watch your adjusted cut.

Tap any mark key when a trim is looping to quickly adjust the cut.

You can also tap the trim buttons from the keyboard while the loop is playing. Hit them as many times as you like during one circuit of the loop. All your key presses will be added together, and the next time the loop comes around the cut will be adjusted.

Numerical Trim

If you have a good idea of the trim length you're looking for, you can simply enter it numerically. Select your rollers, and then, using the numeric keypad, type a plus or minus sign followed by a number. MC trims the transition by that amount. Don't type any punctuation. The system will add it for you, based on the tracking data displayed above the record monitor. To force the system to interpret what you type as total frames, follow your entry with the f key. To repeat the last trim you made, hit the Enter key. (For details on how to enter numbers and how they'll be interpreted, see "Moving by Footage or Time" on page 58.)

Trim Lights/Dual Image Play

When you're trimming both sides of a cut using the three-button player (that is, with rollers on both sides of the transition), the system normally plays only one side—but it allows you to quickly select the side you want to play. Just position your mouse cursor, *without clicking*, over either of the video images. A green Trim Light under the counters will illuminate, indicating the side of the cut that will be seen and heard.

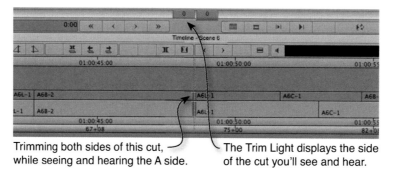

Trimming both sides of this cut,
while seeing and hearing the A side.

The Trim Light displays the side
of the cut you'll see and hear.

Media Composer also has the ability to play both sides of a cut at once. If you're rolling a cut, and you use the three-button player to trim, you'll see both sides play simultaneously in the Composer window. Turn it on by selecting Trim Settings > Features Tab > Dual Image Play.

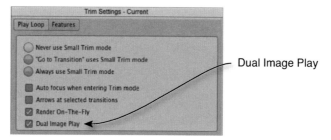

Dual Image Play

Since both sides are playing, the trim lights won't affect video shown in the Composer. But they will affect audio, as well as the side of the cut shown on the client monitor. (Due to system limitations, this setting may produce a frozen frame on the client when trimming both sides.)

The Watch Point

When several transitions are selected for trimming, you can choose to watch and listen at any one of them. This feature can make trimming far more precise and controllable. When an overlap cut is trimmed, for example, you can choose to observe the adjustment at either the video or audio cut point. Move the position indicator by *single-clicking an existing roller*. You'll then be watching and listening to that cut and trimming the others an equal amount to preserve sync. You can trim audio while dragging video along, or you can trim video while dragging audio along. Either way, you'll see and hear what's happening at the position indicator.

In the following diagram, picture and sound will be trimmed together, but the picture cut will be monitored.

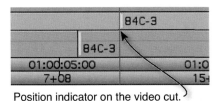

Position indicator on the video cut.

A single click on the audio roller will move the watch point. Both transitions will still be trimmed together, but you'll hear (and see) the audio edit, instead.

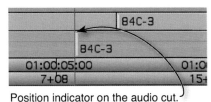

Position indicator on the audio cut.

Summary of Trim Selection Tips

These are the basic rules for selecting and managing rollers.

- Lasso or use a Smart Tool to get into Trim Mode and select rollers.
- Click in the Ruler or a timecode track to exit.
- To trim the A, center, or B side, click in the timeline or on the video images, or use the Cycle Trim Sides button.
- Add more rollers by Shift-clicking or Shift-lassoing.
- Delete rollers by Shift-clicking.
- Single-click an existing roller to move the blue bar and change the watch point.
- Position the mouse cursor over a video image without clicking to move the Trim Light.

Asymmetrical Trimming

So far, we've trimmed all selected tracks in the same direction. But it's also possible to trim in two directions at once. To create such an asymmetrical trim, simply select the rollers you need. Then position the blue bar on the cut you want to observe, and use any trim method you like to make your adjustment: the three-button player, the trim buttons, cut on the fly, etc. Each roller moves in an appropriate direction to keep your sequence in sync. Trimming like this becomes more and more important as you build up multi-track sequences, because it allows you to make complex adjustments in a single step.

In the following example, we'll trim the B side of the video and production audio, while trimming filler at the head of the music in the opposite direction.

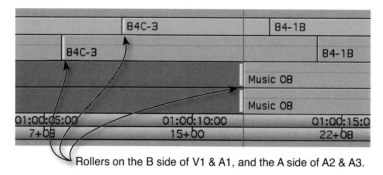

Rollers on the B side of V1 & A1, and the A side of A2 & A3.

Trim using all the usual methods. When you drag or use the three-button player, MC indicates the direction each transition will move with grey trim indicators.

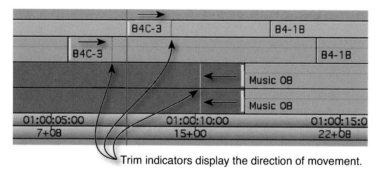

Trim indicators display the direction of movement.

Slip & Slide

Slip lengthens the head of a clip and simultaneously shortens its tail by an equal amount (or vice versa). Slide shortens the tail of the preceding shot and lengthens the head of the following shot (or vice versa), without affecting the current clip.

You can slip or slide by simply clicking on transitions and selecting appropriate rollers. Or you can use one of several shortcuts. Get into Trim Mode any way you like. Then, simply double-click a roller to slip the clip it's on, or right-click the roller and choose Select Slip Trim. With a Trim Smart Tool activated, you don't even have to be in Trim Mode. Just double-click near any transition. Rollers appear at the ends of the clip, ready for slipping.

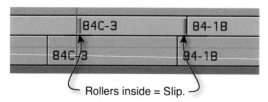

Rollers inside = Slip.

To slide a clip, double-click a roller again (ie. double-click twice) or right-click a roller and choose Select Slide Trim. Rollers appear outside the clip, ready for sliding.

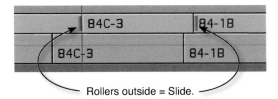

Rollers outside = Slide.

You can also slip and slide clips by lassoing. First, make sure no timeline clips are selected. Then lasso (or option-lasso) a clip from right to left to slip it; Shift-Option-lasso from right to left to slide it. Note that any time you have two rollers in the same track, they're displayed in purple.

Regardless of how you set up the slip or slide, the Composer window changes to display four frames. This is the same display you see when dragging a clip in the timeline: the A and B sides of each of the two cuts you're working on.

A and B sides of first cut.   A and B sides of second cut.

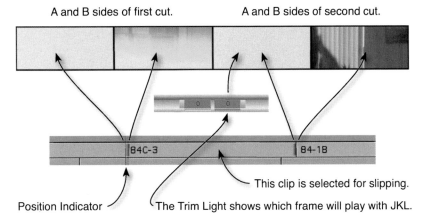

This clip is selected for slipping.

Position Indicator   The Trim Light shows which frame will play with JKL.

You can slip or slide the cut using all the usual trim techniques. If you use JKL, one of the small images will play. To select it, hover your mouse cursor over the appropriate video image; the trim light will display your selection. Note that in this case, the location of the blue bar does not determine the frame that will be played. In the illustration above, for example, the position indicator is at the head of the selected clip, but the trim light shows that the tail of the clip will be played, instead.

Trim Two Heads or Two Tails

There are times when you want to select two head frames, or two tail frames, trim one and adjust the other in the opposite direction to maintain sync. In the past the system couldn't handle this condition; you had to do it in two steps. But now this kind of trim works correctly. You can select two head frames or two tail frames and trim away. The spot where your blue bar is parked will be trimmed and the other head or tail frame will be adjusted appropriately to maintain sync.

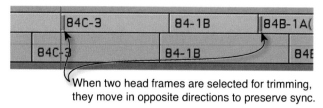

When two head frames are selected for trimming,
they move in opposite directions to preserve sync.

Restore Previous Trim

As you add tracks to your sequences, you'll set up increasingly complex roller combinations to trim them. Sometimes you'll trim something, drop out of Trim Mode to check a cut in context, and then want to return to the trim to make an adjustment. You can restore your most recent trim by holding down the Option key while hitting the Trim Mode button. Your trim comes back just as you left it, with all rollers selected and trim counters showing the amount you trimmed.

To put this function on the keyboard, drag the Trim Mode button from the Command Palette to your Keyboard Settings. Then drag the Add Option Key button on top of the Trim Mode button, adding a small dot to it. When you hit that button, you're hitting Option-Trim.

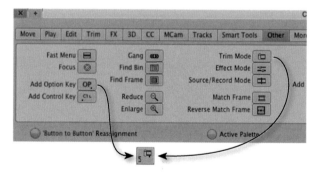

Slip, Trim or Nudge

The trim buttons can be used not only to trim, but also to slip or nudge, depending on context. With the Lift/Overwrite (red) Segment Tool active and with a clip or clips selected, they will nudge the clips, moving them forward or backward in time, as if you were dragging them.

In Source/Record Mode with no clips selected, they will slip the clips under the position indicator in all selected tracks, adding material to the head and removing it from the tail, or vice versa. But note well: *there will be no visual indication of this change.* You can easily alter your sequence this way without knowing it. If you have picture and sound selected you won't even see a sync break.

Extend

The Extend function allows you to quickly lengthen a clip, performing the equivalent of a dual-roller trim, but without entering Trim Mode. Add a single mark in the timeline, select tracks and hit Extend to move the cut nearest the mark, to the mark. If you have two marks in the timeline, Extend will use the mark in. You'll find Extend in the Trim tab of the Command Palette.

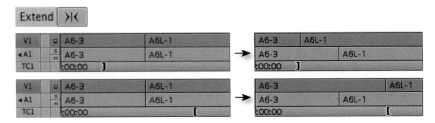

Changing the Trim Loop

By default, the trim loop time is set to four seconds. You can change this in Trim Settings or via the second row of buttons in Trim Mode (see "Play Loop" on page 18). But sometimes you need to temporarily get a longer run at a cut to evaluate it. To do that, just change a single roller. This will fool Trim Mode into playing more of your timeline than it would otherwise. Here's a typical asymmetrical trim:

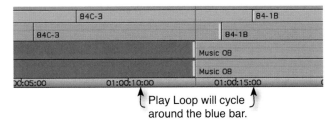

If you want to see the entire previous shot play prior to the cut you've been adjusting, add one roller, by Shift-clicking on an earlier picture cut.

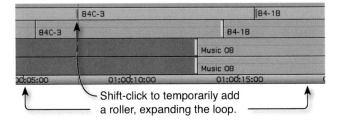

Now the loop plays from before the first picture roller to after the second. When you've seen what you need, deselect the first roller by Shift-clicking it, and you're ready to make additional changes.

Suppress Trim Sides

When you're looping an edit, you'll sometimes hear a short extraneous sound near the cut point. To get rid of it, you have to know which side of the transition it's coming from. You can determine this by temporarily suppressing playback of one side or the other. While the loop is playing, tap the Go To Mark In button (normally the Q key) to loop only the A side; tap the Go to Mark Out button (normally W) to loop only the B side. In either case, the play button under the record monitor will change to indicate the portion of the cut that's playing. Hit Go to In or Go to Out again to return to normal loop play.

The Play button during   Looping the A side.   Looping the B side.
normal loop play.

Dissolves in Trim Mode

One of the easiest ways to create a dissolve is to use Trim Mode.

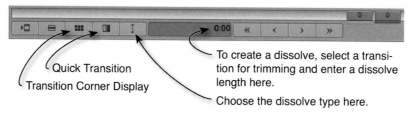

Quick Transition

Transition Corner Display

To create a dissolve, select a transition for trimming and enter a dissolve length here.

Choose the dissolve type here.

Enter Trim Mode on the cut where you want your effect. Then type a length in the field shown above and hit the Return key to create a centered dissolve. If you prefer, open the dissolve type menu and select Ending at Cut, Starting at Cut or Custom Start. (You can make several types of dissolves this way. See "Film Dissolves and Fades" on page 193.)

Transition Corners

To get a better look at the elements of a transition effect, you can display the start, center and end frames for both sides of the effect simultaneously. Enter Trim Mode, create a dissolve or other transition effect, and hit the Transition Corner Display button.

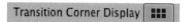

The Composer window changes to display six images.

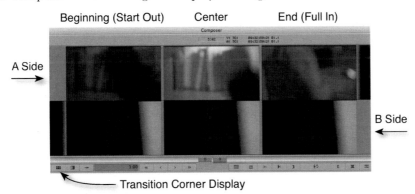

You can trim with the trim buttons, the three button player, or numerically, and the corner frames will update appropriately. Click on the video images to move your rollers from one side of the cut to the other.

In Version 5, Transition Corner Display also allowed you to change the length of a dissolve by dragging. With corners on, position your mouse over a dissolve in the timeline. The cursor will change to look like a cut piece of film. Click and drag to adjust the effect. In later versions, you can do this using the Transition Tool (see page 31).

Trimming Keyframes

Visual Effects

When you trim a visual effect, its keyframes normally move, scaling their temporal positions relative to the amount of the trim. This is often the wrong behavior and forces you to note the position of each keyframe before the trim and then laboriously move each one back where it belongs afterwards. One workaround, if you're making the effect shorter, is to mark the section you want to delete in Source/Record mode and then Extract or Lift rather than trim. That will leave your keyframes where they were and simply delete a portion of the shot, along with its keyframes.

Better yet, you can use the Effect Editor to specify whether your keyframes are Elastic or Fixed. Elastic keyframes move in Trim Mode. Fixed keyframes don't. (See page 181.)

Audio

When you trim away a portion of a clip containing audio keyframes, you don't actually remove them—they remain active on the clip's handles. If you restore the clip to its original length they will come back. This can be helpful in some situations, but the hidden keyframes can also make it harder to set levels on the portion of the clip you're using. (See "Trimming Keyframes" on page 152 for details.)

8   Sync

Sync Breaks

Several features are available to help keep you in sync, the most fundamental of which
is the display of Sync Breaks in the timeline. When synchronized video and audio clips
are edited out of synchronization, each displays the error numerically, along with a white
line indicating the duration of the out-of-sync material. Use the timeline Fast Menu to
turn sync breaks on and off. Note that the numbering format follows the format used in
the top tracking value above the record monitor. If you display timecode, you'll see sync
breaks as total frames. If you display footage or key numbers (in a 35mm film project)
you'll see breaks as feet and frames.

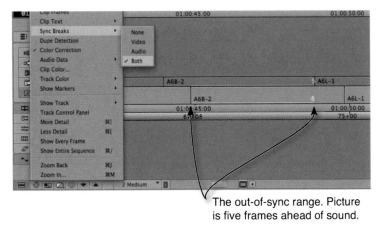

The out-of-sync range. Picture
is five frames ahead of sound.

AutoSync

AutoSync allows you to merge separate video and audio clips into synchronized subclips that behave as if they had been captured together. It's primarily used for syncing dailies.

Capture or import the video and audio clips that you want to synchronize and determine the way you want the system to synchronize them: either with matching timecode or by aligning marks. If you're using marks, play the clips and mark in at the slates. Put the clips in the same bin, select them, and choose Bin > AutoSync.

In the window that opens, select your syncing method: either marks or a variety of time-code formats. Choose the audio tracks you want to include on the synchronized clips. If your video clip contains scratch audio, you can choose to exclude it. Click OK and a new merged subclip will appear in your bin.

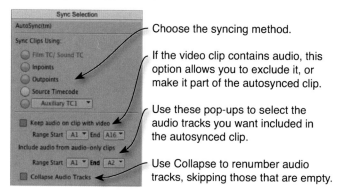

If you're syncing by timecode, you can sync a bin full of clips in a single step, by selecting them all and choosing Autosync. The system batch syncs anything with matching timecode. Note that when video and audio are of unequal lengths, the synced clip will be truncated to the length of the overlap.

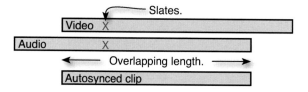

AutoSync can also be used to turn a sequence into a subclip. Cut your video and audio source clips into a sequence, and edit or slip each element until the sequence is in sync, making sure it contains only one clip in each track, with no internal cuts. Then select the sequence in a bin and choose Bin > AutoSync. Your sequence is converted into a subclip.

Slip by Perfs

Timecode-based syncing is quick, but it typically relies on two clocks, one for picture and one for sound. If the clocks aren't synchronized properly, sync can drift during the course of a shooting day. Avid's Slip Left 1 Perf and Slip Right 1 Perf buttons allow you to fix such problems with 1/4 frame accuracy. The feature is only available if you select the Film option when you create your project and choose 35mm 4-perf as the film type. The button names refer to the perforations in 35 mm film: there are four in every frame.

Perf slip only works on subclips, so if your problem clip is a master clip you'll have to subclip it. Mark in a few frames after the head of the clip, mark out a few frames before the tail and create a subclip (see "Subclips" on page 124).

Load the subclip into your source monitor, cue it to a slate or sync point, display the source timeline (zoom it in substantially) and show waveforms. Then hit one of the perf slip buttons. The waveform will shift one-quarter of a frame to the left or right, depending on which button you use. Continue clicking the perf slip buttons until the clip is in sync.

You may find it helpful to show frame images in the timeline. From the timeline Fast Menu select Show Track > Film. Then select Show Every Frame. Frame images will display at the top of the timeline.

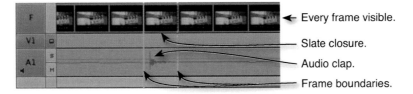

← Every frame visible.
— Slate closure.
— Audio clap.
— Frame boundaries.

Note that you can only slip to the end of the underlying media. That's why it's helpful to create a subclip that's shorter than your master clip. If you need to slip audio two frames to the tail, for example, you'll need to make a subclip that's two frames shorter than the master clip at the head. To see how many perfs a clip has been slipped, display the Slip column in the bin containing it.

Name	Start	Slip	Tracks	Audio S
84-1B	13:16:22:28	-2	V1 A1	48000
848-1B	13:19:09:28	-1	V1 A1	48000
84-3A	13:01:57:23	-2	V1 A1	48000
84-3B	13:17:42:23	-3	V1 A1	48000

The film option creates a couple of limitations. If you edit a subclip into a sequence, you won't be able to trim the sequence clip beyond the edge of the source subclip. And you won't be able to change a master clip's source tape name after the clip is created.

Sync Locks

When you're working with sequences containing many tracks, keeping everything in sync is a constant concern. Avid's Sync Lock feature can help by allowing you to lock tracks together for trimming. Many people leave them engaged at all times. To turn them on, click in the space next to a record-side track selector. If you then trim a track that has its sync lock activated, the system will attempt to trim all other sync-locked tracks equally to maintain sync. If that isn't possible you'll hear a beep. To activate all locks, click the sync lock area in a timecode track.

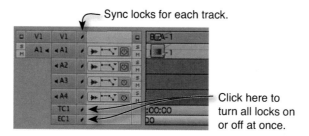

Sync locks for each track.

Click here to turn all locks on or off at once.

Sync locks are particularly helpful when you're trimming tracks containing a lot of filler, because they allow you to ignore any track that contains filler at the position indicator. There's no need to create edits in filler and put rollers on them. And there's no need to get rid of those edits later.

You can go from the image below to the one following it in a single step. Even though trim rollers are only on V1 and A1, everything stays in sync, and all downstream clips move forward.

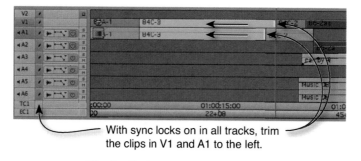

With sync locks on in all tracks, trim the clips in V1 and A1 to the left.

Clips in all other tracks move, as well, even though they're not selected for trimming.

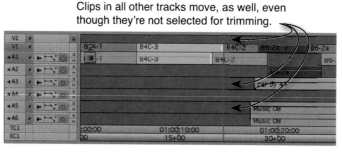

In some cases, the position indicator doesn't necessarily need to be parked over filler for sync locks to work. Nearby filler will be trimmed, if necessary. But it's not always clear what's going to happen, so it's probably better to add rollers in any track or tracks that don't contain filler at the position indicator.

Sync locks also allow you to extract a chunk of material in all tracks without having to turn them all on—all you need to do is enable a single track. When you extract a clip in a track whose sync lock is on, you'll pull material out of all other locked tracks simultaneously.

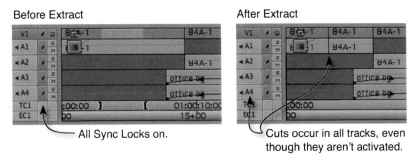

All Sync Locks on.

Cuts occur in all tracks, even though they aren't activated.

Note that Sync Locks are remembered separately for each sequence, so you'll need to turn them on in every new sequence you create.

Sync Locks in Segment Mode

In general, sync locks don't protect you when you're moving material with a segment tool. So you need to be careful about sync when dragging clips around. A setting can help—but it's quirky. It's in Timeline Settings, under the Edit tab: Segment Drag Sync Locks.

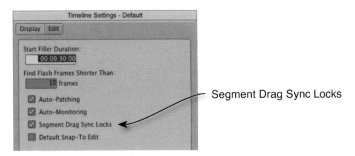

Segment Drag Sync Locks

It will help keep you in sync when you drag clips using Extract/Splice In—the yellow segment tool. (It has no effect on Lift/Overwrite.) This can be useful in certain situations. If you need to rearrange a series of overlapped video and audio clips, for example, you'll be able to do so without chopping everything up—black will be inserted as needed. But in other cases Segment Drag Sync Locks can create surprising behavior. If you rearrange picture clips alone, for example, you'll end up recutting any audio beneath them, even though you didn't select it.

Leaders

If you're working on a multi-track sequence, you may find it useful to create a tail leader and cut it into all your tracks. Then, after making a complicated change, you can jump to the tail of the sequence and zoom in. If you're in sync, all tracks will line up. If you made a mistake, you can measure the offset and figure out what happened.

Editors working in a film environment will want to use standard head and tail academy leaders for this purpose. One point is worth noting: for perfect sync, cut a one-frame sound pop out of ordinary tone. Don't rely on a digitized pre-synchronized pop. It won't be as accurate as one you cut.

You may also want to create your leaders as sequences and then autosync them. When you're out of sync, you'll see a see a sync break on the leader, instantly telling you how far out of sync you are. To do this, cut picture leader into an empty sequence. Then cut a one-frame piece of tone against the video sync mark. Mix down the audio so you have a continuous piece of audio media, with the pop in the correct position (select Special > Audio Mixdown). Then cut this mixed-down audio into every track you expect to use, creating a sequence with the pop at the right position, but without internal cuts. Finally, select the sequence in the bin and choose Bin > AutoSync. Your sequence turns into a subclip. Attach it to the end of your cut sequences. Because it was autosynced, when you're out of sync, the leader will display a sync break.

Note that standard head and tail leaders are symmetrical: there are exactly 2 feet and 15 frames of black *between* the pop and the start or end of your program (not including the pop or the first or last frame of picture).

All Tracks In Sync

Waveforms display a pop in all tracks. ⌐

Out of Sync

A5 and A6 display a sync break of 4 frames. ⌐

Markers as Sync Indicators

It's not possible to display sync breaks for material like music or sound effects that you edit into sync in the timeline. But you can use markers to help keep things lined up.

Edit until you're satisfied with the sync of your extra tracks. Then select V1 and add a marker. Deselect V1, select your audio track, and add another marker. You've now got a sync indicator. Click on the marker and add any text you like. If the clip goes out of sync you can fix it by aligning the markers.

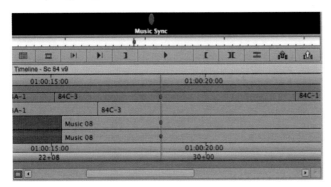

Note that once several markers are lined up this way, you only have direct access to the top one. And using the Delete key, you can only delete markers in order, from top to bottom. To change to a stacked marker in a lower track you'll have to throw the sequence out of sync first, or use the Markers window (see "Markers" on page 62).

Keeping a Client Monitor in Sync

If you use a high definition television as a client monitor, you may have noticed that video and audio appear out of sync on the TV. Most consumer-level sets introduce a video delay—the time it takes the TV's video hardware to do it's job. If you run audio through the TV you won't see the problem—the TV delays audio to match video. But in an editing room, audio is typically coming from Media Composer and isn't delayed.

One solution is to use the Desktop Play Delay setting. (Prior to Version 6, it was in Video Display settings.) Just select an offset: audio will be delayed by the number of frames you enter. You'll have to experiment to get it right: one or two frames usually works.

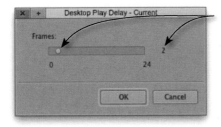

Set the play delay to zero for perfect sync in the Composer window. Experiment with other settings for sync on a client monitor.

Note that when working this way you can't be in sync on both the Composer window and the big screen simultaneously. You'll have to choose: no delay for perfect sync on the Composer, or your preferred offset for perfect sync on the client monitor. Also note that this feature can cause video to jump when you press play or stop, by the number of frames you've selected.

9 Groups

A group is a clip that's made up of other clips, locked together in sync, as if they were in a synchronizer. You select your cameras, mark them at an equivalent spot, and create a new clip: the group. You can then load the group into the source monitor, play it, and at any point, stop and switch to the equivalent position in another element of the group. You can also cut the group into a sequence just like any other clip. Once your group has been inserted, you'll be able to switch a particular clip from one camera to another, without changing your sequence in any other way.

Overview

You'll typically have dailies that include several cameras, all covering the same action. Identify the clips you want to group, and begin by telling the software how to line them up. You can do this with head marks, tail marks or a variety of common timecodes. To use head marks, find a common sync point and mark in at that point in each camera. Then select all the cameras and choose Group Clips from the Bin menu. You'll see the following dialog box:

Select Inpoints and hit okay. A new clip will be created, named with the suffix ".Grp.01". You can rename this to anything you like.

Put the group into the source monitor. Play it, as needed. Then hit the cursor down arrow on your keyboard to switch to another camera. Each additional key press takes you to another camera in the group. Use the up arrow to cycle through the cameras in reverse order.

Previous in Group.

Next in Group.

Cut the group into a sequence. Then, in the timeline, park the position indicator over the group and hit the down or up arrow. The sequence clip will switch to display another camera. You may want to reassign the group buttons, especially if you use the cursor arrow keys for other things. They make it easy to change cameras in a group, but also make it easy to unintentionally recut your sequence.

Editing Group Clips

Once you've cut a group into your sequence you can use Add Edit to cut it up into sections and change the camera in each section. This is particularly useful when cutting material that was shot to playback. Since everything syncs to the same music track, you can often combine all the cameras and takes and build a group clip that contains the coverage for the whole scene.

Put the group in the source monitor. Mark in at the head of the scene and mark out at the tail. Cut the group into a sequence for this entire duration.

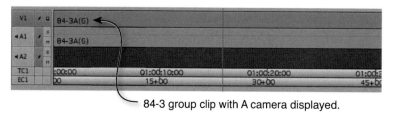

84-3 group clip with A camera displayed.

Then play through the group. When you want to cut to one of the other cameras, press stop. Add an edit in picture at that point.

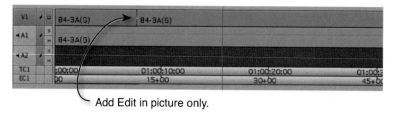

Add Edit in picture only.

Now position the blue cursor after the add edit and tap the up or down cursor arrow.

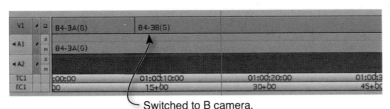

Switched to B camera.

The shot you're parked on will switch to the next camera. Hit the up or down arrow again until you find the camera you're looking for. Continue adding edits and switching cameras until the scene is cut. You can go back at any time and trim up the cuts you've made, using all the usual techniques.

Note how the system creates clip names for groups. It tells you which camera you are looking at, using the clip name from the original clip. But it adds a 'G' in parentheses after the name to indicate that you've actually got the group there and can switch cameras if you choose.

Also notice that hitting the up/down arrow keys doesn't switch the sound, only the picture. In most cases, this is what you want, because the sound is the same for all cameras. But if you prefer, you can switch audio, or jump from one camera to another, by right-clicking a clip in the timeline and making a choice from the resulting contextual menu. You can also use the Group menu in the Composer window.

The Group Menu

Go into Composer settings and make sure Second Row of Info is selected. This makes room for the Group Clip Menu icon. Whenever you're parked on a group its icon will be displayed.

The Group Clip Menu over the source monitor.

Click on the icon to see a list of all the takes in the group; select from the list to switch between them. You can switch sound or picture independently and jump directly from one camera to another.

You can also select Audio Follow Video. Then, every time you swap video (using the menu or arrow keys), audio will be swapped along with it. The group icon will turn green to indicate that you're in this mode.

Using Add Edit Live

When you're editing to music, it's sometimes useful to make several cuts on the fly while music is playing. In a film cutting room this was once done by tapping a grease pencil on the film while it was moving through the Moviola. You can do much the same thing digitally by assigning the Add Edit button to the keyboard. Tapping this button won't stop video playback, so you can hit it as many times as necessary while your material continues to play. When you press stop, all your edits will appear. You can then go back through your sequence, swap the individual cuts and trim them up.

Tap Add Edit from the keyboard while
video plays. Cuts appear when you stop.

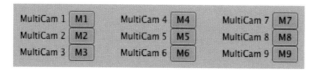

The Multi-Camera Buttons

You can also edit live using the multi-cam buttons. They're available on the Command Palette in the MCam tab. Assign them to the keys of your choice. Then press play. When you want to cut to a specific camera, simply hit the appropriate button. Video will continue to play, your sequence will be cut and the material following the cut will be swapped to the camera you chose. When you press stop the timeline will update and your edits will appear.

MultiCam 1	M1	MultiCam 4	M4	MultiCam 7	M7
MultiCam 2	M2	MultiCam 5	M5	MultiCam 8	M8
MultiCam 3	M3	MultiCam 6	M6	MultiCam 9	M9

Groups in the Source Monitor

To display the first four cameras of a group simultaneously in the source monitor, simply load the clip and click the Quad Split button (you may need to assign it to a button under the monitor). The group will then display as four frames. If you've got more than four cameras, use the Nine Split button.

Press play and all cameras will play together, allowing you to clearly see what's happening in each. A green line under one of the cameras indicates that it is selected. When you edit the group into your sequence, that camera will be displayed. To select another camera, simply click it before making your cut. In all other ways, the group will behave as before. Non-grouped clips display normally—you don't have to deselect Quad or Nine Split to play an ordinary clip.

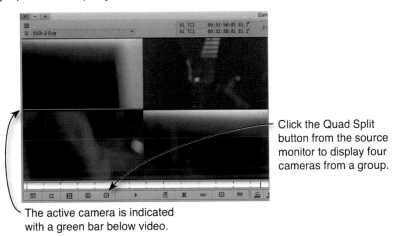

Click the Quad Split button from the source monitor to display four cameras from a group.

The active camera is indicated with a green bar below video.

If your group contains more cameras than can be displayed in the split, use the Swap Camera Bank button to switch from one bank of cameras to the next.

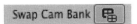

Multi-Camera Mode

Avid also offers what's called Multi-Camera Mode, designed for cutting sitcoms or music videos. To use it, click the Quad or Nine Split button from the *record* monitor, or select Multi-Camera Mode from the Special Menu.

Your screen will change to look like this:

Click the Quad Split button from the record monitor to enter Multi-Camera Mode.

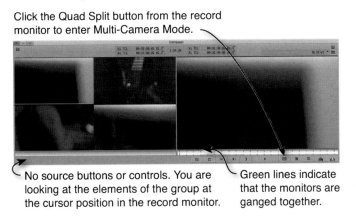

No source buttons or controls. You are looking at the elements of the group at the cursor position in the record monitor.

Green lines indicate that the monitors are ganged together.

The display seems to look the same—with a multi-cam split in the source monitor. But your source-side play controls and other buttons have disappeared. If you press play, the source and record monitors play together as if they were ganged. (A green underline beneath the monitors makes this clear.) The sequence plays in the record monitor and the source of each cut is cued and played in the source monitor.

Start by editing a group into your sequence, for the entire length you expect to use it, regardless of camera choice. Then enter Multi-Camera Mode and play through it. The group will be displayed in the source monitor with all cameras playing. If you press stop and click on one of the source images, you'll put a cut in your sequence and simultaneously switch the material that follows the cut to the camera you clicked on. To switch cameras without adding a cut, Option-click the image. Continue playing and switching cameras until you've cut your entire scene or clip. You can then go back to any cut and trim it up normally.

It's even more intuitive to do this from the keyboard. This allows you to cut groups live while video is playing and watch your cut sequence update dynamically in the record monitor. You can use the M1 through M9 buttons for this, or, if you have one, you can use a numeric keypad. For a Nine Split use all nine number keys. For a Quad Split use 4, 5, 7 and 8. Note that you can use the M1 through M9 buttons when video is paused, but you can use the numeric keypad only while video is playing.

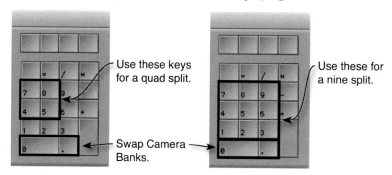

Tap the key that corresponds to the camera's visual position on screen. In a quad split, for example, the 7 key will activate the camera at the top left, the 8 key will activate the camera at the top right, and so on.

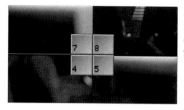

Keys are assigned based on the camera's visual position in the split.

To exit Multi-Camera mode, click the Quad or Nine Split button again or re-select Multi-Camera Mode from the Special menu.

Changing Displayed Cameras

In any multi-camera situation, hold down the Command key to temporarily display clip names over the bottom of the quad or nine split video. Then, with the Command key held down, click on a clip name to pop open a menu of all the clips in the group. Select from this menu to display other cameras or rearrange the split.

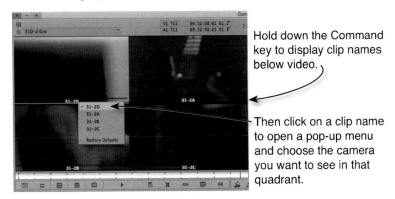

Hold down the Command key to display clip names below video.

Then click on a clip name to open a pop-up menu and choose the camera you want to see in that quadrant.

In Multi-Cam mode you'll see an additional option, allowing you to display the cut sequence in the split, as well. Simply select Sequence from the pop-up menu.

Removing Group Clips

In certain finishing environments, it can sometimes be helpful to remove all group clips from a completed sequence and replace them with the clips that are actually visible in the timeline. To do this, simply right-click the sequence in its bin and choose Commit Multi-Cam Edits. You'll see a warning telling you that all references to the groups will be eliminated. Click Okay, and a copy of the sequence will be generated, labeled with the suffix "NoGroups.Copy.01". All group clips in all tracks (video and audio) will be replaced with the clips actually used. If you made a group from subclips, you'll get the subclip in the timeline. If you made it from a master clip, you'll get the master clip.

10   Bins

How Bin Data is Stored

Media Composer stores a project as a series of separate bin files, rather than as a single unified database. Each bin contains all the numerical data for every clip in the bin (all its metadata), as well as data from every clip used in sequences in the bin. In fact, every bin contains hidden copies of all the source clips used by all the sequences within it, referred to as Reference Clips. You can display them by selecting Set Bin Display from a bin's Fast Menu.

To reveal clips that are used by sequences in a bin, select Set Bin Display from the bin's Fast Menu.

Then click Show Reference Clips.

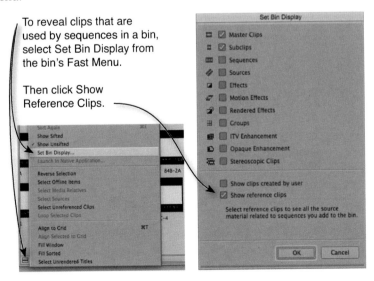

This distributed structure makes it easy to move bins from one system to another and allows several editors to share a project using Avid's Unity server. But it can sometimes present problems. Say you store your master clips in a bin for source clips, and you cut those clips into sequences stored in sequence bins. When you change the name of a master clip, how does that change get propagated to the sequences? The answer is that the master clip bin and sequence bin must be "exposed" to each other—they must be opened at the same time (or during the same editing session).

If you're having trouble with data not propagating correctly, try opening all the bins in question simultaneously. In rare cases you may need to reenter the changed data. Then, be sure you save all bins before closing them.

Bin Management

Folders

To keep your project organized you'll probably want to put your bins into folders. Create a folder using the Fast Menu in the Bins tab of the Project window. Then drag bins into it, as needed. The folder structure in the Project window reflects the structure on disk.

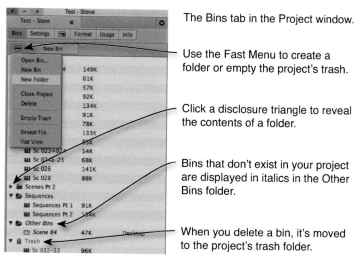

The Bins tab in the Project window.

Use the Fast Menu to create a folder or empty the project's trash.

Click a disclosure triangle to reveal the contents of a folder.

Bins that don't exist in your project are displayed in italics in the Other Bins folder.

When you delete a bin, it's moved to the project's trash folder.

Renaming

To rename a bin, simply click the bin name in the Project window and begin typing. Press Return when you're finished. The new name appears on the bin, in the Project window and in the Mac Finder as well.

Deleting

To delete a bin from your project, select it in the Project window and hit the Delete key. Media Composer automatically creates a Trash folder and transfers the bin to it. But it doesn't delete the bin from your project. If you really want to erase it, select Empty Trash from the Fast Menu.

Bins Outside Your Project

You'll normally work with bins that are stored in your project folder and listed in the Bins tab. But you can open bins that exist anywhere on disk: in other projects or even on the desktop. The system will automatically put such bins in a folder called Other Bins and will display their names in italics along with their location. When you delete such a bin it disappears from your project, but it remains on disk in the original location.

Tabs

Bins and many tools now contain tab bars, allowing you to manage them inside a single frame. To dock one window to another, click on the tab of the window you want to move and drag it anywhere over another window. A colored outline appears around the desti-nation window; when you release the mouse, the window you're moving turns into a tab inside the destination frame.

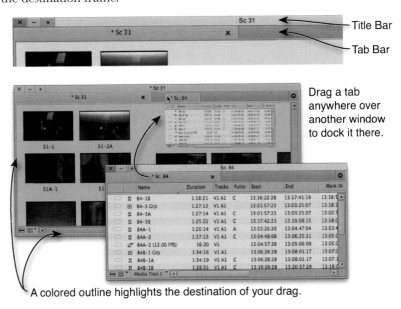

Both bins are then available inside the same frame. Click the tab to switch between them. Drag tabs left/right to change their order. When many bins are tabbed together, it can be easier to switch between them using the Tab Menu.

Drag a tab out of a bin and onto an open area of the interface to detach it and open it as a separate window. The cursor changes into a white circle, indicating that you aren't tabbing it somewhere else. To close a tab, click the X icon in the tab bar.

Drag a tab away from the tab bar to release it.

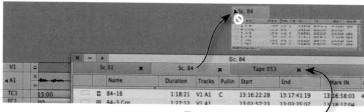

To close a tab, click the X.

To move a clip from one tab to another, click on the clip's icon and drag it to the destination tab. The window switches to display that bin. Release the mouse button to move the clip. To quickly open one or more bins in tabs, simply drag them from the Project window to an open bin.

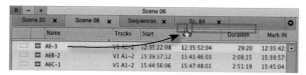

To move a clip from one tabbed bin to another, drag the clip to the tab.

You can also tab tools together, organizing those you use frequently into a single window. Here, the Markers window has been tabbed to the Effect Palette.

#	Name	TC	Track	Comment
0001	● Steve	01:00:07:21	V1	
0002	O Steve	01:00:10:10	V1	

To memorize a group of bins along with their positions and tab arrangements, create a Bin Layout (see page 262).

Clip Selection

In Version 5, the modifier keys for clip selection in bins were changed. To select a clip, simply click on it. To select a series of clips, click the first one and Shift-click the last one (or lasso them). To select (or deselect) several discontinuous clips, click the first one and Command-click the others.

Sort and Sift

To sort the contents of a bin in text view, simply double-click the heading of the column you want to sort by. To sort in reverse order, double-click again. Or click the heading and choose Bin > Sort (Command-E). Add the Option key to sort in reverse order. You can also right-click a heading and select one of the sort options from there. To sort on several columns at once, drag the columns into the order in which you want them sorted, select them all, and then sort. To repeat the last sort, deselect all columns by Shift-clicking their headings and then select Bin > Sort Again.

Right-click on a column heading to sort the bin based on the contents of that column.

To find text in a bin, use the Custom Sift command, available in the Bin menu or in the bin's Fast Menu. Enter a match criterion (contains, begins with, etc.), the text you're looking for and the column you want searched. When you hit Okay, the items that meet your criteria will be shown. To reveal all clips again, select Bin > Show Unsifted. You can also use the Find command to search either the currently active bin or all bins in your project (see page 63).

Script View

You can look at your clips in several ways, selected via the menu at the bottom of every bin. Text View displays clips as rows of data. Frame View displays them as clip frames. Script View is a third way of looking at bin information that many editors aren't familiar with. It allows you to add comments to clips and view the comments along with the clip frames. (It's misnamed and has little to do with shooting scripts.)

The same bin, displayed in Frame, Text and Script views.

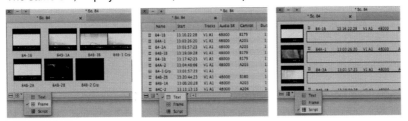

You can easily switch back and forth from Frame View to Script View without losing track of the clip you're working on. Simply select the clip before switching views. The bin will always switch views with the selected clip visible.

Clip Order

Text View won't allow you to arrange clips into anything other than alphabetical or numerical order. But Script View is different—you can simply drag your clips into any order you like. A wavy line moves as you drag, to show you where you're going.

Because Text View mimics the display order set up in Script View, you can use the two views together to create any order you like. Put your bin in Script View, rearrange your clips and then switch back to Text View. The order is preserved.

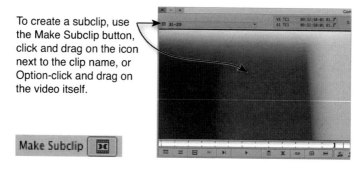

Drag clip frames vertically to change their order. The new order will remain when you return to Text View.

Enter comments here. Numerical information is displayed above the text.

Clip Frames

There are several ways to change the frame used to identify a clip in Frame or Script View. You can click on the clip in the bin containing it and simply use the three-button player to play through it from there. The frame you stop on is the frame that will be displayed. You can also use the Step Forward/Back buttons. Step Forward 8/10 frames is particularly helpful. Just hold it down to move through your material at high speed. Or you can load your clip into the source or record monitor and choose your frame directly. Stop on the frame you want and hit Mark In. Then click on the clip *in the bin* and hit Go To Mark In. The clip frame jumps to the mark.

Subclips

Subclips represent portions of master clips, and for most purposes, can be edited using the same techniques. To create a subclip, load a clip into the source monitor, mark in and out, select tracks, and then hit the Make Subclip button. Your subclip appears in the last selected bin. You can also do this in the record monitor. In that case, you'll create a subsequence—a new sequence containing the marked material. You can also click on the icon next to the clip name above the source or record monitor and drag to a bin to create a subclip there. Or you can Option-click and drag from the video image itself.

To create a subclip, use the Make Subclip button, click and drag on the icon next to the clip name, or Option-click and drag on the video itself.

Make Subclip

Clones and Copies

Simply drag a clip from one bin to another to move it. Hold down the Option key while dragging to copy the clip instead. But note that if you Option-drag a master clip or subclip from one bin to another you are creating a clone of the original clip. If you make changes to either clip, the original or the copy, both will be affected. They are really the same clip—living in different bins. This is different from what happens when you Option-drag a sequence. In that case, a brand new sequence is created, which is not tied to the original.

If you want to make an independent copy of a master clip or subclip, duplicate the clip using Command-D. Then drag the copy to its new destination. To make the difference clear, the system adds the suffix 'Copy.01' to independent copies. It adds no suffix to clones.

Bin Columns

Bins carry dozens of columns of metadata for your clips, but only selected columns are displayed. To change displayed columns open the bin's Fast Menu and select Choose Columns. Or you can right-click anywhere in the bin heading and do the same thing. To quickly hide a column, right click the heading and select Hide Column. To move columns, simply drag them.

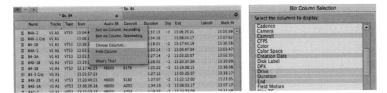

To create a custom column, move your mouse cursor over an empty space in the bin's heading area. It will turn into a text cursor. Click and type to create a column and name it. To edit a custom heading, Option-click it and make your changes.

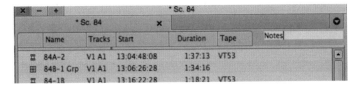

In custom columns you can automatically reenter text. Option-click a cell to open a pop-up list of previous entries in that field. Select an item to automatically enter it.

Horizontal Scrolling

When you scroll a bin horizontally, the clip name will normally remain on screen, allowing you to identify the column data that goes with that clip. But you can choose to hold other columns in place, as well. Simply drag the column divider, a small black square visible under the title bar, to any location you like. Columns to the right of the divider will move when you scroll horizontally. Columns to the left, won't.

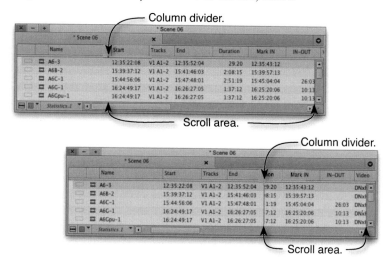

Custom Text Views

If you always like to see a certain column arrangement in your bins, you can memorize it as a view. Set the bin up the way you like it, open the Custom View menu at the bottom left of the bin, chose Save As, and enter a name for your view.

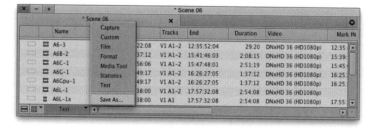

Bin views work like timeline views (page 49). To replace a view, Option-click the menu. To change the name of a view, edit it in the Settings tab of the Project window.

Copying Columns

You can copy and paste entire columns of timecode or text.

1. Select the column you wish to copy from by clicking on its heading.
2. Select Edit > Duplicate (Command-D).
3. A dialog box opens allowing you to specify the column to copy to.
4. Enter a column name and click Okay. The column's contents are overwritten.

To avoid data corruption, only certain columns are legal for this operation.

Entering Text for Several Clips at Once

Suppose you want to enter the same text in a certain column for an entire group of clips. You can do that in a single step. Select the clips, then right-click in any one of them, within the field you want to change. If data entry on multiple clips is permitted in that column, the resulting contextual menu will include the choice, "Set [column name] column for selected clips." Choose that item from the menu and another window will open where you can enter your text. Whatever you type will be entered into that column for all selected clips.

Clip Info Window

To quickly reveal all the metadata logged for a clip in a bin, simply click on it and select File > Get Info (Command-I). You can also right-click the clip and select Get Info. If the clip is loaded into a monitor, either right-click the monitor and select Get Info or hit Command-I. All these techniques will display the fields that actually contain information. To show all fields, including blank ones, use Command-Control-I, instead.

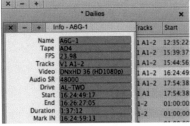

Hit Command-I to display clip information. Add the Control key to show all fields, including empty ones.

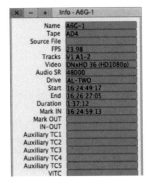

Options for the Save Command

The system will automatically save your work at intervals defined in the Bin settings panel, saving any bin that contains changes. You can have it wait till you pause for a specified amount of time before it saves, and you can also instruct it to force a save after a specified amount of time, even if you never stop working (see "Bin Settings/Save and Auto-Save" on page 269). Bins that contain unsaved changes are marked with an asterisk in the bin's title bar and tab, and a check mark in the Windows menu.

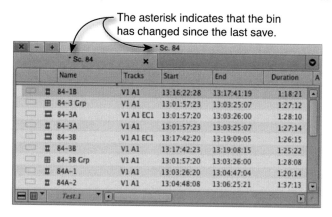

The asterisk indicates that the bin has changed since the last save.

If you want more control over what gets saved, or if you want to save something immediately, you can invoke the Save command manually, by using Command-S or File > Save.

The behavior of the Save command changes based on the window that's active when you select it. The name of the menu pick will adjust to tell you what's going to happen, but the keyboard shortcut remains the same—it's always Command-S. If you generally use the keyboard, be sure to pay attention to which window is active when you save your work.

Active Window	Menu Says	What Will Be Saved
Any Bin Window	Save Bin	The active bin only
Composer or Timeline	Save All Bins	All changed bins
Project Window	Save All	All changed bins and all settings

If you simply want to save a bin, click on the bin to activate it and hit Command-S. If you want to save all changed bins, click in the Composer or Timeline window, instead. And if you want to save all changed bins along with your settings, click in the Project window. (There's no way to save your settings independently of bins.)

Note that Autosave does not save bins that contain certain kinds of minor changes, such as a clip that's been renamed or one that's been moved in frame view. You can rename every clip in a bin, but when the time comes to Autosave, that bin won't be saved. The only way to save changes like this is to do it manually.

The Attic

Every time a bin is saved, the system moves the previously saved version of that bin to a folder called Avid Attic. This allows you to access earlier versions of a bin, and can be helpful if you delete something accidentally or want to review an older version of a sequence. The Attic is typically located here:

> Mac OS X:
> Macintosh HD/Users/Shared/AvidMediaComposer/Avid Attic

> Windows Vista & Windows 7:
> C:/Users/Public/Public Documents/Avid Media Composer/Avid Attic

Inside the attic folder you'll find a folder for each of your projects, and inside each of those you'll find a folder labeled Bins. The Bins folder contains a folder for each bin you've saved, within which are copies of the bin in question, each numbered with a suffix; the highest number is the most recent. Display the Date Modified column to see when each version of the bin was saved.

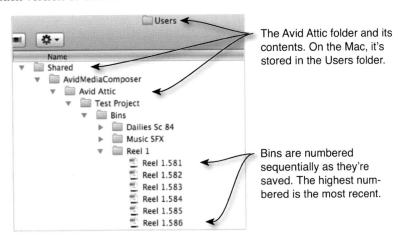

The Avid Attic folder and its contents. On the Mac, it's stored in the Users folder.

Bins are numbered sequentially as they're saved. The highest numbered is the most recent.

Media Composer won't allow you to open two copies of the same bin simultaneously. Nor will it allow you to open a bin from within the Attic Folder. To avoid confusion you'll need to make a new bin and drag sequences and clips there, from the attic.

Locate the bin you're looking for in the Attic, making sure that the current copy of the bin is closed. Then copy the bin from the Attic to your desktop, or to any other convenient place (Option-drag is a good way to do this). Double-click the copy. It will open in MC with its name displayed in italics in the Project window, indicating that it does not reside in your project folder. Create a new bin and copy the material you need from the attic bin to it. If you want to put that material into the current copy of the bin, close the attic bin, open the current bin and drag the material there.

Using Bin Settings, you can control the number of saved bins for each project in the Attic, as well as the number of copies saved for each individual bin. See page 269.

Measuring Sequences

If your show consists of a single sequence, you can measure it easily in the timeline. Mark in and out at the head and tail and use Center Duration, or simply display an appropriate data value in the tracking information above the record monitor: Duration (Dur) continuously displays the length of your sequence, In/Out (I/O) displays the distance between marks, and Remaining (Rem) displays the distance from the position indicator to the end of the sequence (if you clear your marks, Center Duration displays remaining time, as well).

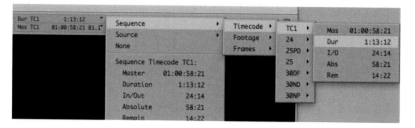

To quickly total the duration of several sequences, use Avid's Get Bin Info command. Select the sequences in question (they must reside in a single bin), right-click one of them, and choose Get Bin Info. The Console window will open and display the total length of the sequences, in both timecode and footage formats.

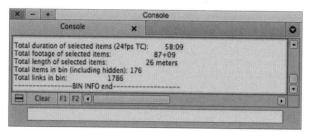

The Calculator

You can also use the Avid Calculator, available in the Tools menu. Start by hitting CL to clear the display. Then click the Format menu and select a data type to work with.

Select timecode and footage formats from the Format menu.

Enter data here or with the keyboard.

Your entries are displayed in paper-tape format.

Add your numbers as you would with an ordinary calculator, using either the keyboard or the on-screen buttons. You don't need to enter punctuation; the calculator will do it for you. To enter a double zero, hit the period key. Enter the length of each sequence followed by a plus sign. To generate a total, hit the equal sign or the Return key.

To convert film footages to time, start by selecting the appropriate film format. For 35mm film, select "16 Frames/Edge." Then enter and total your numbers to produce a result in feet and frames. To convert to 24-fps timecode select "24 FPS."

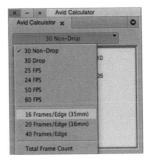

To add film footages, select 16 Frames/Edge, add your numbers and convert to time by selecting 24 FPS.

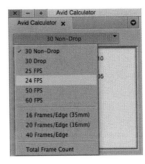

Do not select a 30-fps value, or you'll get an incorrect result. Though the calculator can correctly convert between most other timecode formats, it can't accurately convert footages to 30-fps timecode, nor can it convert between 24-fps and 30-fps timecode (see "24-fps Timecode" on page 235).

Bin Background Color

To change a bin's background color or font, activate the bin by clicking it, and make sure no clips are selected. Then make a selection from the Edit menu. (Be sure that Allow Custom Bin Backgrounds is selected in Interface settings.) The color applies to all bin views: text, frame and script. Hold down the Option key while selecting a color to bring up the system color picker, where you can choose from a wider range of colors. To restore the default color, select Set Bin Color to Default or choose None from the palette.

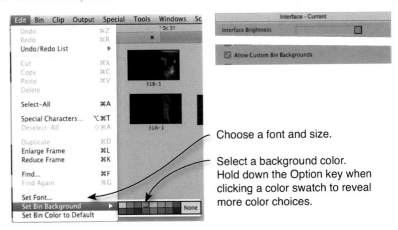

Choose a font and size.

Select a background color. Hold down the Option key when clicking a color swatch to reveal more color choices.

Bin Shortcuts

New Sequence

You can create a new sequence from the Clip menu, or from the button at the top of the Bins tab in the Project window. But it's quicker to use Command-Shift-N. This will put a new sequence into the currently selected bin. If no bin is selected, it will bring up a dialog box asking you where you want it.

Opening and Closing Several Bins at Once

To select a group of bins in the Project window, click and drag in the area to the left of the bin icons, creating a lasso that touches all of them. Or click the first bin and then Shift-click the others (use Command-click to select a discontinuous group). Once the bins you want are selected, double-click any selected bin to open them all, or select File > Open Selected Bins, or drag them all to an open bin to open them in tabs. To close all open bins, click any bin to activate it, then select Windows > Close All Bins.

Maximize Bins

Click the green maximize button at the top of a bin to size it just large enough to show all the items within. Option-click it to make the bin fill the screen. Option-click the button again to return it to the previous size.

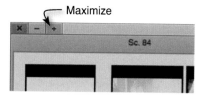

Tab and Return

When typing text into bin columns, Tab moves you to the next column and Return moves you to the next row. Shift-Tab and Shift-Return take you to the previous column and row, respectively.

11   Script Integration

Introduction

Avid's script integration features allow you to import a script into Media Composer and then assign video material to it, identifying locations in your shots that line up with marks you'll make in the script. You can then instantly cue a shot to a particular line of dialog or quickly play through all the available coverage for that portion of the scene. You can also make rough edits directly from the script.

An imported script works much like a bin. It's listed in the bins tab of the project window, is autosaved like a bin and is backed up in the attic. Script text forms the background of the window. Shots are superimposed over it much like they would be in a standard lined script. Each slate or setup is represented with a clip frame, and each take of that setup is represented by a vertical line running through the portion of the script the take covers. Off-camera dialog can be indicated with a wavy line, and you can add color to line sections to help identify them.

Avid offers you three ways mark takes: manually, identifying each line of dialog and adding a mark for it; live, marking the script while video plays; or automatically, with its extra-cost ScriptSync technology, which listens to your dialog and adds marks based on script text.

Once your script is lined and marked, you can double click a mark to cue video to that point in the script, or you can select a series of takes and a section of the script and play that material in a loop. You can use the technology when roughing out a scene or when recutting, or both, quickly locating the coverage for any portion of your scene.

Importing Your Script

Prepare your script in the word processor of your choice. Then export it as a plain text file with the extension txt. You want a file that uses spaces rather than tabs to create indentation. That might be called "formatted text" or "text with layout." You may find an export setting in your word processor designed specifically for Media Composer. If necessary, check the file in a plain text editor, such as Apple's TextEdit, and make any changes necessary. All indented lines should begin with a run of spaces. You can work with the entire script in a single file, but you may want to break it into sections more appropriate for editing, typically one scene, or a few scenes, per file.

In Media Composer select File > New Script and point the dialog box to your text file. It will open in a new window.

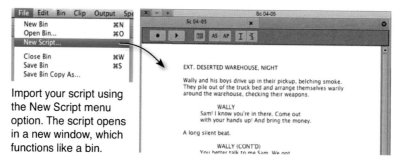

Import your script using the New Script menu option. The script opens in a new window, which functions like a bin.

Keep in mind that Avid's script interface is designed to focus on full lines of text—the material between carriage returns. If you click on the script, you'll highlight a full line; if you click and drag you'll create a selection rectangle, and highlight a group of lines. (Or you can click on the first line and Shift-click the last.) You can't select individual words or characters.

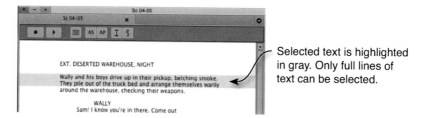

Selected text is highlighted in gray. Only full lines of text can be selected.

At the top of every script window you'll find the Script Toolbar. It allows you to mark the script, find a source bin, color portions of lines, and add scene and page numbers.

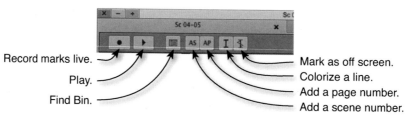

Record marks live.
Play.
Find Bin.

Mark as off screen.
Colorize a line.
Add a page number.
Add a scene number.

Media Composer does not recognize automatic page breaks or scene numbers unless they appear as plain text. To add them in MC, use the Add Scene and Add Page menu options in the Script menu or the equivalent buttons in the Script Toolbar. Click the line where you want a scene or page to begin and hit a button to mark that line.

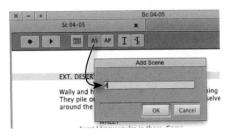

To add a scene number, select a line of text and click the Add Scene button.

Scene numbers appear in the left margin, page numbers in the right. Both also appear at the bottom of the script window. Click a number there to activate the Go to Scene or Go to Page dialog boxes and jump to another scene or page. To change a scene or page number, select the appropriate line, click a button and enter a new number.

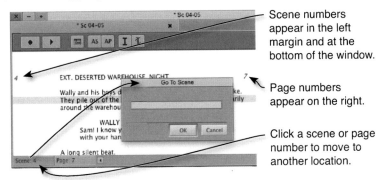

Scene numbers appear in the left margin and at the bottom of the window.

Page numbers appear on the right.

Click a scene or page number to move to another location.

You can do limited text editing of an imported script via the standard Cut and Paste commands. To delete a line, select it and hit Command-X. To replace lines of text, create the text in a text editor and copy and paste, one line at a time. MC will ask if you want to paste before or after the currently selected line. Be sure to include leading spaces. You can also import your material as a new script and cut and paste sections from there. You can make changes before or after you've added coverage to your script. But be careful; the undo command doesn't apply to changes you make in script windows.

Adding Coverage

Load your source material into a bin using all of the normal techniques. Organize it and enter data as needed. Keep in mind that you may end up editing with both the script and the bin. Create normal clip names. In addition, display the Take column in the bin and enter a take number for each clip.

You'll add clips to the script one setup at a time, dragging all the takes of that camera angle into the script at once. First, identify the portion of the script a setup covers and select it by clicking and dragging over it, turning the script background gray. Then select all the takes for that setup and drag them to the gray area. Media Composer creates a Slate (clip frame) with vertical lines emanating from it and spanning the portion of the script you selected. Each line represents a take. At the top of each line you'll see what Avid calls Take Tabs, identified with the number you entered in the Take column.

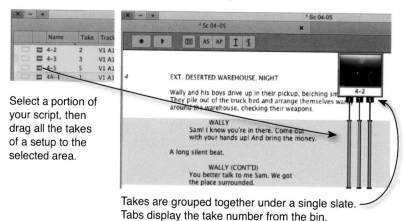

Select a portion of your script, then drag all the takes of a setup to the selected area.

Takes are grouped together under a single slate. Tabs display the take number from the bin.

You can select any take line by clicking on it or by clicking on the take tab at the top of the line. This highlights the line. The clip frame is labeled with the clip name of the currently selected take. You can move slates anywhere you like; the take lines move with the slate. To change the beginning and end of one or more takes, select them and Command-drag the beginning or end vertically. To change the clip frame displayed for a slate, select its tab and then use the Step Forward/Backward buttons to move through the shot. Use Command-L and Command-K as you would in a bin, to enlarge or shrink clip frames.

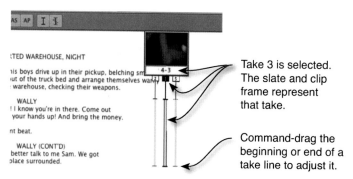

Take 3 is selected. The slate and clip frame represent that take.

Command-drag the beginning or end of a take line to adjust it.

Continue adding coverage until all your source material for the scene has been included. To remove a take, select the take number and hit Delete. To remove a slate, select all of its takes and hit Delete.

You can add group clips the same way. But note that the Take column doesn't function for groups, and take numbers on the individual shots within a group won't appear in the script. To identify the group, select its take line—the clip name appears on the slate.

Marking the Script

Once coverage has been added to your script, you'll mark it up, adding color and off-screen indicators, and associating locations in your video with lines of text.

Color & Off-screen Indicators

You can change the color of any section of a take line, or you can add a wavy line over it, indicating that the underlying dialog is off-camera. Start by selecting a portion of a line by lassoing it. When you release the mouse button, a section of the script text will be highlighted along with one or more take lines. It is the intersection of these highlights that you'll be affecting.

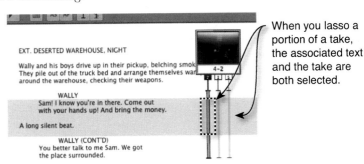

When you lasso a portion of a take, the associated text and the take are both selected.

First, choose the color you want to use by selecting Script > Color. Then hit the Set Color button to colorize the selected region. To mark it as off camera, select it and hit the Set Offscreen button. To remove color or off-screen indicators, lasso the affected portion of a line and hit the button again.

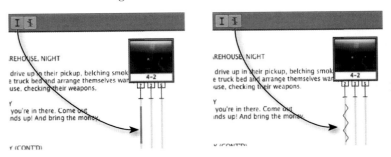

Script Marks

The most important part of your task in preparing a script is to add what Avid calls Script Marks, which tie the script to locations (ie. timecode) in your video. You can add marks three ways: manually, live while video is playing, or automatically with ScriptSync. To mark manually, you'll use the Add Script Mark button. It's not assigned to the default keyboard, so before you begin marking, assign it to the key of your choice.

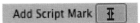

Identify the line of dialog you want to mark by selecting it in the script. Then double-click a take tab, or double-click at the intersection of the dialog line and the take line. The selected shot loads into the source monitor. Play it as you would any other shot, until you find the beginning of a the line of dialog you're marking. You may find it helpful to show the source timeline (page 42) and turn on waveforms, so you can locate the beginning of a line of dialog visually (page 36).

Then, with the take and line of dialog still highlighted in the script, click the Add Script Mark button. (You can do this while video is playing, but playback will stop when you hit the button.) A double headed arrow appears at the intersection of the take and the dialog line you selected. After that, if you double-click the mark, the shot will be loaded into the source monitor, cued to the frame you identified. As with other script actions, you can't undo the creation of a mark. To remove it, click on it (or lasso several) and hit the Delete key.

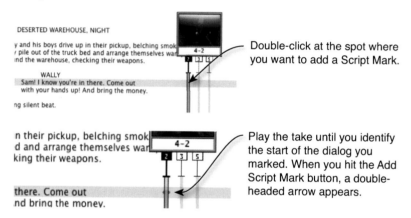

Double-click at the spot where you want to add a Script Mark.

Play the take until you identify the start of the dialog you marked. When you hit the Add Script Mark button, a double-headed arrow appears.

Real-Time Marking

To mark while video is playing (Avid calls this Real-Time Marking), select one or more takes by clicking and Shift-clicking their take tabs, or by lassoing a group of takes. Then hit the Record button in the Script Toolbar. The first take cues in the source monitor, begins to play, and it's take line turns green. As it plays, double-click the appropriate line in the script window. Script marks appear and video continues to play.

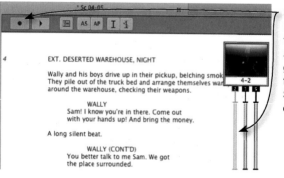

Select takes and hit the Record button to play them. The currently active take is shown in green. Double-click on the green line to add Script Marks while video continues to play.

If necessary, scroll the script window; this won't affect playback. When the first selected take has played, the second will be cued. Selected takes will continue to play in a loop until you hit Stop. You can use the J and L keys in this mode to jog back and forth through your material. But you can't hit K or you'll abort live marking. Use the Tab key to jump forward to the next selected take and Shift-Tab to jump back and continue playing.

ScriptSync

ScriptSync is the quickest and most efficient way to add marks to a script because it actively listens to your audio, correlates it with the script, and then assigns marks automatically with excellent accuracy. Avid's script integration features come with every Media Composer, but ScriptSync requires an additional license fee. Like PhraseFind, you'll activate it with the Avid License Control application (see page 15).

Once ScriptSync is installed, simply select one or more takes in a script window and choose Script > ScriptSync. The ScriptSync window opens.

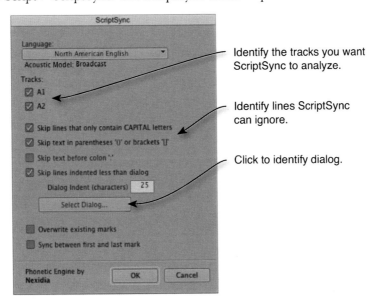

Identify the tracks you want ScriptSync to analyze.

Identify lines ScriptSync can ignore.

Click to identify dialog.

Start by hitting the Select Dialog button. This allows you to directly point to dialog in the script and have the application determine the number of spaces used to indent it. Identify the audio track or tracks you want the ScriptSync engine to listen to. To replace existing marks, select Overwrite Existing Marks. Sync Between First and Last Mark restricts the ScriptSync engine to listen only in that range. If you don't want it to listen to the entire take, add marks manually and chose this option.

When you click Okay, the ScriptSync engine quickly scans your audio and adds a mark for every line of dialog in the script. A progress bar appears showing you what's happening. If you want to stop automatic marking hit Command-Period.

ScriptSync enters a mark for every line of text. If a speech spans multiple lines, each will get a script mark. You may want to go back through your material and check the marks or clean them up. Note that ScriptSync looks for dialog in script order, finding both on camera and off camera lines. Dialog that doesn't match the script, or repeated dialog, will typically be skipped.

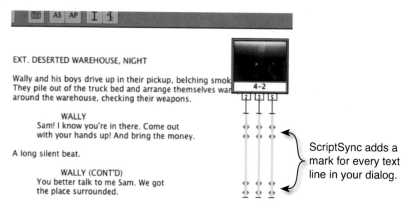

ScriptSync adds a mark for every text line in your dialog.

Resets and Improvisation

To deal with production resets ("let's start over from the top" or "do that line again") you have two choices. You can subclip the repeated material and treat it as an independent take, adding it to the script and then marking it manually or with ScriptSync. Or you can hand mark the repeated material within a single take, adding an extra mark for each repeat. Keep in mind that marks do not necessarily have to appear in chronological order; they can point anywhere within a clip. When working this way, you won't be able to play all the repeats in a loop. But you can easily double-click each mark to compare readings. You may find it helpful to add blank lines within dialog, to make room for multiple marks.

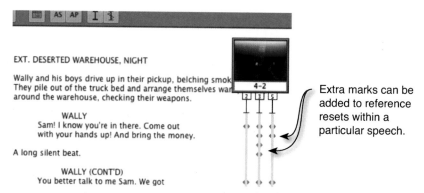

Extra marks can be added to reference resets within a particular speech.

Improvisation presents a similar problem. Hand marking can be one solution. Or you may want to have your improvised material transcribed, and then import it as a script. You can then use ScriptSync to analyze it, deriving marks precisely and automatically. This can be helpful in documentary work.

Editing

Once your script is entered and coverage has been added and marked, you're ready to begin editing. You can cut directly from a script, ignoring the relevant bin, or you can move back and forth between the bin and script. Or you may want to do your first cut from the bin and later, when you are recutting, use the script to identify alternate readings and coverage.

A marked script allows you to do three key things. First, it lets you quickly find a line of dialog within a take. Simply double-click a script mark and the take it references is loaded into the source monitor cued to the script mark. A Mark In is automatically added, and you're ready to edit it as you would with any other clip. You can double-click a series of readings in this way and quickly compare them. When you find the shot you want, edit it normally.

Second, you can play across lines of dialog, comparing performances in a series of takes. Select a line or lines and a group of takes by lassoing. Note that selected lines are indicated in dark gray.

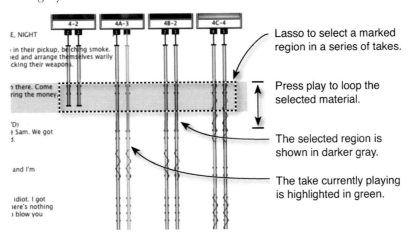

Lasso to select a marked region in a series of takes.

Press play to loop the selected material.

The selected region is shown in darker gray.

The take currently playing is highlighted in green.

Then hit any Play key. (The Play button in the Script Toolbar is convenient, but any will work, including the space bar.) All the selected takes load in the source monitor and the section you highlighted plays in a loop. The currently playing take is identified in green. When you find the material you want, hit Stop and edit normally. Within each take, you can use J and L to jog back and forth, and you can jump from take to take using Tab and Shift-Tab.

Finally, you can edit directly from the script into the timeline. When you hold down the Command and Option keys and hover your mouse over a portion of a take, the cursor turns into a yellow Insert icon. Double-click to insert that line of dialog into the timeline at the current in mark, or if no mark is present, at the position indicator.. If multiple takes are selected, all of them will be inserted sequentially. One way to use this is to go through your material, looping and playing coverage as needed, and then selecting and inserting your preferred shots into the timeline, moving through the script until you've assembled a rough cut. Or you might want to mark your preferred material in color and then, in a second step, edit each line into a growing timeline.

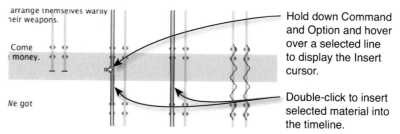

Hold down Command and Option and hover over a selected line to display the Insert cursor.

Double-click to insert selected material into the timeline.

Find Script

Once you've got a sequence assembled, you can use the Find Script button much like you'd use Find Bin, to locate the script containing a particular shot. Load the shot into the source monitor. Then hit Find Script. The script opens with the shot selected and the Script Mark closest to the position indicator shown in dark gray. (If a script is already open, Find Script will not bring it forward.)

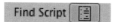

If you need to locate a script for material in the timeline, first use Match Frame to open the relevant clip in the source monitor; then hit Find Script. Note that if you include resets within a take, Find Script may have trouble locating them accurately.

Find Text

To find text within a script, activate the script window and choose Edit > Find (Command-F.) The Find window opens. You can choose to search the current script or all scripts in the project. If you select the current script, you'll be taken to the first instance of your search term. Hit Command-G to find additional instances. If you select Scripts in Project, you'll get a list of instances. Double-click each one to open the relevant script with the search term highlighted. (For more about the Find window see page 63.)

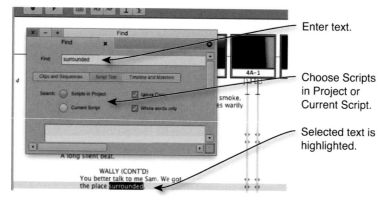

Enter text.

Choose Scripts in Project or Current Script.

Selected text is highlighted.

Settings

You can make several useful interface adjustments with the Script Settings panel. Most options are also available in the Script menu, and the choices you make in the menu override those in the settings panel. Show All Takes is on by default. If you turn it off, you'll only see one take line per slate. Show Frames turns clip frames on or off. When off, slates are displayed with clip names but without images. (Note that Media Composer can only display 4x3 clip frames. 16x9 images are automatically squeezed.)

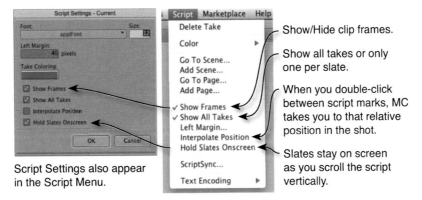

Script Settings also appear in the Script Menu.

Show/Hide clip frames.

Show all takes or only one per slate.

When you double-click between script marks, MC takes you to that relative position in the shot.

Slates stay on screen as you scroll the script vertically.

Interpolate Position causes MC to interpolate your location when you double-click between marks. When it's off, you're cued to the mark ahead the spot where you double-clicked. When it's on you're cued to a place in video between the two marks. If you were halfway between two marks in the script, you'll be cued halfway between the marks in the shot. Hold Slates Onscreen moves slates with you as you scroll through your script. As long as a script line is visible, the slate will be visible, too.

Font and Size apply only to the next script you import. To change the font in an existing script, activate the script by clicking in it and choose Edit > Set Font.

12 Audio

Overview

Media Composer offers a wide range of audio controls, and each recent software update has added new capabilities. The system provides two primary ways of controlling audio levels: clip gain and volume automation. Clip gain permits you to adjust the overall level for an entire clip. Volume automation allows you to move levels up and down within a clip using keyframes. Clip adjustments can be made either to source or sequence clips; automation works only in the timeline. Each approach has advantages, and they can be used together or separately. If you apply both, the adjustments are added together when a sequence is played.

Pan works in much the same way. You can pan an entire clip, or you can create pan keyframes to make changes as a sequence is played. Volume and pan keyframes are independent of each other. Each can be viewed in the timeline, but you can't see both simultaneously.

Mono, stereo, 5.1 and 7.1 surround sound are all supported. To make this possible, Media Composer allows you to create clips, tracks and sequences in a variety of types. By default, sequences are stereo, which means that sound can come from the left or right speaker or can be panned between them. Sequences can also be 5.1 or 7.1, so that you can listen to and pan sources anywhere around the room. Clips are mono by default and contain a single audio voice, but they can also be stereo, 5.1 or 7.1, wrapping two or more voices into a single object in the timeline. Clip and track types must match; you have to edit mono clips in mono tracks, stereo clips in stereo tracks, and so on. But sequences are agnostic; they can contain tracks of all types.

You'll need the right output hardware and speakers to listen to surround audio. Media Composer allows you to work with surround material in a mono or stereo environment, automatically mixing down your tracks, but for most purposes, you'll want hardware matched to your mix. For details, see the help system.

Keep in mind that while you can edit 24 audio tracks in a timeline, Media Composer can currently play back only 16 voices. A stereo clip uses two, a 7.1 clip uses eight, etc. If you cut more tracks than can be played, some will automatically be inactivated. Their status will be displayed in the Track Control Panel (see page 34).

Audio Keyframes

Audio keyframes are a crucial tool for sound work, but their display in the timeline is turned off by default. You won't be able to add or change keyframes until they are enabled, either from the timeline Fast Menu or the Track Control Panel.

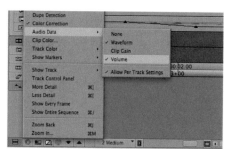 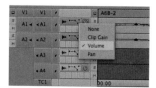

Use the Timeline Fast Menu or the Track Control Panel to select audio display options.

When keyframe display is turned off, clips that contain them reveal only a single colored keyframe, centered on the clip, indicating that there are one or more keyframes present.

Keyframe display turned on. ——

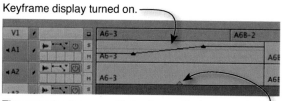

The same keyframes, with keyframe display turned off.

Adding Keyframes

You'll typically add keyframes with the Add Keyframe button, either from the keyboard or from your screen. By default, it's on the quote key. This is the same button that's used to create visual effects keyframes. Park your position indicator on the frame where you want a keyframe, select tracks and tap the button to create keyframes in those tracks. You can now also use the mixer to both add keyframes and adjust their levels. When you make a level change, a keyframe is automatically added (see page 149).

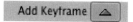

The Add Keyframe button creates both audio and visual effects keyframes.

Adjusting Keyframes

Keyframe volume adjustments obey marks and track selection. To change a single key-frame, clear timeline marks, select a track, and click and drag a keyframe vertically. The decibel level you set is displayed at the bottom of the timeline as you drag. To manipulate multiple keyframes simultaneously, select their tracks and mark in and out. When you drag, all keyframes within the marked range move up and down together, with the same volume change applied to all of them.

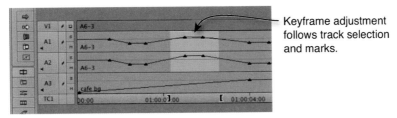

Keyframe adjustment follows track selection and marks.

Because of the way keyframe adjustments work, you should use caution when adjusting them—you are always affecting all keyframes between marks, in all selected tracks. A lot of damage can be done this way, very quickly! In general, it's best to get in the habit of checking or clearing marks before adjusting levels this way.

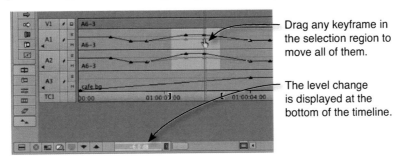

Drag any keyframe in the selection region to move all of them.

The level change is displayed at the bottom of the timeline.

You can also set levels using the Mixer in Automation Mode, explained below. Click on a keyframe, be sure its track is selected, and drag the appropriate fader, or enter a numeric value in the decibel display. This allows for .1 db precision and, since you can only adjust one keyframe at a time, there's less chance of error.

To move a keyframe in time (left/right), hold down the Option key and drag the key-frame, as needed. Note that you cannot move more than one keyframe at a time. Marks are ignored, but keyframes at the same timeline position in all active tracks will be moved together.

Deleting Keyframes

To delete a keyframe, select its track, clear marks, click the keyframe and hit the Delete key. To delete multiple keyframes, mark a range, click on any keyframe within the range and hit Delete.

The Audio Mixer

Avid has combined several previously separate audio tools to create a unified Audio Mixer. To open it, select Audio Mixer from the Tools menu. Then use the Mode button to cycle between Automation Mode (formerly Automation Gain), Clip Mode (formerly Audio Mix) and Live Mix Mode. You can also hold down the mode button, which will turn it into a pop-up menu, from which you can make the same choices.

Click the Mixer Mode button to cycle through its three modes, or hold the button down to turn it into a menu.

The modes are visually quite similar, differing primarily in the background color behind the faders, so be sure you know where you are before making adjustments. The mixer now displays live level meters and can show four, eight or sixteen tracks simultaneously.

When a clip is playing, the mixer now displays active level meters.

Mixer modes are distinguished by the background color behind the faders. Automation Mode.   Clip Mode.

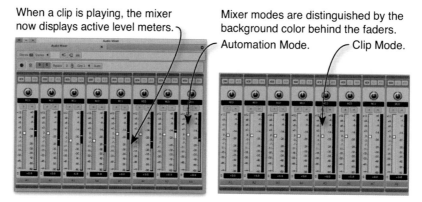

Clip Mode

Use Clip Mode to set a gain or pan value over the entire duration of a clip, either for source clips or clips in sequences. To adjust a clip, load it into the appropriate monitor. (If it's already there, be sure the monitor is active by clicking on it.) Select Audio Mixer from the Tools menu and make sure it's set to Clip Mode. Then simply drag the appropriate fader or enter a decibel value in the text entry field under it. To set a fader to zero, Option-click it. If you're making adjustments on a source clip, note that when you edit the clip into a sequence, clip gain and pan settings are carried over. But once in the sequence, they can be adjusted independently of the source.

You can also make clip-level adjustments in a bin. Select a clip or clips and choose Clip > Apply Gain. You can then make additional changes, if necessary, with the Mixer.

In addition, you can automatically set clip gain to a specified value when audio clips are imported. Go to the Audio tab of the Import settings panel and enter the decibel level you prefer. If you're only concerned with CD imports, select CD Only.

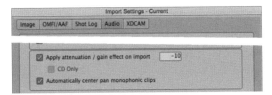

Automation Mode

Automation Mode allows you to mix with keyframes, gradually ramping levels up or down within a clip. As described above, you can conveniently adjust keyframes by dragging in the timeline, but the mixer offers more precision and additional controls. Unlike timeline adjustments, when you use a fader to set a level, you are always operating on a single keyframe. To make an adjustment, activate the appropriate track, park on a keyframe (or click on it) and then drag a fader. You can also click the green number at the bottom of a fader, and enter a value numerically from the keyboard. Hit the cursor arrow keys to move a fader in .1 db increments; add the Shift key to move in 1 db increments.

New in Version 6, if you are not parked on a keyframe when you make an adjustment, one will automatically be added for you. This makes it easier to quickly add keyframes and precisely set their values.

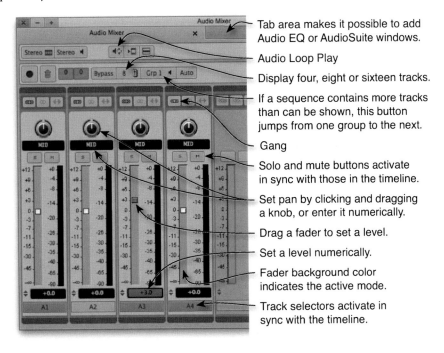

Tab area makes it possible to add Audio EQ or AudioSuite windows.

Audio Loop Play

Display four, eight or sixteen tracks.

If a sequence contains more tracks than can be shown, this button jumps from one group to the next.

Gang

Solo and mute buttons activate in sync with those in the timeline.

Set pan by clicking and dragging a knob, or enter it numerically.

Drag a fader to set a level.

Set a level numerically.

Fader background color indicates the active mode.

Track selectors activate in sync with the timeline.

To reassign channels in the mixer, click and hold on a track selector button. A pop-up menu appears, letting you assign that fader to any track in the timeline.

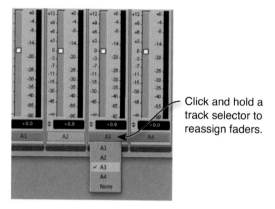

Click and hold a track selector to reassign faders.

Clip Gain and Automation Gain can be displayed simultaneously in the timeline, either with the timeline Fast Menu, or with the Track Control Panel. Options you select with the Fast Menu are saved in timeline views and apply to all tracks (see "Timeline Views" on page 49). Options you select with the Track Control Panel apply to each track individually and are saved with the sequence. Hold down the Option key when making a selection in the track panel to apply the selection to all tracks. To temporarily override the selections you make in the Track panel, deselect Allow Per Track Settings in the Fast Menu.

Clip gain is displayed as a horizontal line, automation gain, as a line connecting keyframes.

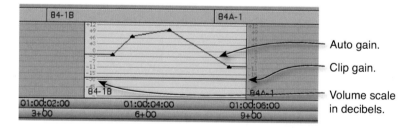

Auto gain.

Clip gain.

Volume scale in decibels.

To loop clip playback, click the mixer's Audio Loop Play button. If you've got marks in the timeline, it loops around them. If not, it loops between the audio edits nearest the position indicator.

Recording Keyframe Automation

You can also use Automation Mode to record volume changes while your sequence plays, allowing you to listen while making adjustments. To begin recording, click the red Record button on the mixer. Your sequence begins to play, either from your mark in, or, if you've cleared your marks, from the cursor position. Drag your faders up or down as needed. Keyframes are recorded and will appear when you hit stop or get to your mark out. To drag several sliders together, click their gang buttons, then move any one of them.

To record a mix while your sequence plays, select Automation Mode and click the Record button.

To mix two tracks simultaneously, click their gang buttons.

Then drag faders, as needed.

Meters display audio levels as the tracks play.

Keyframes appear when you stop sequence play, either by reaching your mark out, clicking the Record button again or hitting the Play key.

To change a mix, simply use Automation Mode to record over it. As you mix, you'll replace keyframes that are present in the track you're adjusting. When you stop, keyframes following that point are preserved.

Live Mix Mode

Live Mix allows you to temporarily override existing keyframes and experiment with levels, without recording automation. One way to use it is with a dedicated external control surface, allowing you to mix live during a screening, for example. But note well—as long as the mixer remains in Live mode, the adjustments you make apply to any sequence you load into the record monitor. If you drag a fader to the bottom and leave the mixer in that mode, you won't be able to hear audio.

In Live Mode, fader backgrounds turn red.

The Mixer Fast Menu

The Mixer's Fast Menu lets you make adjustments that would be difficult or impossible in the timeline. Options in the menu change depending on the mode it's in. In Automation Mode, use Adjust Pan/Volume on Track – In/Out to raise or lower a group of keyframes between marks, in selected tracks. A window will open allowing you to enter an offset to the volume or pan of the keyframes in that range. Note that if there are no marks in your sequence, the menu pick will change to Adjust Pan/Volume on Track – Global. Any change you make will apply to all keyframes in every selected track.

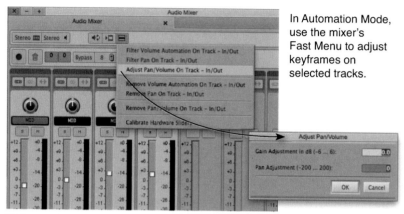

In Automation Mode, use the mixer's Fast Menu to adjust keyframes on selected tracks.

Filter Volume Automation on Track allows you to thin out keyframes in a marked region. You may find that recording automation gives you so many keyframes that you can't easily manage them. By repeatedly selecting this item you can slowly thin out the keyframes, as needed.

In Clip Mode, you can use the Fast Menu to make clip-level and pan adjustments to a series of clips in a single step. Mark in and out, and select appropriate tracks. Then use Adjust Pan/Vols on Track to raise or lower clip gain or pan in the marked region. Or set a level on a clip, park on it, and use Set Level on Track to adjust all clips to match.

The Fast Menu in Clip Mode

Trimming Keyframes

When a clip containing audio keyframes is trimmed shorter, Media Composer retains its keyframes. If you later trim the clip back to its original length, the keyframes will still be present. If these hidden keyframes get in your way you'll have to trim the clip out, remove them and then trim it back. Or you can hit Match Frame followed by Replace Edit to replace the clip with a clean copy and then add the keyframes you need.

When you trim a clip, keyframes are retained.

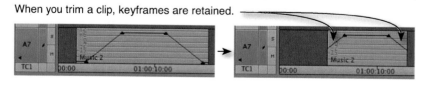

Stereo and Surround Tracks and Clips

To simplify the editing of multi-track material, Version 5 introduced stereo audio clips and tracks, and Version 6 added 5.1 and 7.1 surround formats. The underlying technology is the same. Multi-track clips, regardless of format, package two or more tracks of audio into a single clip for editing, and each must be edited into a track type that matches the clip. Tracks display appropriate icons in the Track Selector Panel so you can tell which is which.

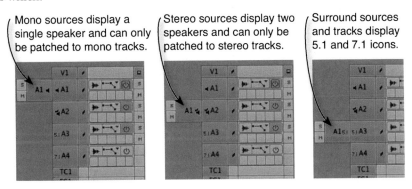

Mono sources display a single speaker and can only be patched to mono tracks.

Stereo sources display two speakers and can only be patched to stereo tracks.

Surround sources and tracks display 5.1 and 7.1 icons.

In most respects, multi-track clips and tracks behave like their monophonic equivalents. You can cut, trim, drag and mix, just as you would with mono. Stereo clips display two sets of waveforms on a single clip, but they carry only a single row of keyframes, making them easier to handle in mixing. 5.1 and 7.1 clips display six or eight waveforms, respectively. Audio effects are applied to multi-track clips in the same way they would be to mono clips. (Sequence types are set in the mixer and are explained on page 157.)

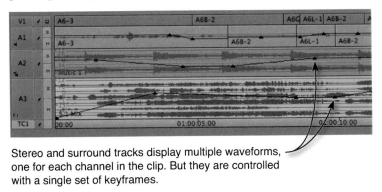

Stereo and surround tracks display multiple waveforms, one for each channel in the clip. But they are controlled with a single set of keyframes.

Clips

You'll create multi-track clips with the Multichannel Audio dialog box, available in several locations. Right-click a master clip or clips that contain two or more tracks and choose Modify (or select Modify from the Clip menu). Then open the pop-up in the Modify dialog, select Set Multichannel Audio, and use the menu under the tracks to treat them as stereo or surround. The same options appear in the Audio tab in Import Settings and in the Capture tool, allowing you to adjust imported or digitized audio in the same way.

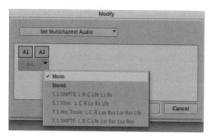

Click the Link icon to adjust a clip's multichannel status. Grey represents mono, green represents stereo. You'll see a yellow icon if you select several clips that don't match each other.

Multi-track sources can be treated as a series of mono clips, stereo pairs or a single surround clip.

Note that if you change the multichannel format of a clip after using it for editing, existing sequences will not change; only material you edit after the change is affected. To reveal the audio format for a source clip, display the Track Formats column in the bin containing it.

	Name	Tracks	Track Formats	Audio SR	Audio Bit
	Handcuffs	A1-2	Stereo: A1A2	48000	16
	Music 1	A1-2	Stereo: A1A2	48000	16
	Music 2	A1		48000	16
	Music 3	A1-2	Stereo: A1A2	48000	16
	5.1 Mix	A1-6	5.1 Surround: A1A2A3A4A5A6	48000	24

Tracks

To create a stereo track in the timeline, select Clip > New Audio Track and choose the kind of track you want from the sub-menu. You can also right-click anywhere in the timeline and do the same thing. Then edit normally, cutting multi-track clips into matching track types.

When you create a new audio track, it's normally added at the bottom of the timeline. But there are times when you'll want to add new tracks elsewhere. For example, say your sequence contains two mono tracks, A1 and A2, and two stereo tracks, A3 and A4. You want to add an additional mono track after A2. To do so, use the Add Track dialog box. Hold down the Option key and select any option in the Clip > New Audio Track menu, or simply hit Command-Option-U. Then choose the track type and position you want.

Your track will be created and other tracks will be renumbered, as needed. (You may see a message telling you that the track already exists, letting you know that some tracks are going to be renumbered.)

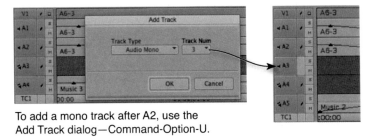

To add a mono track after A2, use the
Add Track dialog—Command-Option-U.

As a convenience, you can rename your tracks by right-clicking the track selector and choosing Rename Track. This changes the text label on the track, but the underlying track number remains the same.

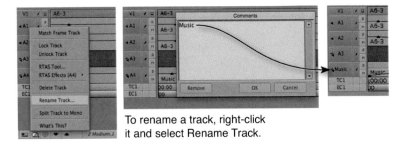

To rename a track, right-click
it and select Rename Track.

When you create a new sequence it normally contains one video track and two mono audio tracks. If you prefer that new sequences contain stereo tracks, you can make the change in the Edit tab of Timeline settings.

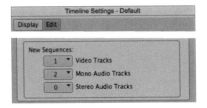

Splitting Stereo and Surround Tracks

Stereo and surround clips, tracks and RTAS effects can be exported from Media Composer to recent versions of Pro Tools via AAF. But prior to PT 9, you'll have to break tracks up in MC before exporting. Select the track you want to split, right-click the track selector, and choose Split Track to Mono. To split all tracks in a sequence, load it into the record monitor and choose Clip > Split All Tracks to Mono. Each stereo or surround track is converted to a series of mono tracks and all clips within it are split, as well. RTAS effects will be removed. AudioSuite effects are converted to their mono versions, but will need to be re-rendered. Clip gain and keyframes will be copied to the new mono clips.

Stereo and Surround Panning

Just as with volume, Media Composer offers two ways to pan your material. You'll use Clip Mode to pan entire clips, and Automation Mode to pan clips using keyframes. As with volume, clip level pan is initially carried across when clips are edited into a sequence, but unlike volume, Clip and Automation pan adjustments are not additive. Instead, pan keyframes override clip-level panning. Once you add panning keyframes, you won't be able to further adjust clip level panning until you remove the keyframes using the Mixer's Fast Menu.

Panning Source Clips

Mono and stereo source clips can be panned in the source monitor using the mixer's Clip Mode. Mono clips display a single panner, stereo clips display two, allowing independent adjustments. But you don't have to pan your source clips. By default, mono clips that haven't be explicitly panned are treated as if they were centered, or played out of the left and right channels equally; stereo clips are panned left/right.

Media Composer also contains a legacy feature that will play unpanned mono clips out of the left or right channel, depending on which track they are cut into. Clips in odd-numbered tracks are played out of the left; clips in even numbered tracks are played out of the right. The treatment of unpanned mono clips is determined in the Audio settings panel. Be sure it's set to All Tracks Centered. To be safe, you may want to explicitly pan your clips with the mixer.

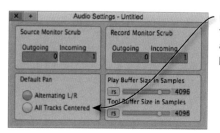

By default, mono clips that haven't been panned are treated as if they were panned to the center.

Avid also offers a shortcut that makes Clip Mode center panning quicker. Simply select a group of clips in a bin and choose Clip > Center Pan. To remove pan settings choose Clip > Remove Pan. You can do the same things by right-clicking the clips and making your selection from the contextual menu.

Pan Automation

To display pan automation in the timeline, use the track control panel to display pan keyframes for the tracks you're interested in. Then add keyframes and adjust the pan value at each one, either with the mixer or in the timeline. To pan a clip to the left, drag it to the top of the track; to pan it to the right, drag it to the bottom. Note that you can't display Pan and Volume simultaneously.

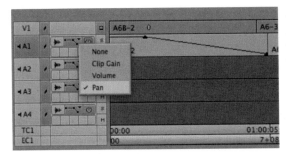

To adjust pan values, display them with the track panel or use the Mixer. The clip displayed is panned from left to right.

Sequence Formats and Surround Mixing

Pan controls are dependant on your sequence format and monitoring environment, which are controlled via two adjacent pop-up menus in the mixer. By default, sequences are stereo, but if you've got the hardware and speakers for multi-channel audio, you can make surround mixes and pan your audio around the room.

Load your sequence into the record monitor, open the mixer and choose your sequence type from the Sequence Mix Format pop-up. Then choose a monitor configuration from the Monitor Mix Format pop-up. Media Composer automatically mixes down your tracks and plays them out of the hardware channels available, based on the Monitor Format you choose.

Sequence Mix Format.   Monitor Mix Format.

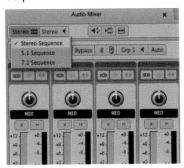

The sequence format determines how tracks can be panned, and the mixer adjusts accordingly, providing either mono, stereo or surround panners. In a stereo sequence, mono clips display a single panner, allowing you to pan the clip left, right or anywhere in between. Stereo clips display two panners, one for each channel. Option-click a panner to quickly set it to a standard position, centering a mono panner or moving a stereo panner 100% left or 100% right.

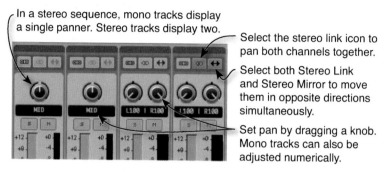

In a stereo sequence, mono tracks display a single panner. Stereo tracks display two.

Select the stereo link icon to pan both channels together.

Select both Stereo Link and Stereo Mirror to move them in opposite directions simultaneously.

Set pan by dragging a knob. Mono tracks can also be adjusted numerically.

In a 5.1 or 7.1 sequence, stereo and mono tracks display surround panners, allowing you to pan them anywhere you like. (Note that surround tracks in a surround sequence are fixed and don't display adjustable panners. For full control, separate your tracks into mono elements by right-clicking them in the timeline and choosing Split Track to Mono.)

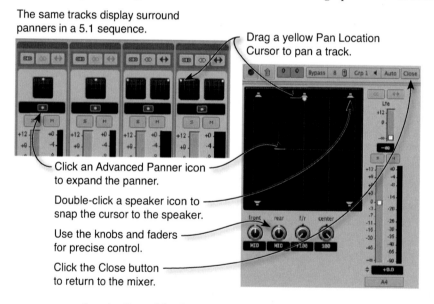

The same tracks display surround panners in a 5.1 sequence.

Drag a yellow Pan Location Cursor to pan a track.

Click an Advanced Panner icon to expand the panner.

Double-click a speaker icon to snap the cursor to the speaker.

Use the knobs and faders for precise control.

Click the Close button to return to the mixer.

Keyframes are created and adjusted in the same way they are for audio levels. Note that pan keyframes can only display limited data in a two-dimensional timeline track. Choose the data you want displayed in the Track Control Panel.

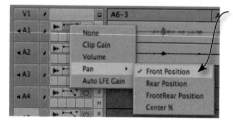

In a 5.1 sequence you can display pan data from one of several dimensions in the timeline.

Audio Output

You'll determine the way multi-channel audio is handled by your hardware with the Output tab in the Audio Project settings panel. With native, built-in audio, all you can do is set an overall output level and chose whether to output in stereo or mixed mono. But with Avid's Nitris hardware you're offered a host of options via pop-up menus, including Direct output, which routes every track in the timeline to a separate hardware channel.

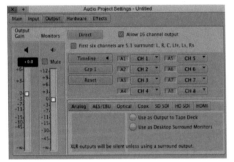

Audio EQ

The Audio EQ Tool allows you to add real-time, three-band equalization to audio clips. To use it, park on a clip in the timeline and select the appropriate track or tracks. Then select the EQ Tool from the Tools menu and make adjustments by dragging the sliders, raising or lowering the volume in each frequency range: low, middle and high. You can also enter values numerically in the text fields. As soon as you make an adjustment, EQ icons appear on the appropriate clip or clips.

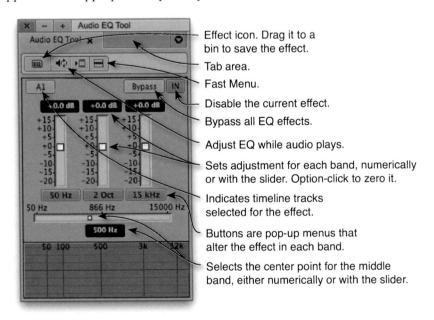

Effect icon. Drag it to a bin to save the effect.

Tab area.

Fast Menu.

Disable the current effect.

Bypass all EQ effects.

Adjust EQ while audio plays.

Sets adjustment for each band, numerically or with the slider. Option-click to zero it.

Indicates timeline tracks selected for the effect.

Buttons are pop-up menus that alter the effect in each band.

Selects the center point for the middle band, either numerically or with the slider.

The Audio Loop Play button has a special role here, allowing you to adjust equalization live, while audio continues to play. (It may take a second or two before you hear an adjustment take effect.) Click the In button to disable the effect you're working on. Click Bypass to disable all EQ effects, including those you've created previously. To save an effect for later use, drag the Effect icon to a bin. Then drag the icon onto another clip to apply it.

The labels below the sliders are pop-up menus, allowing you to change the range of frequencies affected by each band.

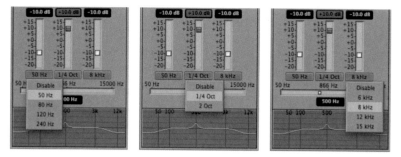

The left and right sliders create a "shelf," meaning that the adjustment boosts or attenuates all frequencies above or below the specified value. The center slider is "parametric," meaning that its effect can be spread over a wide or narrow area, determined by the pop-up. The horizontal slider beneath it allows you to select a center frequency where the adjustment is focused.

To help you visualize what you're doing, the EQ window includes a graph that displays the amount of boost or attenuation applied across the spectrum.

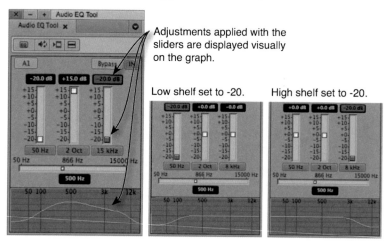

Adjustments applied with the sliders are displayed visually on the graph.

Low shelf set to -20.   High shelf set to -20.

Avid provides a group of useful EQ presets, available in the Fast Menu. Most can't be altered—when you select them the sliders disappear. Others are adjustable. The intended purpose of each preset is indicated in its name, but you may find them useful in other contexts, as well. To remove an EQ effect, use the Delete Effect button or select the effect in the timeline and hit the Delete key.

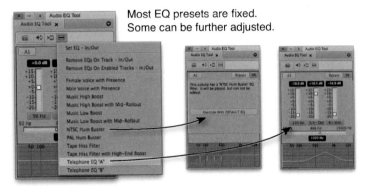

Most EQ presets are fixed. Some can be further adjusted.

AudioSuite Effects

AudioSuite allows you to apply a wide range of sophisticated audio effects, either to individual clips or to entire tracks, using plug-ins designed for Pro Tools systems. Many are included by default, and you can purchase more from Digidesign and other vendors. When applied to clips, these effects must be rendered, but they can be previewed before rendering. Only one effect is permitted per clip. When applied to tracks, they do not need rendering, and up to five can be applied to each track.

To apply an effect to a clip, park on it, select the track containing it and choose Tools > AudioSuite. Then choose the appropriate plug-in from the Selection pop-up menu. Click the plug-in icon to activate it and display its controls.

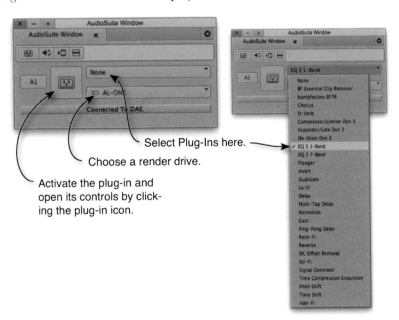

Select Plug-Ins here.

Choose a render drive.

Activate the plug-in and open its controls by clicking the plug-in icon.

There are far too many plug-ins to be described in detail here. Instead, I'll briefly cover two, in order to introduce some basic AudioSuite concepts and controls. Descriptions of the other supplied plug-ins are available in the Media Composer Help system. Track-level effects will be explained in the RTAS section on page 164.

D-Verb

D-Verb produces digital reverb, simulating various kinds of room acoustics. Select it from the AudioSuite plug-in menu and click the activation button to reveal its controls. The top of the window is shared by all AudioSuite effects and includes buttons that allow you to Preview, Render and Bypass the effect. When you click Preview, the clip will be looped, and you can make adjustments while it plays (like the EQ tool, it may take a moment for a change to take effect). To temporarily listen to the clip without the effect, click Bypass. When you're satisfied, click Render.

Note that the clip will display a blue "unrendered" dot until you hit OK, exit the Audio-Suite window and return to the timeline. You can also render from the timeline, as you would with a visual effect. To delete an AudioSuite effect, select it in the timeline and hit Delete, or use the Remove Effect button.

The lower area of the AudioSuite window contains controls for the plug-in itself. D-Verb provides several reverb algorithms. Each one can be further adjusted to mimic three different room sizes. Experiment by clicking the buttons and previewing the effect. Then make additional changes, if needed, using the sliders. Adjust the Mix parameter to vary the balance between the treated (wet) and untreated (dry) signal.

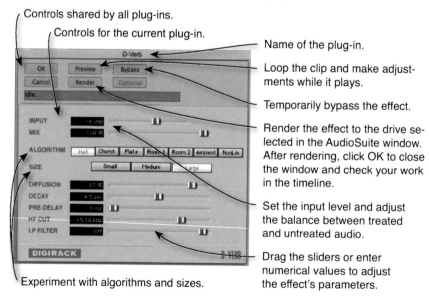

Controls shared by all plug-ins.

Controls for the current plug-in.

Name of the plug-in.

Loop the clip and make adjustments while it plays.

Temporarily bypass the effect.

Render the effect to the drive selected in the AudioSuite window. After rendering, click OK to close the window and check your work in the timeline.

Set the input level and adjust the balance between treated and untreated audio.

Experiment with algorithms and sizes.

Drag the sliders or enter numerical values to adjust the effect's parameters.

1-Band Equalizer

Media Composer now offers improved compatibility with Digidesign plug-ins, and many of the newer ones have a more graphical look. Knobs replace sliders, but they work in much the same way. The EQ III 1-Band Equalizer is a good example. Use it to adjust a single frequency band.

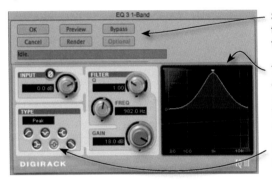

Standard AudioSuite controls to preview and render the effect.

The frequency graph displays the results of your adjustments. Drag the control point or make changes using the knobs.

Select an effect type with the buttons.

It offers these controls:

Control	Effect
Input	Raises or lowers the volume of the source signal.
Q	Adjusts the spread or bandwidth of the effect.
Frequency	Specifies the center frequency where the effect is focused.
Gain	Adjusts the amount of compensation. (Shelf and Notch filters are set to the maximum automatically.)

Choose the effect type by clicking a button in the Type area. Some examples are shown below.

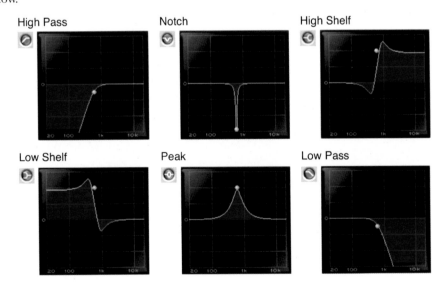

High Pass

Notch

High Shelf

Low Shelf

Peak

Low Pass

Then either click and drag the control point in the graph or click and drag on a knob. You can drag knobs either vertically or horizontally—there's no need to drag in an arc. Option-click a knob to return it to its default value. Shift-click a control point to invert its effect.

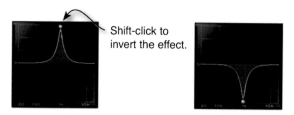

Shift-click to
invert the effect.

The setting for Q bears special mention. It stands for Quality Factor, a mathematical description of the spread or bandwidth of your effect. A low Q disperses the effect over a wide range of frequencies. A high Q focuses it tightly. To change the Q visually, hold down the Control key, then click and drag the control point.

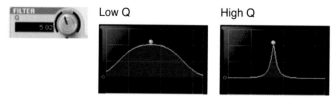

Low Q   High Q

As you work, click the Preview button to audition your changes. When you're satisfied, click Render and OK and check your work in the timeline. If you need more control, try using the EQ III 4-Band or 7-Band Equalizer. They feature a similar interface but allow you to make adjustments to four or seven frequency bands.

Real-Time AudioSuite Effects (RTAS)

You can now add AudioSuite effects in another way: by applying them to a track in the timeline. This allows you to do things that were difficult or impossible before, such as ringing out music into silence, or adding equalization to an actor's entire performance. But the technology has limitations, because effects can't be automated—whatever you do applies to an entire track. These plug-ins, known as Real-Time AudioSuite effects, or RTAS effects, play in real time. No rendering is needed, and you can make adjustments live while audio plays. Media Composer ships with a wide assortment of them and many more are available for purchase from third parties. (You'll often get both AudioSuite and RTAS versions of an effect in the same package.)

RTAS effects are added to tracks using the RTAS insert buttons in the timeline Track Control Panel. You can apply up to five effects per track, labeled "a" through "e." Multiple effects are processed in order, from left to right.

To add an effect, choose Tools > RTAS, or simply click an RTAS button. The RTAS Tool opens, where you can select the effect, the track, and the insert where you want it installed. RTAS effects also appear in the Effect Palette, and you can drag them from there to an insert button, as well.

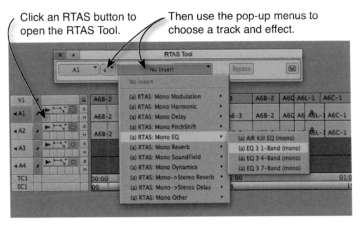

Click an RTAS button to open the RTAS Tool.

Then use the pop-up menus to choose a track and effect.

When you make a selection, the plug-in appears in the RTAS Tool, where you can audition it and make changes to its parameters. Effects are provided for mono, stereo and surround tracks; you'll be offered those designed for the track you're working on. Once you've added an effect to an insert, simply press play. You'll hear the effect and you'll be able to make adjustments as it plays. If you have marks in the timeline, and the RTAS window is active, clip play will loop between the marks. When you're satisfied, close the RTAS window.

To make changes to an effect at a later time, click the appropriate insert button. The RTAS window opens with your effect selected. To remove an effect, select No Insert from the plug-in pop-up. To move an effect to different insert, drag it there. To copy it to another track, Option-drag it.

To save an effect with all your adjustments, drag the insert button, or the Effect Icon in the RTAS window, to a bin. To reapply it elsewhere, drag it from the bin to an insert. Note that RTAS effects are not copied when one sequence is edited into another. To preserve your effects, copy them to a bin and reapply them to the destination sequence.

The RTAS Tool with the 1-Band EQ effect applied.

To save an effect, drag the insert or the Effect Icon to a bin.

Enlarging the Timeline

When you're working primarily with audio, and you've got a client monitor, it can be helpful to shrink the Composer window by hiding video, and simultaneously expand the timeline. (See page 61.) You can then enlarge your audio tracks, display waveforms and keyframes and control everything with more precision.

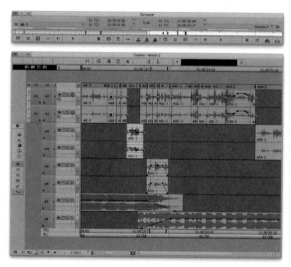

Composer video hidden.

Timeline window enlarged.

Short video tracks.

Tall audio tracks with waveforms and keyframes displayed and waveforms enlarged.

You can memorize such a window arrangement and associate it with a timeline view using a Workspace. (See page 260).

Two Kinds of Audio Dissolves

To smooth out audio transitions, you can quickly create real-time audio dissolves by simply selecting a transition and then entering a dissolve length in the Trim Mode dissolve field. (You can also use the Quick Transition dialog box. See page 192.)

Sometimes you'll hear an audible dip in the center of a dissolve. To deal with that, the system lets you make two kinds of effects: Linear, which is the default, and Constant Power, which adds a 3 db boost at the center. You'll find the option in the Effects Tab of Audio Project settings. Note that the setting is applied to new dissolves only. Any dissolve you make after changing it will reflect the change, but dissolves made beforehand remain as they were.

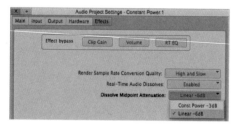

Once you've made a dissolve, there's no way to determine what kind it is. If you don't like how a dissolve sounds, change the setting and remake it. To make it easier to switch from one type to the other, create two Audio Project settings, one with each type of dissolve selected. (See page 256.)

iTunes for Music and Effects

If you work with a lot of music and sound effects, it can be helpful to organize your audio library using a standalone browser. iTunes works well for this, comes with every Mac and is a free download for PCs. Once you get used to the way it works, you may wonder how you got along without it.

One of the problems with importing sound effects into Media Composer is that you have to add descriptions by hand. But most of the commercial sound effects libraries are now part of the Gracenote database, so when you load those CDs into iTunes, the disk is recognized and tracks can get labeled automatically. Once your effects are loaded into iTunes, you'll be able to do a keyword search and find everything with the word "splash" or "gunshot" or "wind" in the description and listen with a simple hit of the space bar. And unlike Media Composer, iTunes keeps playing even as you move around in a clip, which makes it great for browsing.

More important, iTunes can play material while you play something else in Media Composer. This makes it a good tool for experimenting with temp music. Park in a sequence where you need music and press play. Then switch to iTunes and press play there. You'll be playing music against picture, and you can move your cursor around in either application and try different sync positions easily.

If you're using external audio hardware for your Avid, be sure the audio output of your computer is routed through it as well. You don't want to listen to iTunes through the tiny speakers on your computer when everything else is coming from a bigger system.

Importing

To make the import into Media Composer easier, have iTunes name your files with the Gracenote track name. Before loading, select iTunes Preferences > Advanced > Keep iTunes Music folder organized. iTunes will use descriptive filenames, which will end up in your bin as clip names. Media Composer can handle most formats that iTunes can create, but to be safe, check that your preferred format will import before loading a lot of audio.

Media Composer won't import from iTunes directly. Instead, drag from iTunes to your desktop (or, to keep things neat, to a folder). This creates a copy of the sound file and leaves the original in iTunes. Then drag the copy into a bin. Once the file has been successfully imported you can delete the copy in the Finder. You can also right-click a clip in iTunes, select Show in Finder and drag from there into a bin. Or you can select a bin in Media Composer and choose File > Import.

If you make an interim file on the desktop, you may want to edit the filename before importing. When files are named to match descriptions from Gracenote, they sometimes end up with long names containing unnecessary punctuation. Better to keep them short and simple. Finally, consider your sample rate options before importing. See page 215 for details.

13

Visual Effects

Avid's visual effects capabilities have grown significantly over the years, and it's well beyond the scope of this book to cover all available effects. Instead, I'll offer a detailed overview and describe some key features that have been added recently or seem underutilized.

Applying Effects

Visual effects are listed in two places: the Effects Tab of the Project window and the Effect Palette. The Project tab is always available, the Effect Palette is accessed from the Tools menu, but there's little difference between them. Effect categories are listed in the left column, effects within that category are listed on the right. Avid makes a distinction between Segment Effects, which are applied to clips, and Transition Effects, which are applied to cuts. But some effects can work for both.

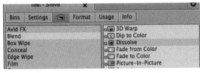 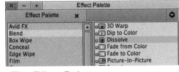

The Effects tab in the Project Window.   The Effect Palette.

The system uses a top-down effects metaphor. If an effect in an upper track is transparent, you'll see through it to the clip below. Each video track contains a monitor button. If you monitor the top track you'll see everything. If you monitor a lower track, you'll see that track and the ones below it. To solo a track, Command-click its monitor button.

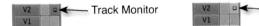

To add an effect, simply drag it to a clip or cut in the timeline. (If an effect is already present, this will replace it.) You can also apply effects by selecting a clip or transition and then double-clicking an effect icon. To apply an effect to several clips at once, select them all before double-clicking. Dissolves and fades can also be applied using the Quick Transition dialog box (page 192), or the dissolve field in Trim Mode (page 100). To delete an effect, select the clip and hit Delete or use the Remove Effect button.

Effect Mode

To adjust an effect, select it in the timeline, or park on it and select its video track. Then click the Effect Mode button in the timeline. The Effect Editor opens and the record monitor changes into an Effect Preview Monitor. The system employs two keyframe models: Standard and Advanced. Standard keyframes are displayed in a single, unified row under the preview monitor. Advanced keyframes are displayed in separate rows in the editor window, one for each parameter, and can also be adjusted graphically. This offers much more control, but adds complexity. Most effects now use the advanced model.

If you double-click a sequence created in an older version of the software, one containing outdated standard effects, the system offers to copy it and promote its effects to advanced keyframes. You can also promote a sequence manually by right-clicking it and selecting Update Effects. (If you need to open a newly created sequence in an older Media Composer, use Revert Effects.)

The standard effects editor is shown below; advanced effects are covered on page 174. Basic operations work the same way with both types. Standard effects contain keyframes at the first and last frame, advanced don't, but you can add them with a menu pick. Click a keyframe to select it. Shift-click to select more than one. Then make changes using the sliders. Tools and buttons appear along the right and bottom of the Effect Editor.

Effect Name. Effect Icon.   Effect duration. ──────   Position in the effect.

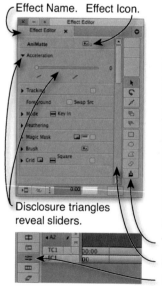
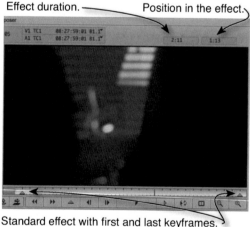

Disclosure triangles
reveal sliders.

Standard effect with first and last keyframes.
Toolbar shows tools appropriate for selected effect.
Scroll bar lets you move through all parameters.
Effect Mode button opens the Effect Editor.

Select a slider by clicking on its handle, then drag as needed, or enter values with the numeric keypad. Use the cursor up/down or left/right arrow keys to adjust the slider one unit at a time. (When no slider is selected, left/right will move the position indicator.) Add the Shift key to adjust by ten units. In Effect Mode, the trim left and trim right buttons can also be used to adjust slider values.

Use the Tab key to move from one effects slider to the next. Use the Fast Forward and Rewind buttons to move to the next or previous keyframe. Option-drag a keyframe to move it in time (left/right).

To copy all parameters from one keyframe to another, click the source keyframe under the preview monitor and select Copy. Then click the destination keyframe and paste. To save an effect, drag the effect icon from the Effect Editor to a bin. To reuse it, drag it from the bin to a clip in the timeline. Bins that contain effects saved this way appear at the bottom of the effects tab or effects palette, allowing you quick access to them.

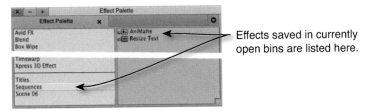

Effects saved in currently open bins are listed here.

Effects that will play in real time display a green dot in the effect tab and palette and in the timeline. Effects that must be rendered display a blue dot (and no dot in the palette).

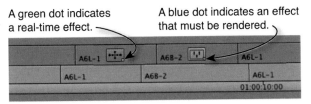

A green dot indicates a real-time effect.

A blue dot indicates an effect that must be rendered.

Render your effects, if needed, using the Render options in the Clip menu. To render everything in a range, select tracks, mark in and out, and choose Render In/Out. You can also use ExpertRender In/Out, which will analyze your effects and render only what's necessary to let them play properly. To render an individual effect, park on it, select tracks, clear marks and choose Render at Position, or use the Render Effect button.

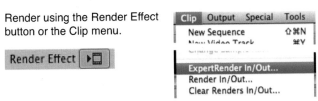

Render using the Render Effect button or the Clip menu.

Note that you can preview any effect in the Effect Editor by simply hitting Play. Effects that must be rendered will play slowly, but you'll get a sense of how they work in motion.

Nested Effects

To explore the contents of an effect, use the Step In and Step Out buttons at the bottom of the timeline. Park on a visual effect, select the track containing it, and click Step In to reveal its contents. For a simple effect you'll just see the raw source clip, without the effect applied. This allows you to replace the source without changing the effect itself. Edit normally within the stepped-in timeline, patching if necessary, then click Step Out to look at the clip with the effect applied.

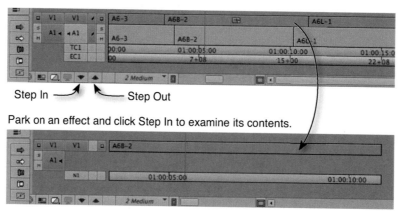

Step In ⟶   ⟵ Step Out

Park on an effect and click Step In to examine its contents.

More important, you can use these functions to add multiple effects to the same clip, without adding layers in the timeline. Avid calls this Nesting. Apply your first effect to a clip. Then Option-drag another effect to the same clip, or select the clip in the timeline and Option-double-click an effect in effects tab or palette. The first effect seems to disappear, but it's still there, nested underneath. Hit Step In to see it. To reveal the raw source clip, step in again. This allows you to manipulate the elements of a complex effect individually, one layer at a time.

You can also see nested effects by expanding them in the timeline. Activate a segment tool and then double-click a clip containing an effect. The timeline opens to show the layer under the effect. If you've got more than one nested layer, double-click each one to reveal its contents, until all are visible. They'll be displayed in reverse order, with the last effect you applied on the bottom of the stack and the unaffected source clip on top.

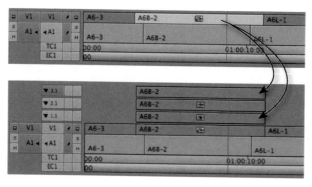

Double-click a nested effect to reveal the layer beneath it. Here, a resize was applied first, then a flop and finally a color correction.

You can patch, edit and make changes in this mode; even trimming is permitted. To add additional effects, drag or Option-drag them to the appropriate clip. To create an additional layer, select a layer, then right-click in the timeline and choose New Video Track. The new layer is created above the one you selected.

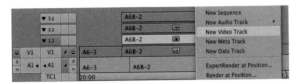

When you're finished, double-click each clip to close the layer above it. Note that when you work in this mode, you'll be monitoring the entire effect stack in the record monitor. If you need to see the layers separately, use the Step In and Step Out functions, instead.

You can also view and manipulate all nested effects on a clip simultaneously, as a single, unified effect stack, as long as they all employ advanced keyframes (see page 175).

Collapse/Submaster

Another way to simplify your timeline is to take a stack of effects in separate video layers and collapse them into a single clip. Select the clips you want to collapse, or select tracks and mark in at the beginning of the effect and out at the end. Then click the Collapse button. The stack turns into a single clip with the Submaster effect applied.

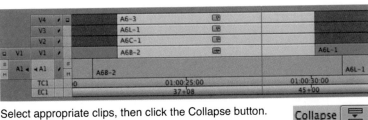

Select appropriate clips, then click the Collapse button.

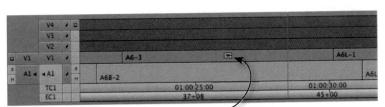

The clips are merged into a single object, with the Submaster effect applied.

To reveal the contents of the Submaster, simply double-click it with a segment tool, or use the Step In button. But note well: Submaster effects can't be parsed by FilmScribe, and you'll get an error message if you try to make lists for sequences containing them. If you need to make film lists, don't collapse your effects, or plan on re-editing the effects to remove the nest, when you need to make lists.

Advanced Keyframes

Because Avid's standard effects model displays all keyframes in a single row, there's no way to isolate keyframes for individual parameters. Advanced keyframes work differently, displaying values for each parameter separately. This provides more control, and allows you to do things that were once impossible. For example, it lets you to change the way the system interpolates values between keyframes. The old model simply drew a straight line—if a value moved from 0 to 100 and back to 0, it seemed to bounce harshly at the center keyframe. The new model allows you to create and manipulate curves between keyframes, and thus it helps you make effects that feel smoother and more organic.

A simple resize effect, used for blowing up or repositioning a shot, is shown below, with the Effect Editor positioned over the preview monitor. Each parameter displays a separate row of keyframes. (If you don't see them, click the Show Keyframe icon.)

Effect Track (Resize).   Group Track (Scaling).   Parameter Tracks (X/Y).

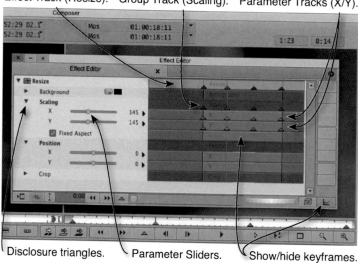

Disclosure triangles.   Parameter Sliders.   Show/hide keyframes.

You can move keyframes around in the position bar under the preview monitor or with the unified Effect Track at the top of the Effect Editor, which serves the same purpose. But you can also control each parameter individually. Disclosure triangles are used to cluster parameters into Groups, such as Scaling, Position or Crop. This allows you to manipulate all keyframes in the group, or to set values for individual parameters. For example, in the illustration above, clicking on a keyframe in the Scaling group will select keyframes in the X and Y tracks simultaneously.

Moving Multiple Keyframes in Time

One nice feature of the advanced model is that it allows you to move adjacent keyframes together in time (left/right). Click the first keyframe you want to move and Shift-click the others. Then hold down the Option key and drag any selected keyframe to move all of them at once.

Keyframe Graphs

The advanced keyframe interface also allows you to display each keyframe parameter as a graph, making it easy to see how values change between keyframes. You can manipulate one or more keyframes simply by dragging them.

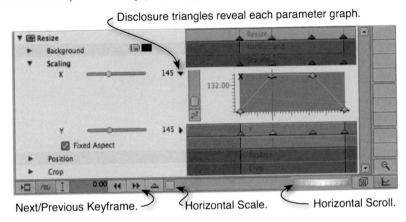

Disclosure triangles reveal each parameter graph.

Next/Previous Keyframe.   Horizontal Scale.   Horizontal Scroll.

In the graph, keyframe movement is normally constrained to the vertical dimension, changing the parameter value. If you want to move the keyframe position in time (horizontally) hold down the Option key while dragging. To move a keyframe horizontally without moving it vertically, hold down Option and Shift simultaneously.

Nesting Effects with Advanced Keyframes

If all the effects in a nest employ advanced keyframes, you can view and adjust them as a single stack in the Effect Editor. In the illustration below, three effects have been nested and are visible simultaneously.

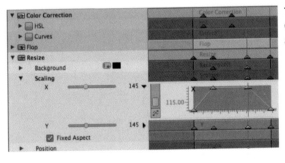

Three nested effects: Color Correction, Flop and Resize.

To change the order of the effects in the nest, simply click and drag an effect icon up or down.

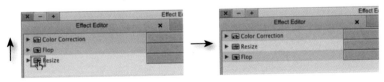

Adding Keyframes

Standard effects require keyframes. But with advanced effects, if you don't plan to vary parameter values, they aren't necessary. For example, if you're simply blowing up a shot, without zooming or moving, you can adjust the scale and position parameters, setting a base value that will be maintained over the duration of the effect. A green line appears in the parameter graph, highlighting the value you've selected. If you then add a keyframe, it will initially be set to that value and will appear on the green line.

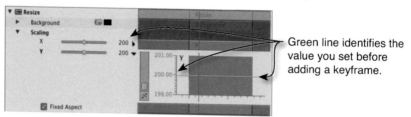

Green line identifies the value you set before adding a keyframe.

But most effects work requires keyframes. Media Composer offers you several ways to add them. With advanced keyframes, the most direct way is to park the position indicator on the appropriate frame, right-click a track or graph and choose Add Keyframe. If you right-click in a parameter track, you'll create a keyframe in that track; if you do it in a group track, you'll create keyframes in all parameters in the group. And if you do it in the effect track, you'll create keyframes in all tracks in the effect. When you right-click in a track, a text message appears identifying the track you've selected.

Adjust the position indicator, then right-click in a track to add a keyframe.

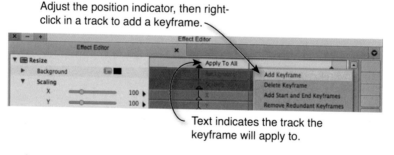

Text indicates the track the keyframe will apply to.

Note that when you add a keyframe to a single parameter, three keyframes are typically created: one in the parameter track, one in the group track containing it and one in the effect track.

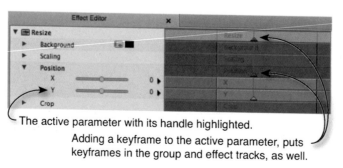

The active parameter with its handle highlighted.

Adding a keyframe to the active parameter, puts keyframes in the group and effect tracks, as well.

Once an initial keyframe is created in an effect, and as long as no keyframes are selected, moving any parameter slider will automatically create a keyframe at the position indicator. To deselect a keyframe, Shift-click it; to deselect all keyframes in a track, right-click in the track and choose Deselect All Keyframes.

You can also add keyframes using the purple Add Keyframe button (the only way to add keyframes to a standard effect). If you click it in the Effect Editor, it opens the Add Keyframe Mode Menu, allowing you to choose tracks for your keyframes.

The menu makes a distinction between Active, Open and Enabled groups and parameters. The Active parameter is the one you're currently working on, identified by a highlighted slider handle, and, if a graph is open and you've clicked in it, a lighter graph background. The Active Group is the group containing that parameter. An Open group is any group in which the disclosure triangle is facing downwards, revealing its parameters.

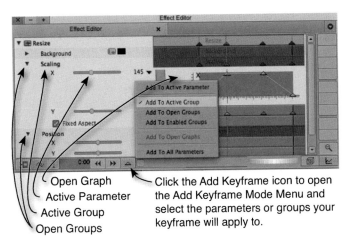

Open Graph
Active Parameter
Active Group
Open Groups

Click the Add Keyframe icon to open the Add Keyframe Mode Menu and select the parameters or groups your keyframe will apply to.

An Enabled effect is the one you're working on, indicated with light gray shading behind its sliders. When two or more effects have been nested, clicking anywhere on an effect's controls will enable it, and selecting Add to Enabled Groups will put a keyframe in all the parameters of that effect. When you're working on a single, un-nested effect, Add to Enabled Groups simply puts keyframes in all parameters.

The menu will only allow you to do things that make sense. If no groups are open, for example, Add to Open Groups will be greyed out. If you add a keyframe from the keyboard, or with the Add Keyframe button under the preview monitor, it will be applied as if you'd used your most recent selection from the menu—the one with the check mark next to it.

To select all keyframes within a track or graph, right-click the track or graph and choose Select All Keyframes. To remove unnecessary keyframes, where parameter values don't change, Right-click in a track or graph where you want to remove keyframes and select Remove Redundant Keyframes.

First and Last Keyframes

Standard effects require keyframes on the first and last frame. But advanced effects don't. Instead, the system lets you control the way parameter values change before the first, and after the last, keyframe you create, wherever they are. Right-click in a track or graph to reveal its contextual menu.

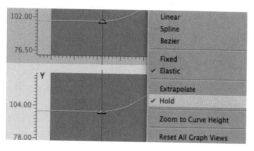

You have two choices: Hold and Extrapolate. Hold makes values at the first and last keyframe persist until the end of the effect, creating a horizontal line in the graph. Extrapolate extends the curve. Hold is the default.

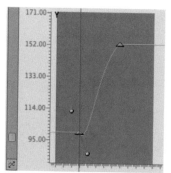
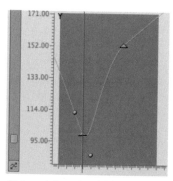

Hold preserves the values at the first and last keyframe.

Extrapolate extends the curve.

If you prefer to use first and last keyframes, you can add them with a quick contextual menu pick. Right-click in the track or graph where you want the keyframes created and choose Add Start and End Keyframes.

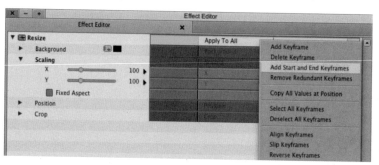

Keyframe Interpolation

Using the same contextual menu, you can change the way the system interpolates values between keyframes.

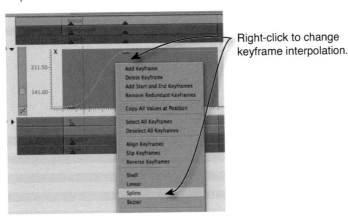

Right-click to change keyframe interpolation.

You have four options: Linear, Spline, Bézier and Shelf. The resulting curves are shown below. The choice you make will apply to all keyframes in a track.

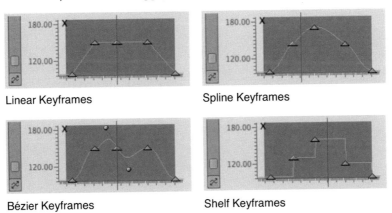

Linear Keyframes

Spline Keyframes

Bézier Keyframes

Shelf Keyframes

Linear is now the default and represents the way interpolation worked with standard keyframes, connecting them with a straight line. To smooth out keyframe transitions, select Spline, instead. Shelf keyframes hold values until the next keyframe, creating sharp transitions. Bézier keyframes offer the most control. When you click on one, handles appear, allowing you to precisely adjust the way interpolated values change at the keyframe. Click and drag the handles to alter the shape of the curve.

You can adjust Bézier handles in three ways: symmetrically, asymmetrically or independently. When you drag a handle symmetrically, both handles move in equal and opposite directions. When you do it asymmetrically they move in opposite directions, but you can control the *distance* of each handle separately. Independent adjustments allow you to freely change the angles and positions. Option-click and drag the handles repeatedly to cycle through these options.

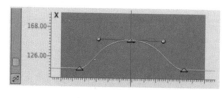

Click on a Bézier keyframe to reveal its handles. Then click and drag a handle to move the control points symmetrically.

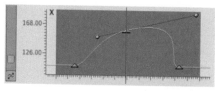

Option-click and drag to make asymmetrical adjustments.

Option-click and drag again to make independent adjustments. Continue to option-click and drag to cycle through these choices.

Vertical Scaling

When you first open a keyframe graph you're likely to see something like the image on the left, below. Your keyframes are visible, but they're closely spaced vertically. To make them easier to see, adjust the scaling of the graph using the vertical scale bar. To quickly expand the graph to fill the viewing area, click the Zoom to Curve Height button, or select that option from the graph's contextual menu.

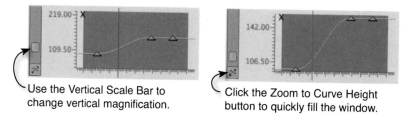

Use the Vertical Scale Bar to change vertical magnification.

Click the Zoom to Curve Height button to quickly fill the window.

To enlarge the graph window vertically, click and drag its bottom edge. If you can't see all your keyframes, Option-click anywhere in the window (but not on a keyframe) to display the hand tool and drag the graph around, as needed.

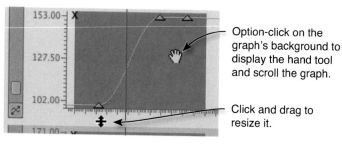

Option-click on the graph's background to display the hand tool and scroll the graph.

Click and drag to resize it.

Aligning and Slipping Keyframes

Using a track's contextual menu, you can move one or more keyframes in time so that they line up with the position indicator, or you can slip an entire keyframe graph, moving the selected keyframe to the indicator and all others the same distance. Select a keyframe; then move the position indicator to the desired location. Right-click in the track or graph and choose Align Keyframes to move that keyframe to the indicator. Select Slip Keyframes to shift the entire graph.

Trimming Keyframes

With standard keyframes, if you change the length of an effect by trimming, all its keyframes move in time (left/right), scaling their positions relative to your trim. This is helpful in certain cases, but more often than not, it means moving all your keyframes back where they were before the trim. With advanced keyframes you have a choice. Elastic keyframes will move proportionally when an effect is trimmed. Fixed keyframes won't. Right-click in a track or graph and make your selection from the track's contextual menu. Your choice applies to the effect, the track, or the group, depending on where you right-click. If you want all the keyframes in an effect to stay where they are when you trim it, right-click in the Effect track and select Fixed.

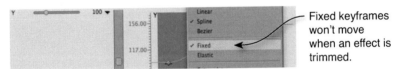

Fixed keyframes won't move when an effect is trimmed.

The two keyframe types have different icons, but you'll only see them in the keyframe graph. Elastic keyframes display the traditional pink triangle. Fixed keyframes are similar, but add a bump on the bottom.

Elastic   Fixed

Effect Editor Shortcut Menu

If you right-click on the background of the Effect Editor, you'll reveal a pop-up that allows you to change its options. (Some choices are also available in Effect Editor Settings.)

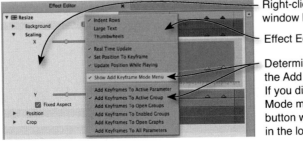

Right-click on the window background.

Effect Editor options.

Determines the behavior of the Add Keyframe button. If you disable the Keyframe Mode menu, the Keyframe button will obey the selection in the lower half of this menu.

Update Position While Playing causes the position indicator to move in the Effect Editor when you press play. Real Time Update displays the result of a change as you drag a slider or keyframe rather than when you release the mouse button. Show Add Keyframe Mode Menu allows you to suppress the pop-up that appears when you click the Add Keyframe button. If you deselect it, the Add Keyframe button will perform the action specified in the list below it.

Reduce and Enlarge Tools

Most effects display zoom in and out buttons in the effect toolbar, allowing you to scale the image in the preview monitor. (Avid calls the buttons Reduce and Enlarge.) You can also use keyboard shortcuts to do the same thing. With the preview window active, Command-L will zoom in and Command-K will zoom out. Or you can hold down the Command key to display a magnifier icon and then click the image to zoom in, moving progressively tighter until you jump back to 100%.

As long as you are zoomed in to a size greater than 100%, holding down the Command and Option keys will turn on the hand tool, allowing you to drag the image vertically or horizontally.

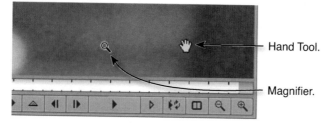

— Hand Tool.

— Magnifier.

Some effects reveal additional controls when you are zoomed out. For example, the Resize effect will display scale handles on the image. Drag them to quickly resize a shot, and simultaneously create a keyframe when you do so. You can also drag the image to reposition it.

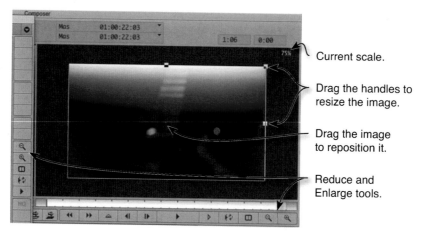

Current scale.

Drag the handles to resize the image.

Drag the image to reposition it.

Reduce and Enlarge tools.

3D Warp / Promote to 3D

Though they've been around for some time, 3D effects are often underutilized by editors. The basic effect is called 3D Warp. It's in the Blend category and offers a wide range of controls for manipulating the 3D geometry and perspective of your video. Some are visible below.

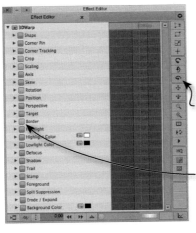

The 3D Warp effect, with all its parameter groups visible. Click the disclosure triangles to open and adjust individual parameters.

Or select a tool and then click and drag on the video image to make adjustments interactively.

Enable buttons turn groups on and off. Option-click a button to reset its parameters to default values.

You can also promote many standard effects to 3D and thereby add all the controls in the 3D Warp effect to them. For example, say you are using a Picture-In-Picture effect to place video in a monitor. To precisely fit the video to the TV, promote the effect to 3D by clicking the 3D icon at the bottom right of the Effect Editor.

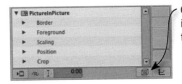

Click the Promote to 3D icon to add 3D parameters to many effects.

The Picture-in-Picture effect is converted to a 3D Warp, and you can then use the geometry controls to change the shape and orientation of the superimposed video. Try using the rotation parameters to rotate the image in space. Or use corner pinning to precisely position each corner of the video. Select the Corner Pin tool and simply drag the corners to position them, as needed. Or open the Corner Pin group and use the sliders to move each corner.

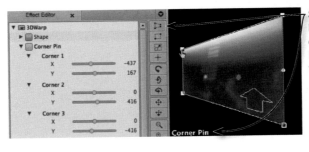

Select the Corner Pin tool and drag each corner. A text label indicates the tool you're using.

Stabilize

Media Composer now allows you to stabilize a shaky shot automatically at high quality. Simply drag the Stabilize effect to a clip in the timeline. The Effect Editor opens, and the shot is played, tracked and cropped, using FluidStabilizer and Steadiglide (see below). All you need to do is watch it happen. Avid calls this AutoStabilize.

If you need more control, click anywhere to stop automatic tracking and undo once to clear the automatic tracking data. Then make selections from the menus. The stabilize effect is very deep and there are a host of options. The following should get you started. For details, check the help system.

One tracker is created automatically and named T1. If necessary, activate it in the Position or Tracking group. The tracker measures movement in your shot so it can be counteracted. The Tracking Window opens automatically. If you don't see it, click the Tracking Tool Button to bring it forward.

Select Tracking Data from the Display pop-up. Then make a selection from the Tracking Engine pop-up. FluidStabilizer is the simplest option because it intelligently analyzes movement in the entire shot. The Correlation Tracker and the FluidTracker analyze movement in one area, instead. You'll choose the area of analysis using two superimposed yellow rectangles. The center rectangle should surround an object that would not move if the shot were stabilized. The outer rectangle represents the search area and should be large enough to capture the existing movement. You can move the tracker, and you can change the size of the rectangles, as well.

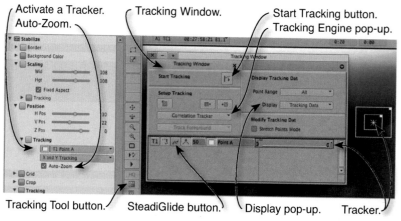

You'll probably want to select SteadiGlide. This permits some movement in the shot (a smooth camera move, for example) while still removing jittery motion. If you want to simulate a locked off shot, choose the Correlation Tracker and leave SteadiGlide off. Then click the Start Tracking button. The shot is played from head to tail and analyzed. Tracking data, a series of dots, will be displayed over video. Play the shot and check it. It will be stabilized, but black will appear at the edges. You'll need to blow it up and reposition it to remove the black. To have this done automatically, select Auto-Zoom.

Paint and Animatte

The Paint and Animatte effects allow you to create vector-based shapes over a shot. Paint is a single-layer effect and applies changes within that layer. Animatte cuts a hole in a shot, allowing video on the track below the effect to be seen through or around the hole. Both effects offer similar tools, and both employ standard keyframes. You can move shapes around the screen, or change their geometry, as the shot plays.

Start by applying the effect to a shot, and enter Effect Mode. Then create one or more shapes, using the shape or brush tools. With the Brush tool active, you can choose brush options to modify its characteristics. Use the Selection Tool to activate each shape and alter it, as needed. You can create rectangles, circles, polygons and free-form curves. Use the Reshape Tool to manipulate individual control points; Option-click with the Reshape Tool to access Bézier handles. Use the Mode Menu to determine the action of a selected shape: blur, sharpen (unsharp mask), colorize, mosaic, and many more options are available. Magic Mask allows you to turn any shape into a mask based on a selected color. Drag an eyedropper from the color well to choose the color.

Then make adjustments, moving or resizing shapes, as needed, to follow the motion of your shot. Keyframes are created automatically when you change a shape, or you can add them manually. Keep in mind that an object must carry the same number of control points throughout a shot.

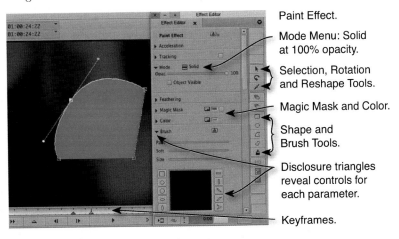

Paint Effect.

Mode Menu: Solid at 100% opacity.

Selection, Rotation and Reshape Tools.

Magic Mask and Color.

Shape and Brush Tools.

Disclosure triangles reveal controls for each parameter.

Keyframes.

Animatte offers much the same tools, but allows you to combine two images. For details on all of the many options for these two effects, see the help system.

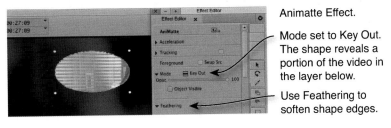

Animatte Effect.

Mode set to Key Out. The shape reveals a portion of the video in the layer below.

Use Feathering to soften shape edges.

Timecode Burn-In

Avid's Timecode Burn-In effect has been significantly improved and now represents an important workflow enhancement for any editor who has to deliver cut material to other departments. You can add four separate fields of data, including timecode at various frame rates or a running footage counter (Avid calls footage "edgecode"), as well as all kinds of source data extracted from bin columns, such as key numbers, timecodes or clip names, which will automatically change from shot to shot. You can add a title (Avid calls it a Note), and you can change the size and position of any element, adjusting the color or transparency of your text or of the bounding box around it. Surprisingly, all this plays in real time. You'll find the Timecode Burn-In effect in the Generator category in the Effect Palette.

Click the disclosure triangles to add and configure data.

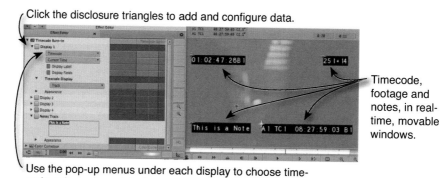

Timecode, footage and notes, in real-time, movable windows.

Use the pop-up menus under each display to choose timecode, edgecode or data from a source bin column.

Motion Effects

Traditional

Avid's traditional motion effects are created from source clips and stored in bins. Speed changes are made by duplicating or dropping frames or fields, so these effects can sometimes look jerky. But because they can be loaded into monitors and played like other clips, they are useful in many situations.

To create a motion effect, load a master clip or subclip into the source monitor and mark in and out to identify the portion of the clip you want to use. Then, with the source monitor activated, click the Motion Effect Editor button. You'll find it on the Tool Palette, but you may want to assign it elsewhere. (See page 66.)

The Motion Effect Editor button in the Tool Palette.

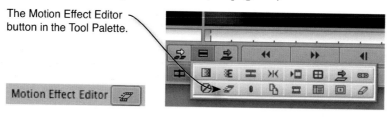

Motion Effect Editor

The Motion Effect window will open. Use the Variable Speed options to specify the speed or duration of your effect. The simplest way to do this is by entering a percentage in the Percent Speed field. To create reverse motion, enter a negative value. If you are trying to fill a specific duration, mark it in the timeline and select Fit To Fill. The marked material in the source monitor will be speed-adjusted to fit the timeline duration. To create a strobe effect, enter a value in the Strobe Motion field. Frames will be held for the duration indicated, skipping forward or backward to match the speed you selected with the Variable Speed options.

Note that though they once had to be rendered, simple, forward-speed motion effects now play in real time (reverse-speed and strobe effects require rendering).

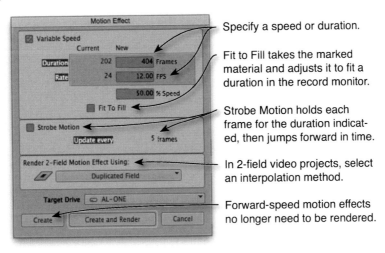

Specify a speed or duration.

Fit to Fill takes the marked material and adjusts it to fit a duration in the record monitor.

Strobe Motion holds each frame for the duration indicated, then jumps forward in time.

In 2-field video projects, select an interpolation method.

Forward-speed motion effects no longer need to be rendered.

When you click Create, the system asks you to select a destination bin, where the motion effect clip will be stored. To help you identify the new clip, the adjusted speed is appended to the clip name.

	Name	Duration
	84A-2 (12.00 FPS)	16:2
	84A-2	1:37:1
	84B-18	1:28:0

Timewarp and Fluidmotion

The Timewarp effect is Avid's advanced way to create motion effects, and because it intelligently creates new frames, it produces results that can look much smoother than the traditional motion effects described above. It also allows you to ramp from one speed to another in the middle of a shot, or even move from forward to reverse motion or create a freeze, all within a single effect. Depending on the options you choose and the complexity of the resulting effect, it may play in real time. If playback hesitates, you'll need to render.

Unlike traditional motion effects, Timewarps are applied directly to clips in the timeline. You'll find Timewarp in the effects tab or palette, in a category also called Timewarp. Drag the effect to a clip in the timeline. Then park the position indicator on it and select the track containing the clip (or select the clip using a segment tool) and click the Motion Effect Editor button on the left side of the timeline. The Motion Effect Editor opens, allowing you to configure the effect.

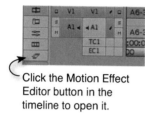

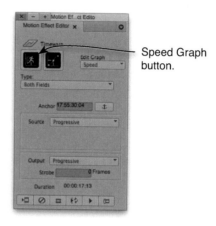

Click the Motion Effect Editor button in the timeline to open it.

Speed Graph button.

Click the Speed Graph button to reveal the graph below. Start by selecting an interpolation option from the Interpolation Type pop-up. This determines the way the effect creates new frames. The most flexible approach is to start with something that is likely play in real time, such as Both Fields, or Blended Interpolated, which can be a bit smoother. This allows you to quickly manipulate the effect and set speed values without stopping to render.

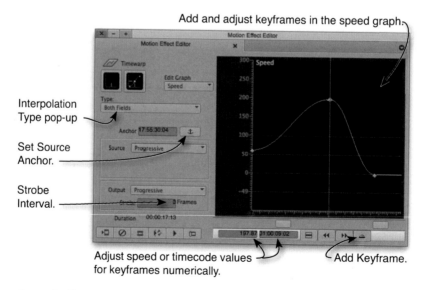

Add and adjust keyframes in the speed graph.

Interpolation Type pop-up

Set Source Anchor.

Strobe Interval.

Adjust speed or timecode values for keyframes numerically.

Add Keyframe.

Then make and adjust your keyframes. The simplest effect has only one keyframe, located automatically at the first frame of the clip. Click on that keyframe to activate it and drag it up or down to change speed, or type a value in the Percent Speed text box at the bottom of the graph. The entire clip will now play at this new speed. Check your work by playing it.

Though the duration of the clip hasn't changed, its out point has been adjusted, because the shot is playing at a new speed. You may need to trim the shot longer or shorter to get the result you want. Note that the Motion Effect Editor differs from the standard Effect Editor in that you can continue to work in the timeline without closing it. You can even trim the effect with the Motion Effect Editor open.

If you want to vary the speed within your effect, add additional keyframes and adjust them, as needed. To move a keyframe horizontally, Option-drag it. To move it horizontally without moving it vertically, use Shift-Option-drag. To create a strobe effect, enter a value in the Strobe field. Note that strobe effects won't play in real time.

Once you've got the basic motion working, you can experiment with interpolation options by selecting them from the Interpolation Type pop-up. Fluidmotion usually looks smoothest, but it needs to be rendered and can sometimes create artifacts.

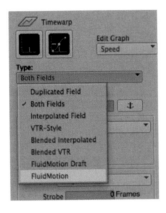

Promoting a Traditional Motion Effect

If you've got a traditional motion effect edited into your sequence and want more control, you can easily convert it to a Timewarp. Park on it, select the appropriate track and open the Motion Effect Editor by clicking either the Motion Effect or Effect Mode button. Hit Promote to convert the clip.

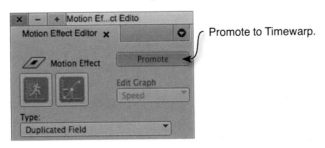

Promote to Timewarp.

Anchor Frame

Timewarp effects normally lock down the position of the first frame of your clip, adjusting the out point based on the speed changes you make within the effect. But it's possible to lock the position of any other frame and move the rest of the clip instead. For example, you could lock the last frame and allow the start frame to be adjusted. Or you could lock down any other frame internally. It's easiest to select your anchor frame before you start to make adjustments. Otherwise you'll find frames moving around unpredictably.

Move the position indicator to the frame you want to lock down. Add a keyframe at that position. Then hit the Set Source Anchor button. The anchor icon under the speed graph moves to the selected keyframe. Now make your adjustments, changing speeds or adding additional keyframes, as needed.

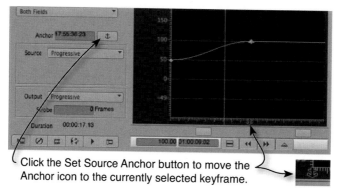

Click the Set Source Anchor button to move the Anchor icon to the currently selected keyframe.

If you simply intend to change the speed of a shot without ramping it, but want an anchor frame within the body of the shot, add your anchor frame and then delete the automatic keyframe at the beginning of the effect.

Keyframe Options

Timewarp effects employ advanced keyframes and can be manipulated like other advanced effects. For example, you can select and move several keyframes at the same time. Right-click on the keyframe graph, or click the Motion Effect Editor's Fast Menu, to see many of the advanced keyframe options described earlier (page 174). Note that by default, Timewarp effects employ fixed keyframes.

Right-click on the keyframe graph to select keyframe options.

Timewarp Presets

The Timewarp effects category also includes several simplified motion effect presets, including 0-100%, 100%-0%, Reverse Motion, Speed Burst, and Speed Bump. These represent pre-built Timewarps that can quickly be applied to a clip without creating keyframes. Once they're applied, you can modify them any way you like. Note that the presets use elastic keyframes, so if you trim, keyframes will move proportionally. Also note that they start with interpolation set to Both Fields. As with other Timewarp effects, once you've adjusted the shot to your liking, you can alter the interpolation method.

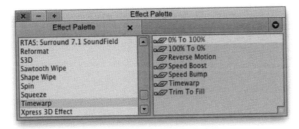

Trim to Fill

Trim to Fill is perhaps the most useful of these presets. When you first apply it to a clip, nothing changes. But when you trim the shot, the head and tail frames don't change—the speed of the clip changes instead with the new speed displayed next to the clip name. You'll see the same action on the clip, but it will run slower or faster depending on how much you trim.

Freeze Frames

You can create a frozen frame two ways, either traditionally, or using a Timewarp effect. Traditional freeze frames create clips and media for a single frame held for a duration you specify. Load a clip into the source monitor and park on the frame you want to freeze. Then select Clip > Freeze Frame. You'll be asked to select a target drive and bin. Once your clip is created, you can edit it just like any other clip.

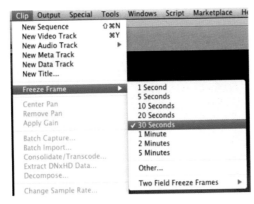

To create a freeze with a Timewarp, apply the effect to a clip in the timeline and add a keyframe on the frame you want to freeze. Then, right click on the speed graph background and select Shelf keyframes (see page 179). Set the speed at the keyframe to 0%. This causes motion at the keyframe to stop instantly. With interpolation set to Both Fields, freeze frames typically don't require rendering.

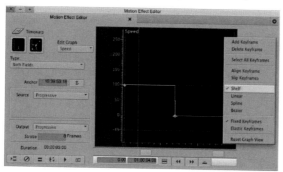

Fades and Dissolves

The system provides several ways to create fades and dissolves. You can use the Quick Transition dialog box, you can drag an effect from the effect palette, or you can use the dissolve field in Trim Mode. (See "Dissolves in Trim Mode" on page 100. You can also manipulate transition effects with the Transition Tool. See page 31.)

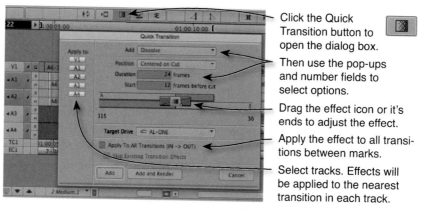

Click the Quick Transition button to open the dialog box.

Then use the pop-ups and number fields to select options.

Drag the effect icon or it's ends to adjust the effect.

Apply the effect to all transitions between marks.

Select tracks. Effects will be applied to the nearest transition in each track.

Any of these methods will create fades, but you may find it quicker to use the Head Fade and Tail Fade buttons. You'll find them by default in the timeline button bar. They work differently than other effect creation tools, in that they use the position indicator to identify one end of the fade.

If you're making a fade in, position the blue bar where you want the effect to end, select the tracks you want to fade, including audio tracks, and hit the Head Fade button. MC

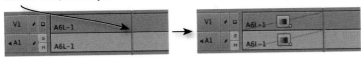

will add a video dissolve to selected picture tracks and an audio dissolve to selected sound tracks, starting at the head of the current clip and ending at the position indicator. You can do the same thing at the end of a clip using the Tail Fade button. In that case your fade will start at the blue bar and end at the tail of the clip.

To create a fade in, park the position indicator where you want the fade to end, select your tracks, and click the Head Fade button.

Cuts Against Fades

Fades that are cut directly against other clips can create problems, sometimes turning into dissolves. If possible, it's a good idea to put at least one frame of filler between your fade and the next segment. If you're making a fade out/fade in, insert a frame of filler between the fades or use the Dip to Color effect.

Film Dissolves and Fades

Media Composer was unique in its ability, early on, to simulate the look of analog film effects, the kind created in an optical printer. When made this way, dissolves and fades appear shorter than they actually are. A six-foot (four-second) dissolve, for example, will appear to be about five feet long. Fades are typically even more truncated. Video effects work differently. A four second dissolve is visible for a full four seconds.

The discrepancy is due to the "S" shape of the film exposure curve—in video the curve is a straight line. This gives it a different feel, more gradual when starting and ending. The Film Dissolve effect simulates this by recreating the film exposure curve. It's based on the interpositive/internegative stock that was in use in the early '90s and was pretty accurate in its time. The Film Fade effect was designed to mimic another issue, as well: the way an optical camera shutter works for fades. It was somewhat less successful in accurately simulating film.

At one time, feature films and long-form television were universally finished on film, and all dissolves were created optically. Today, few people finish their effects that way, and most editors should probably avoid film effects. If, on the other hand, you prefer the feel of the these effects, you should be able to up-res them accurately in an Avid finishing environment. Standard effects and film effects are displayed with different icons, as follows:

Dissolve

Fade From Color

Fade To Color

Film Dissolve

Film Fade

Note that when you create a dissolve in Trim Mode, the type of dissolve you create will be determined by the last dissolve you made in the Quick Transition dialog box. By default that should be a standard dissolve, but if you're unsure, open Quick Transition and create one. After that, any dissolve you make in Trim Mode will be a standard dissolve.

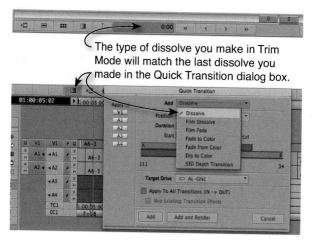

The type of dissolve you make in Trim Mode will match the last dissolve you made in the Quick Transition dialog box.

Effect Summary

With a Sequence Report, you can generate a useful summary of all the effects in a sequence. This can be particularly helpful in identifying nested effects, because they are normally hidden and you have to step in to see them.

Right-click your sequence in a bin (or load it into the record monitor and right-click the monitor). Then select Sequence Report. In the window that opens, you can choose to list the effects in a marked range or in enabled tracks. You can have the list tell you where all your effects are or have it only show nested effects. Click Generate Report and select a destination. The report is a standard txt file and will open automatically in a text editor.

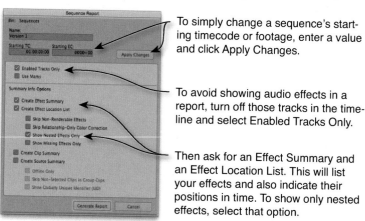

To simply change a sequence's starting timecode or footage, enter a value and click Apply Changes.

To avoid showing audio effects in a report, turn off those tracks in the timeline and select Enabled Tracks Only.

Then ask for an Effect Summary and an Effect Location List. This will list your effects and also indicate their positions in time. To show only nested effects, select that option.

Note that in film projects, timecode locations in the report are sometimes listed in Avid's NP (No Pulldown) timecode format. To locate the effects in your sequence, you may have to display 30 NP Master Timecode above the record monitor.

Measuring Effects with I/O

You can't display center duration in Effects Mode, and that makes it hard to measure the distance between keyframes. Making your marks and then jumping back to Source/Record Mode in order to measure something gets old very quickly. But there's an easier way. Just display I/O in the tracking information above your record monitor (see "Monitor Tracking Data" on page 56). The display will be visible in Effects Mode and will show you the distance between your marks. One way to use it is to make only one mark in the timeline. I/O will then show you the distance from the mark to the position indicator, and it will update as you move the blue bar.

Render on the Fly

When you park on an effect or drag the position indicator through it, the system normally attempts to present the effect as if it were rendered. If you have a complicated but unrendered effect in the timeline, it can cause performance to suffer as you drag through it. With today's processors this is rarely a problem, but if you notice a slow-down, you can turn this feature off by deselecting Render on the Fly in the Special menu.

Render on the Fly is also available in Trim Settings. There it is off by default and only applies when you are stopped in Trim Mode.

Effect Editor Settings

The Effect Editor has its own settings panel. If you're having trouble seeing numbers and text on the editor screen, select Large Text to blow it up a bit. Choose Update Position While Playing to have the position indicator in the Effect Editor move when you are playing (with complex effects this can slow down playback). If you'd rather not see the Add Keyframe Mode Menu (page 177), you can turn it off, as well.

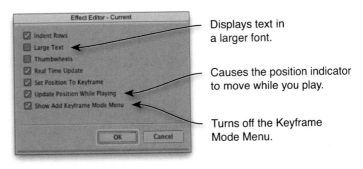

14

Color Correction

Color correction is an art, and a full treatment of the subject could easily fill this entire volume. Instead, I'll lay out a brief introduction to get you started, along with a few important tips.

Controls Overview

Color Correction effects are normally applied from within Color Correction Mode, invoked via the mode button in the timeline.

Color Correction Mode ▦

Hit the button and the Composer window changes to reveal three monitors. By default, the center monitor displays the clip you're parked on, the left, the last frame of the previous shot, and the right, the first frame of the following shot. This allows you to compare color from shot to shot. You can also customize the monitors to display several kinds of scopes and other options. Click the title of each pane to open a menu and configure it.

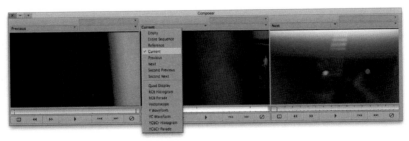

Below the clip frames you'll see three hue offset wheels, one each for shadows, midtones and highlights.

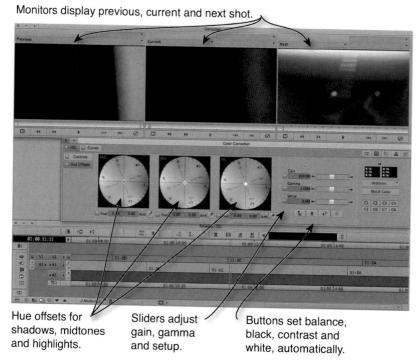

Monitors display previous, current and next shot.

Hue offsets for shadows, midtones and highlights.

Sliders adjust gain, gamma and setup.

Buttons set balance, black, contrast and white, automatically.

To create a basic color correction, select the video track containing the clip you want to work on, and then simply make an adjustment, either by dragging the white cross-hair in the middle of one of the wheels, or using any of the other controls. A Color Correction effect will be applied to your shot. For the simplest corrections, the central, midtone wheel may be all you need. Just drag the cross-hair around until you see what you like. But many other controls allow you to fine-tune your work.

Buttons under the three monitors move you from shot to shot and should be self-explanatory. The Dual Split button divides the image in half, displaying the shot both with your correction and without it. It's a toggle: click to turn it on, click again to turn it off. Use the four white triangles in the dual-split display to change the dimensions of the split.

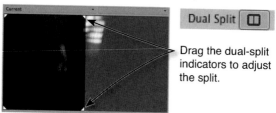

Dual Split

Drag the dual-split indicators to adjust the split.

Notice the controls to the right of the color wheels. The sliders allow you to make adjustments to Gain, Gamma and Setup numerically, and the buttons add automatic adjustments for color balance, contrast, white level and black level. Like other effects, you can save a correction by dragging the effect template icon to a bin.

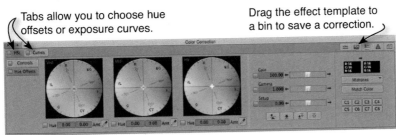

Tabs allow you to choose hue offsets or exposure curves.

Drag the effect template to a bin to save a correction.

Tabs at the left side of the window organize the various controls into logical groups. The HSL tab offers two sub-tabs. The Hue Offsets sub-tab is shown above. Additional numerical controls are available via the Controls sub-tab, below.

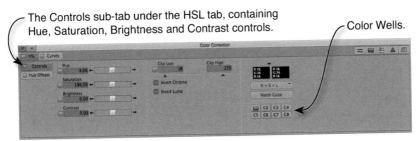

The Controls sub-tab under the HSL tab, containing Hue, Saturation, Brightness and Contrast controls.

Color Wells.

Buttons on the lower right side of the window, labeled C1 to C8, represent color wells. Once you make a correction, hold down the Option key and click a well. Your correction will be recorded in that well. When you find another shot that requires the same correction, simply click the well to apply it. Note that the contents of the wells disappear when you quit Media Composer. To save them, click on a well and drag to a bin. This creates a template icon in the bin. To restore, drag the template back to a well.

All tabs and controls include Enable buttons, allowing you to quickly toggle a correction on or off and observe its effect. Option-click a button to reset a control or group to default values.

Enable buttons.

If you're more comfortable with Photoshop-style color curves, click the curves tab. Create control points by clicking on the graphs and move the points around to adjust the look of the shot. Note that the various tabs work together. Adjustments in one are added to adjustments in the others to produce an overall correction. The exceptions are the

Gain, Gamma and Setup sliders, which appear in both the Curves and Hue Offsets tabs and move together.

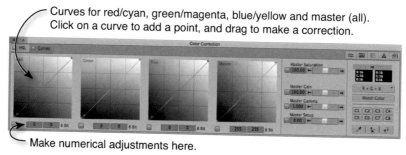

Curves for red/cyan, green/magenta, blue/yellow and master (all).
Click on a curve to add a point, and drag to make a correction.

Make numerical adjustments here.

Eyedroppers under the HSL wheels, or at the bottom right of the Curves tab, allow you to adjust overall color by removing a color cast in a chosen part of a shot. In the HSL tab you have eyedroppers for shadows, midtones or highlights. In the Curves tab a single eyedropper adjusts red, green and blue values simultaneously.

Eyedroppers in the HSL tab.

Locate an area in your image that should be neutral in color. Click the appropriate eyedropper to activate it, move your cursor over the image, and click on the area you identified. The color of the shot will be adjusted, removing any color cast in the area you clicked on.

Matching Color

To the right of the other controls, you'll find buttons that allow you to match a section of one shot to another. You may find them helpful, for example, when matching the skin color of an actor in two nearby shots. Click the Match Type pop-up to specify the values you want to match. Each tab offers different options. When matching skin tones, try using NaturalMatch in the Curves tab. This helps compensate for different lighting conditions in the two shots.

Next, select your source and destination. The two groups of adjacent RGB values are actually buttons. Position your mouse cursor over the right column of values and it will turn into an eyedropper. Click and drag the eyedropper and release the mouse button over a portion of an image that contains the look you prefer (the reference color). The button color will change to the color of the pixel you clicked, and the RGB indicators will change, as well, indicating the numerical values for that pixel.

Then click the left column of values and release the mouse over a portion of the image you want to correct. That button changes color, updating in the same way. Finally, click Match Color to correct the shot.

Color match controls. Each column of RGB values is a button. Click, drag and release over an area in a shot you want to match. The right column is the reference, the left is the color you're adjusting.

HSL Options   Curves Options

Note that when working in the Curves tab, dragging the match eyedropper over an image graphically displays RGB values in the curves, making it easy to figure out where a particular pixel falls in a graph.

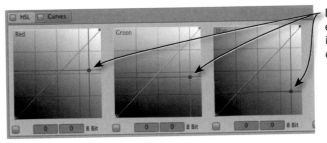

Drag the match eyedropper over an image to graphically display pixel values.

Playing Across Cuts

If you hit the play button in Color Correction Mode, clip play will stop at the end of the clip you're working on. You can drag or jump from cut to cut, but if you want to play the sequence, you have to return to Source/Record Mode. That's awkward, but there's a workaround. In Color Correction Mode, the Play Loop button will play across cuts. Put it in your timeline button bar or on the keyboard so it's available when you're working on color.

You can also use the Edit Review button to play the end of the preceding shot, the current shot and the beginning of the following shot.

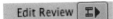

Correcting Several Shots at Once

You can adjust several contiguous shots with a single correction by applying the correction to filler. Create a new video track above the clips you want to correct and add an edit before and after them. Select the track, go into Color Correction Mode and make your correction. It will appear in the track you selected and will apply to all clips underneath it.

Start by creating add edits in filler before
and after the clips you want to correct.

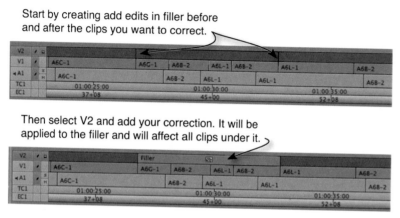

Then select V2 and add your correction. It will be
applied to the filler and will affect all clips under it.

Keyframing Color Corrections

It's now possible to create color corrections that change dynamically within a shot, making it easy to compensate for lighting changes. To take advantage of this feature, you'll need to open the Effect Editor and use it alongside Color Correction Mode. Color effects employ advanced keyframes and work much like other advanced keyframe effects. The trick is in using both modes at once.

Start by creating a correction on a shot you want to keyframe. Once you've got a basic look, open the Effect Editor by clicking the Effect Mode button in the timeline or in the Color Correction window.

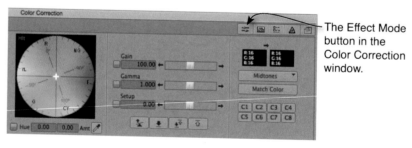

The Effect Mode button in the Color Correction window.

With the Effect Editor open, locate the frame where you want your color change to begin and add a keyframe. Move to the spot where you want the change to end and add another keyframe. Then click on the keyframes and make your adjustments, using the controls in the Color Correction window or the sliders in the Effect Editor.

Once you've created a keyframe in an effect track you can create others automatically by moving the position indicator to a new location and making an adjustment in the Color Correction window or with an effect slider. But be sure to deselect your last keyframe by Shift-clicking it before doing this. Otherwise you may end up inadvertently adjusting the selected keyframe, instead.

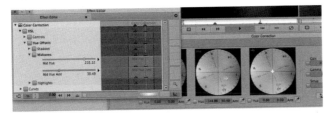

The Color Correction window and the Effect Editor open at the same time. Two keyframes are visible.

If you're using the Curves tab to make corrections, note that all keyframes must contain the same number of control points. If you add or delete a control point at one keyframe, it will be automatically added or deleted at the others, potentially changing the corrections in all of them.

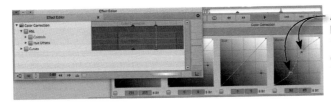

Adjusting curves in a keyframed color effect. Each keyframe must contain the same number of control points.

Color Correction Mode and Workspaces

Depending on your monitor configuration you may find that the standard window placements in Color Correction Mode are not to your liking. To memorize custom window positions, use a workspace (see "Workspaces" on page 260). Your windows will go where you want them, and if you've associated a timeline view with your workspace, that will be activated, as well.

15 Titles

Creating a Title

Avid's Title Tool is now a separate application, but otherwise it functions much as it did before. To launch it, select Clip > New Title, or Tools > Title Tool Application. The program opens, displaying the current frame in the record monitor, with the Text Tool activated. (You can also make titles with Avid Marquee, but that's beyond the scope of this book.) Click on the image, type your text, and use the Selection Tool to move it. Add effects, including color and drop shadow. Use the Alignment and Object menus to move and group elements. To view your work at full quality, select Object > Preview. Then select Save Title and choose a bin, resolution and drive for your title media. A clip appears in the bin, ready for editing. To create a series of similar titles, use Save Title As instead of Save.

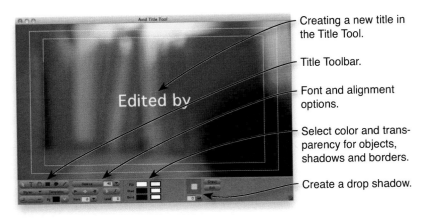

Creating a new title in the Title Tool.

Title Toolbar.

Font and alignment options.

Select color and transparency for objects, shadows and borders.

Create a drop shadow.

To superimpose a title over video, edit it into an upper video track, above the background clip. Once edited, you can select the title in Effect Mode and make additional changes, moving it around, changing its size, adding fades, etc. You can also promote the title to 3D for additional control.

Title Toolbar

The Title Toolbar allows you to create and manipulate title elements. The function of most tools should be self-evident. Use the Text Tool to create and edit text and the Selection Tool to move it. The title window can be resized smaller than the full video frame, so the Hand Tool allows you to move video under the title. You can suppress the video background so it won't display when a title is edited, or you can add a plain colored background.

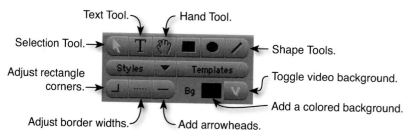

Text

To quickly activate the Text Tool, double-click an existing title. The text cursor appears at the spot where you double-clicked. To toggle between the Selection Tool and the Text Tool, Option-click anywhere in the Title Tool window. To nudge a title, activate the Selection Tool and tap a cursor arrow key. (You can do this when the Text Tool is active by holding down Control.) Note that leading and kerning apply to everything in a text box, and leading can only be applied when the box has been selected with the Selection Tool. To add a text stroke, select a text box and use the border width pop-up in the Title Toolbar.

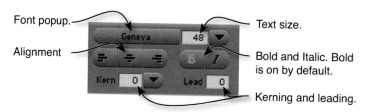

Colors

You can change the fill, stroke, and shadow color for any selected object by clicking the swatches next to the text controls. You can adjust transparency for all these elements, as well. Select an object and then click and drag on a swatch. A popup color picker appears. Then click on a color or drag over the color palettes. Your selected object's color will change when you release the mouse button.

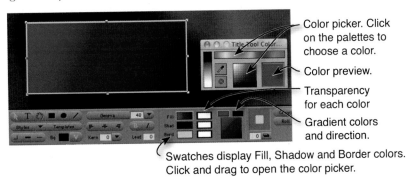

Color picker. Click on the palettes to choose a color.

Color preview.

Transparency for each color

Gradient colors and direction.

Swatches display Fill, Shadow and Border colors. Click and drag to open the color picker.

Shadows

You can add a drop shadow to a title or object using the shadow control box at the bottom right of the Title Tool. Select an object by clicking on it and then add the shadow using the controls below. To adjust shadow size and direction using the keyboard, hold down the Shift key and tap the cursor arrow keys.

Drag the shadow outline to change size and direction.

Or adjust the size numerically, here.

Choose a drop or depth shadow.

The button at the bottom right allows you to toggle between a drop and depth shadow. Drop shadows appear to project a shadow on a surface. Depth shadows appear to be extruded from the title.

Drop Shadow

Depth Shadow

To make your shadow look more organic, soften it by selecting Object > Soften Shadow. Enter the amount of softening and hit Apply to preview the effect. Then hit Okay to add it. You can also soften a shadow using the cursor arrow keys. Select the title and hit Shift-Option-Up Arrow to increase softening or Shift-Option-Down Arrow to decrease it.

Soften a shadow using the dialog box or the keyboard.

Changing an Existing Title

To make changes to an existing title in the timeline, park on it, open the Effect Editor and click on the Edit Title button to open the title in the Title Tool. When you're finished, hit Save to update the title in the timeline. A new clip will be created in the bin containing your active sequence and new media will be created, as well. If you want to put the new title clip elsewhere, select Save As.

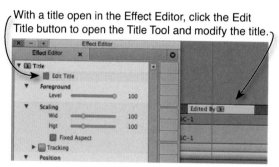

With a title open in the Effect Editor, click the Edit Title button to open the Title Tool and modify the title.

You can also load an existing title into the Title Tool by Command-double-clicking it in a bin. But note that when you save, you'll create new media and also overwrite the title icon in the bin. This won't affect copies of the title already edited into sequences, but it will make it harder to locate and manage the old version's media. To retain access to the original version you may want to select Save As, instead. This will create a new title clip without changing the old one.

Presets

Once you've adjusted a title in the timeline you can save it as a preset, with all effect parameters included, by dragging the effect icon to a bin.

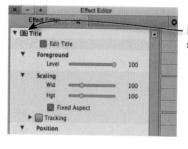

Drag the effect icon to a bin to save the title with all keyframes.

You can also save the preset values, but without the title itself, by Option-dragging the effect icon. This saves everything you did to the title in the Effect Editor—that is, all of its keyframes—but not the text or graphics created in the Title Tool. Once the preset is in the bin you can apply it to another title by editing the title into a sequence and dragging the preset on top of it. Or you can apply it to a series of titles by selecting them all and double-clicking the preset.

Styles

Style sheets permit you to collect a group of character attributes and then apply them with a single click. Create your title, click the Save Style pop-up menu next to the Styles button and select Save As. The style sheet window opens where you can select attributes from the current title to include in the style sheet. You can also choose a function key shortcut for this style. This will replace any command you may have assigned to that key—but only in the Title Tool.

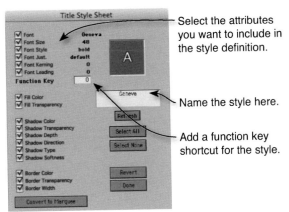

Select the attributes you want to include in the style definition.

To create a style, click the Style pop-up and open the Style Sheet window.

Name the style here.

Add a function key shortcut for the style.

Once you've created your style, you can apply it by selecting a title, or text within a title, and then choosing the style from the Style pop-up. You can also click the Styles button to open a floating button bar displaying samples of your styles.

Click the pop-up to apply a style.

Click the Styles button to open a button bar with your saved styles.

To replace a style with the parameters of the current title, Option-click it. Title Styles are saved in the Settings tab of the Project window. Double-click a style in the Project window to open it. Hit the Delete key to remove it.

Option-click the pop-up to replace a style.

Note that unlike styles created in desktop publishing programs, when you change a style's definition, previously created titles using that style do not change.

Templates

You can also create Title Templates that can be used as starting points for a series of similar titles. You'll incorporate the template into a new title and then, if necessary, replace the template's text. Other elements won't change.

Start by building your title, creating text boxes and any other elements you need: lines, shapes, etc. Select colors, drop shadow and other treatments. Then click the Templates button (it's really a pop-up menu) and save your template. The default location for templates in OS X is Applications/Avid Media Composer/Settings/Title_Templates.

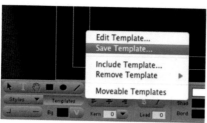

When you're ready to use the template, open the Title Tool, click the Template button and select Include Template. Choose a template and its elements will be added to your title. Change the text, as needed. You won't be able to alter the size of text boxes or any other graphic elements brought in with the template, but you can move them around on screen by selecting Moveable Templates from the Templates menu.

Layout Grid

Avid's flexible layout grid can be overlaid on the source or record monitor or displayed in the Title Tool. Activate it by clicking the Grid button, available in the FX tab of the Command Palette.

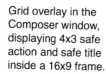

Grid overlay in the Composer window, displaying 4x3 safe action and safe title inside a 16x9 frame.

To configure it, open Grid settings. There are many options, and you'll probably have to do some experimenting to create the grid you need. Use the Coordinates tab to adjust the aspect ratio and the Display tab to choose content and color options. Using the Type popup, select Square for standard video coordinates.

Grid Settings Tabs with menus closed and popped open.

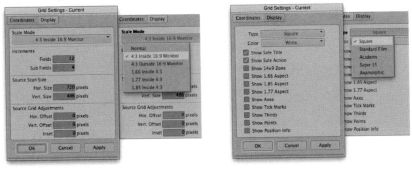

To display your customized grid in the Title Tool, select Object > Safe Title Area > Global Grid.

You can also display an alignment grid in the Title tool by selecting Alignment > Show Alignment Grid. To have objects snap to the alignment grid as you move them around, select Align to Grid.

Fades

You can quickly add real-time fades to your titles using the Fade Effect button. First create your title normally and cut it wherever you like. Then put the position indicator on the title, select its track and click the button. In the dialog box that follows enter the lengths of your fades. They will be created with keyframes. To examine or change them, enter Effect Mode. To simply adjust the fade length, hit the Fade Effect button again. But note that the resulting dialog does not display the current length of the fade. It shows you the length of the last fade you entered there.

16

Projects and Media

Project Types

Media Composer now offers considerable flexibility in project creation. Not only can you create a wide range of project formats, but, in a limited way, you can change a project's format after beginning to work. Project types are shown below. Make your selection based on the format and frame rate of the majority of your source clips and, more important, your sequences. It's well beyond the scope of this book to go over each project type in detail. Check the help system for in-depth descriptions. (For more about film projects, see "Avid Project Types for 24-fps Media" on page 241.)

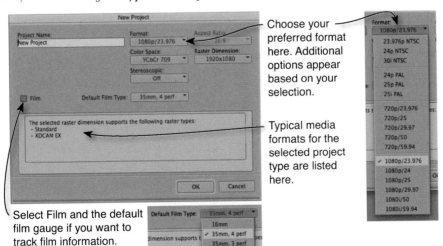

Choose your preferred format here. Additional options appear based on your selection.

Typical media formats for the selected project type are listed here.

Select Film and the default film gauge if you want to track film information.

To help make this clearer, the project window now contains a detailed Format tab, providing information about the current project. You can change certain parameters of your project (but notably not its frame rate). For example, you can switch your project from standard definition to high definition, allowing you to offline in SD and conform in HD. But you should use caution when changing things in this tab. Format changes will affect any sequences you create after the change.

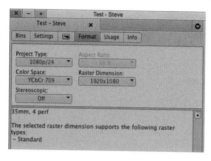

Media Creation

Media options are now mostly centralized in the Media Creation settings panel. (It's also available in the Tools menu.) Go through the various tabs, paying attention to the drives you choose for different types of media. A little care with this task at the beginning of a show will keep your media where it belongs and avoid problems later. Start with the Media Type tab. In standard definition projects you have a choice of MXF or OMF. With high def., MXF is the only option. Select a resolution in the Transcode or Capture tab.

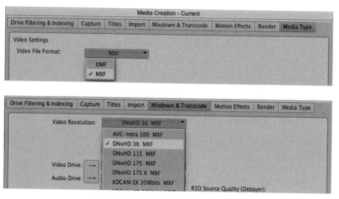

If you want to copy settings from one tab to another, use the Apply to All buttons.

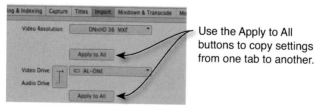

Use the Apply to All buttons to copy settings from one tab to another.

Audio Media

Audio formats are selected with a separate panel: Audio Project settings. The old standard, AIFF, has been supplanted by MXF, which is now the default. But your sound editors may prefer WAVE. It's best to check with them before you start a project.

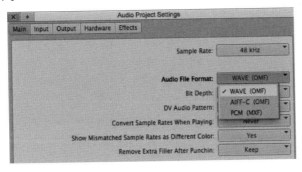

The same setting panel allows you to select a playback sample rate for your project: either 48K or 44.1K. (Depending on your project type you may see the pulled-down variants instead: 47.952K and 44.056K.) You can also choose a bit depth: either 16 or 24.

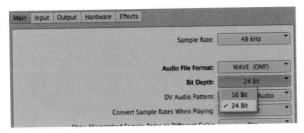

The Media Tool

The Media Tool is Avid's primary access point for managing media, available in the Tools menu. It allows you to select projects and drives, as well as the kinds of clips you want to see: media files, master clips, or precompute clips (render files, including title media).

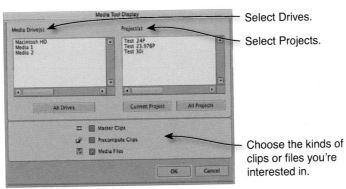

Select Drives.

Select Projects.

Choose the kinds of clips or files you're interested in.

Note that you won't see all your projects in the Media Tool's project list. Only projects with online media, along with the current project, whether its media is online or not, will appear in the list.

Make a selection and hit return, and you'll be presented with a list of media files or clips. The window is designed to function like a bin, with most of the same controls. You can display your material in the views you're familiar with, you can sort and sift in the same ways (page 130), and the Fast Menu behaves like it does in bins, as well.

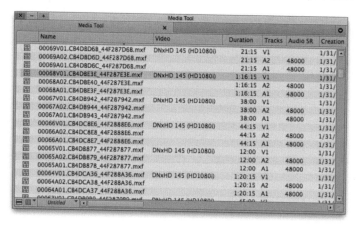

Show Media Files

To locate media for a clip, right-click the clip in a bin and choose Reveal File. The software will take you to the operating system, with the clip highlighted. If more than one file is involved (video and audio, for example) both will be highlighted, but you may have to scroll to find them. Note that this only works with master clips. If you're interested in sources for a subclip or sequence, load the clip in a monitor and then use Match Frame and Find Bin, as needed, to locate the original master clip (see page 42).

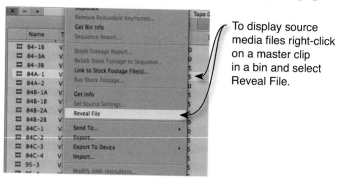

To display source media files right-click on a master clip in a bin and select Reveal File.

You can also use the Media Tool. Open it from the Tools menu, select your project and appropriate drives and choose Media Files. The tool opens with your media files displayed. Then open the bin with the clips you're interested in, select them, and choose

Bin > Select Sources. All media files for the clips you selected will be highlighted in the Media Tool (you may have to scroll to find them).

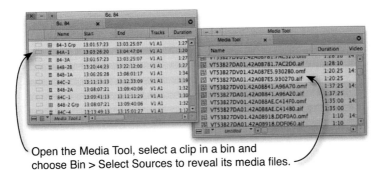

Open the Media Tool, select a clip in a bin and choose Bin > Select Sources to reveal its media files.

Delete Unused Render Files

Render files tend to accumulate like weeds. One way manage them is by identifying "unreferenced clips." Open the Media Tool and select Precompute Clips. Choose your project and drives. Then, open all bins containing sequences or titles that reference render files you want to *keep*. Click on the Media Tool and choose Bin > Select Unreferenced Clips. All render files that *aren't* used in sequences in currently open bins will be selected. Hit the Delete key to remove them.

Show Offline Items

To see whether all the clips in a sequence are online, open the bin containing it and choose Bin > Select Offline Items. (It's also available in the bin's fast menu.) It will highlight any offline clips, or any sequences that contain them. To identify offline clips within a sequence, colorize them in the timeline (see page 51). The Offline bin column can also be used to help you find problem clips. It works on source clips (not sequences), and indicates which tracks are offline. If a clip is online, the field will be blank.

Deleting Media Databases

Media is indexed using two database files, with the extensions pmr and mdb, located in every MediaFiles folder. Media Composer normally updates these files whenever it adds or deletes media to the folder. If you're having trouble linking media, try forcing MC to rebuild the indexes. First quit the system. Then locate the database files and delete them using the Finder. Then restart MC. As it starts, it will rebuild the files, showing a progress bar as it does so.

MC normally adds new media to this folder: Avid MediaFiles > MXF > 1. You can rename it, in which case MC will create a new "1" folder and add newly created media there. But it will not re-index renamed folders if their names contain alphabetic characters—only numbers are recognized.

Importing and Exporting

Importing Media

Before the advent of Avid Media Access (described below), importing was the standard way to load file-based media such as stills, audio or Quicktimes and convert it to media in a MediaFiles folder. This approach has partly been supplanted by AMA, but it still has a place in many editing environments. Open a bin and make sure it's active. Then select File > Import. Choose a resolution and target drive (defaults are set in the Media Creation settings panel). Then click the Options button to open the Import Settings panel (also accessible from the Project window) and choose the import options you want. The Image tab is used to adjust settings for both stills and video.

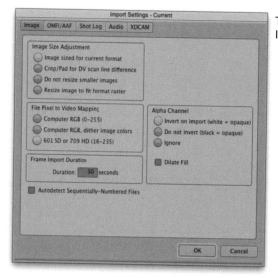

The Image Tab in the Import Settings panel.

When you import a Photoshop file, you can choose to bring in each layer separately, merge them, or import only the layers you specify. Each layer comes in as a separate clip, at the length you've chosen in Import settings, and a sequence is automatically created with the clips edited into layers. Empty layers are ignored.

Exporting a Sequence

You'll typically export by selecting a sequence and then choosing File > Export. You can export in a variety of formats, including AAF and many flavors of Quicktime. Media Composer comes pre-configured with a group of named Export settings. You can use them as is, change them or create new ones. Export settings are listed in the Settings tab of the Project window. When you select Export, you're first presented with the currently selected setting in the project window (for a newly created User, this will be an untitled setting).

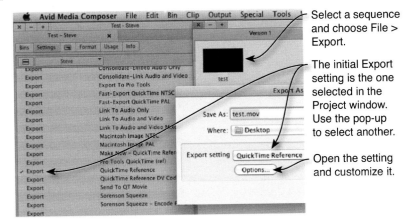

Select a sequence and choose File > Export.

The initial Export setting is the one selected in the Project window. Use the pop-up to select another.

Open the setting and customize it.

Click the Options button to open and customize the setting (or do it in the Project window). First, make a selection in the Export As pop-up. Then go through the other options and make adjustments as needed. When you choose Quicktime Movie (or use the Send to QT Movie setting), you'll see the Format Options button, which opens additional Quicktime settings. To quickly test your settings, mark a short section of your sequence, and select Use Marks. You'll export only the material between the marks and can examine the resulting Quicktime for problems. Note that when you hit Save in the Export dialog, you aren't saving your sequence, you're saving the currently selected setting. To create a new setting, use Save As and give your custom setting a name.

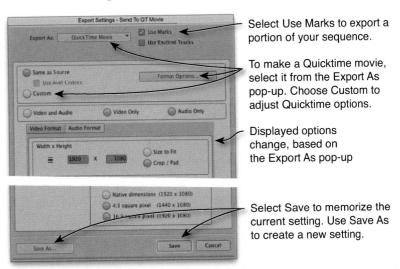

Select Use Marks to export a portion of your sequence.

To make a Quicktime movie, select it from the Export As pop-up. Choose Custom to adjust Quicktime options.

Displayed options change, based on the Export As pop-up

Select Save to memorize the current setting. Use Save As to create a new setting.

Select Same as Source in the Export setting to create a Quicktime that uses your Avid media without transcoding. Keep in mind that the Avid Codecs must be installed in order to play the file you'll create. They're installed with Media Composer, but you'll need to add them on other machines. You can download the codecs from Avid's web site.

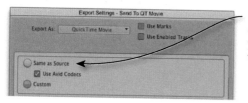

Use Same as Source to create a Quicktime that uses your Avid media in its native format.

Quicktime Reference Movies

You may find it easiest to off-load export transcoding to a third-party conversion application, which can work in the background. To do this, create a Quicktime reference movie. Instead of making new video media, a reference movie points to the media you're already using, in your MediaFiles folder. As a result, the export typically happens much more quickly. MC will render your effects and create a mixdown of your audio. Open the Quicktime reference movie in the compression application of your choice (Sorenson Squeeze may have been bundled with your copy of Media Composer) and compress or convert from there. Note that you can't currently make a Quicktime reference from AMA-linked sequences.

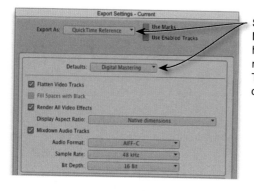

Start with Digital Mastering to create a high quality Quicktime reference movie. Then make additional changes, as needed.

Send To

Avid also provides a set of templates to make exporting easier. Each one uses a setting found in the Project window, specifies a destination on disk, and can launch an application with your exported sequence preloaded. You can use an existing template, or make new ones. You'll find Send To in the File menu.

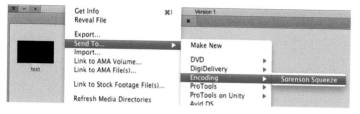

Avid Media Access (AMA)

Media Composer relies on tight control of audio and video files to produce a bullet-proof editing environment. Media is segregated into specific folders managed by the application, and "Media Offline" messages are rare. That approach has worked well for years, but because it's based on Avid's proprietary file formats, it has made the system less successful for modern file-based cameras. Avid Media Access (AMA) aims to change that. The technology is based on a set of plug-ins that allow the application to deal with a wide range of file formats in their native state. Some plug-ins are included, but most must be installed separately. (Be sure you have the latest versions. For a complete list, enter AMA_ListPlugins in the Console.)

AMA allows you to edit directly from the memory cards used in these cameras, or it can work from Virtual Volumes—copies of the cards' contents on local drives. Thus it leaves the task of media organization to the user. You can mount and play new formats easily, but if you move media around and rename folders, clips can go offline. AMA's flexibility allows productions to adopt a wide range of workflows. Rather than try to cover all of them here, I'll offer a brief conceptual overview to get you started.

Basics

Your media will either exist on a memory card or on local storage. As long as AMA is turned on in Media Composer, a recognized card will be opened as soon as it's plugged in. You can also copy the contents of a card to a drive and tell the system that the drive is a virtual volume. Either way, all the media will be automatically imported into a bin. The camera's metadata will be imported into bin columns, and markers created in the field will become Media Composer markers. Clips will be imported with the names assigned in the camera, but can be changed in the bin. In earlier versions, online AMA clips were highlighted in yellow in text view. They are now displayed with a unique icon, instead. (If they go offline the icon reverts to a standard master clip icon.)

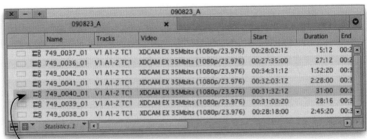

In text view, online AMA clips display a unique icon to remind you that Media Composer is not managing their media.

Settings

You'll select options via the AMA settings panel. The Volume Mounting tab allows you to turn AMA on and off, and it determines the system's behavior when a card is taken offline and then remounted.

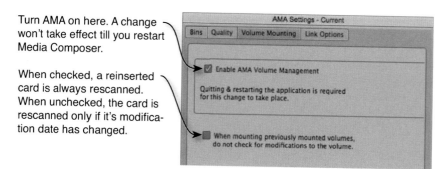

Turn AMA on here. A change won't take effect till you restart Media Composer.

When checked, a reinserted card is always rescanned. When unchecked, the card is rescanned only if it's modification date has changed.

The Bins tab tells the system how you want AMA bins created. You can add media to the currently active bin or make a new bin. The default is to create a new bin named to match the memory card or virtual volume name. This helps to keep you organized.

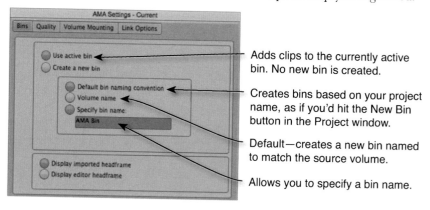

Adds clips to the currently active bin. No new bin is created.

Creates bins based on your project name, as if you'd hit the New Bin button in the Project window.

Default—creates a new bin named to match the source volume.

Allows you to specify a bin name.

Some file-based cameras generate proxy (low-resolution) and full resolution media simultaneously. Use the Quality tab to choose the resolution you want to work with. The Link Options tab allows you to link pairs of audio tracks and treat them as stereo or surround in the timeline.

Virtual Volumes

To create a virtual volume, simply copy the complete contents of your memory card to local storage. Think carefully about how you want to organize your media. It's possible to rename folders after you start editing, but you'll have to remount the volumes and you may run into trouble. It's best to stick with your original folder structure.

To mount a virtual volume, select File > Link to AMA Volume. Then navigate to the folder containing the contents of the memory card. For P2, navigate to one level above the Contents folder. For XDCAM, navigate to one level above the Clip folder. For XD-CAM EX, navigate to one level above the BPAV folder. When you select Open, the contents of the folder will be imported into a bin according to your AMA Bins settings.

If you later move the virtual volume, or rename the folder containing it, your clips will go offline. To reconnect them, simply select Link to AMA Volume and navigate to the appropriate folder, as described above. If your bin was named to match the volume name, Media Composer will open the bin and automatically reconnect the original clips. If you've been renaming your bins, select Use Active Bin in AMA settings and open and activate the relevant bin before choosing Link to AMA Volume.

For convenience, you can mount a group of virtual volumes simultaneously. Create a folder for each one and place them all into a single enclosing folder. Select Link to AMA Volume and point the system at the enclosing folder. You'll see the following dialog box. Choose Bin(s) Based on Subfolders to create a set of bins, each named to match a subfolder.

Transcoding Your Media

You can edit directly off a memory card or from a virtual volume, but timeline performance may suffer. For better results, you'll probably want to transcode your media into a standard Avid format, typically DNxHD. Select Clip > Consolidate/Transcode and choose your options in the dialog box below. Note that if you changed a clip's Reformat attribute, new media will be generated with the format "baked in." (See page 229.)

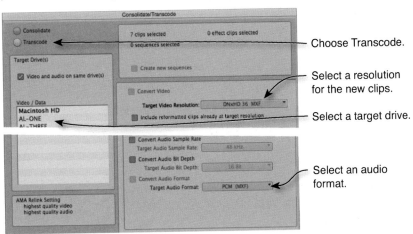

Choose Transcode.

Select a resolution for the new clips.

Select a target drive.

Select an audio format.

It's best to transcode before you start editing, because transcoding creates new master clips. But, if necessary, you can transcode after you begin work, in which case you'll need to relink your edited sequence to the transcoded clips. Select the sequence and choose Clip > Relink. In the Relink dialog box, select Media on Drive and Allow Relinking of Imported/AMA Clips by Source File Name. If you'd like to retain a copy of your sequence linked to the AMA clips, then select Create New Sequence.

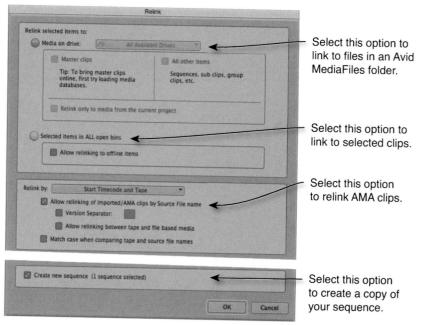

Select this option to link to files in an Avid MediaFiles folder.

Select this option to link to selected clips.

Select this option to relink AMA clips.

Select this option to create a copy of your sequence.

When you're finished editing, you may want to relink a copy of your sequence back to the AMA media. Media Composer normally relinks to media in a MediaFiles folder. To relink to AMA media instead, select the sequence and the clips you want to link to. In Version 4, they had to reside in the same bin. In Versions 5 and 6 this isn't necessary, but be sure all the clips are selected and the sequence bin is active. Then, in the Relink dialog box, choose Selected Items In All Open Bins. This forces the system to link to the selected items. You'll also need to select Allow Relinking of Imported/AMA Clips by Source File Name. Once the sequence is relinked, open it in the timeline and check to make sure all clips were relinked properly.

Note that if you're working with AMA media you'll run into limitations when exporting via AAF. Any sequence track that contains AMA clips (including audio clips autosynched with AMA video) can't be exported this way. You'll have to transcode, instead.

Quicktime

AMA now allows you to work natively with many flavors of Quicktime. This means that if your hardware is up to the task, there's no longer any need to import and convert Quicktime media to an Avid format. You can simply open the clips and go to work.

Begin by organizing your files as carefully as you can, putting them on appropriate drives and setting up a suitable folder structure. (It's best to avoid non-alphanumeric characters in Quicktime filenames, such as slash, ampersand, question mark, etc.) Then link to a folder full of files via the Link to AMA Volume command, or to individual files by creating a bin, selecting File > Link to AMA File(s), and navigating to the appropriate file or files. They will open in the bin ready for editing. Timeline performance will vary depending on the codec and your hardware configuration. For best performance, you'll probably want to transcode. (Note than Quicktime transcoding can be much quicker than importing.) Most Quicktime formats are supported, but not all. For a complete list, check the help system.

If you move Quicktime files after linking to them, they'll go offline and you'll have to reconnect them. You cannot use the Link to AMA Volume command for this purpose—it will create new clips. Instead, right-click each clip, choose Relink to AMA File(s), and navigate to the appropriate file. To relink several clips in the same bin to a batch of Quicktime files in the same folder, sort the bin so that clip names are listed in alphabetical order. Select all the clips you want to relink. Right-click the first one, navigate to the matching media file and select it. All the other files you selected will relink simultaneously. To adjust the field dominance and color range of AMA Quicktime files, use the Set Source Settings contextual menu pick, described below.

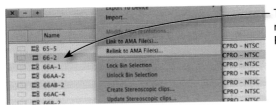

To relink a Quicktime file, right-click it and choose Relink to AMA File(s).

RED

Version 5 permitted you to work with Red R3D files and Version 6 expanded that to include Epic material. You can link to a volume of clips or to individual files using the Link To AMA options in the File menu. Images are scaled to the project's raster size and can be further adjusted using the Reformat option (page 229). You'll control color and debayering with the Set Source Settings contextual menu pick, described below. Camera metadata appears in a series of specialized bin columns. Note that timeline performance will be influenced your Video Quality Setting (page 37).

ProRes

You can link to an individual ProRes file, or a folder full of files, using the same menu picks you'd use with any other Quicktime format. But you can also rewrap your ProRes media into Avid's MXF format and have Media Composer manage the media inside a standard Avid MediaFiles folder. This arguably gives you the best of both worlds: your original media without any quality loss due to transcoding, but handled via Avid's powerful media management.

To do this, you'll use what Avid calls Fast Import. Select a bin, then choose File > Import. From the Resolution pop-up, select the MXF resolution that matches your ProRes source material. Click the Options button to open the Import Settings panel (it's also available in the Project window) and, in the Image category, select the color space used in your source material, typically Rec. 709. Then click Okay. If the media is being rewrapped you'll see the words Fast Import in the progress window.

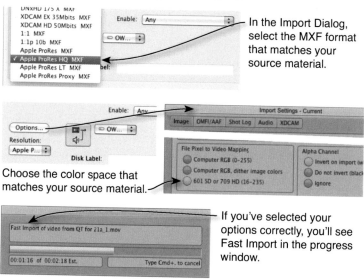

AVCHD

With Version 6 you can use AMA to link to AVCHD media, either an entire card, or one or more individual .mts files. Performance is good, but if you find playback with your hardware to be balky, you'll need to transcode. If media goes offline, relink the volume as explained earlier (page 223). You can also try relinking by right-clicking the offline clips, choosing Link to AMA Files, and selecting the relevant source files simultaneously.

Stills

You can also use AMA to open still images. This works with most formats, including jpegs, pngs tiffs, and even Photoshop files. It's faster than importing, you don't waste space creating Avid media, and you can use the Reformat attribute to adjust the shape of the image (page 229). Note that, as with an import, you don't get access to the full resolution of the source file; the image is resized when it is linked. In Version 6, you can use Source Settings to adjust the image's luminance range.

Source Settings

Media Composer allows you to adjust color and other options for most AMA file types via a contextual menu pick. Right-click an AMA-linked clip and choose Set Source Settings. In the dialog box that follows, you'll see a frame preview and histogram, allowing you to adjust color and debayering for Red material, or apply color settings files. To update previously edited clips with newly applied color settings, right-click the relevant sequence and select Refresh Sequence > Source Settings. For details, see the help system.

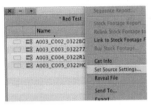
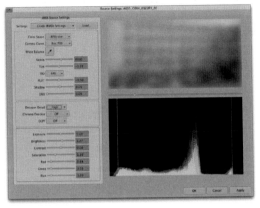

Red source settings allow you to adjust color and debayering, or load a setting file.

Mixing Frame Rates (Mix and Match)

Media Composer can handle source clips at a variety of frame rates in the same sequence, a feature sometimes referred to as Mix and Match. It does this by applying what Avid calls Motion Adapters to clips as they are edited into the timeline. Motion Adapters typically play in real time and generally do the right thing, producing the smoothest motion possible. If you aren't satisfied, you can modify the adapter and try alternatives.

Say you are working in a 29.97-fps project and wish to include 23.98 source material. If the 23.98 material exists on tape, you'll need to load it into a 23.976 project, and then open the resulting bins in your 29.97 project. If the 23.98 material came from a file-based source and can be linked via AMA, you can bring it directly into your 29.97 project, instead. (Note that Avid uses 23.976 and 23.98 labels somewhat inconsistently. Clips digitized into a 23.976 project display a frame rate of 23.98.)

Once the clips are accessible from your 29.97 project, edit them normally, intercutting the sources as needed. Clips that don't match the project frame-rate will display a green dot in the timeline, indicating that a real-time motion adapter has been applied. Their clipnames will be appended with the original frame rate of the clip in parentheses. You can also display mixed rate material in color in the timeline (see page 51).

23.98-fps clips edited into a 29.97 timeline display a green dot, indicating that the clip carries a real-time motion adapter.

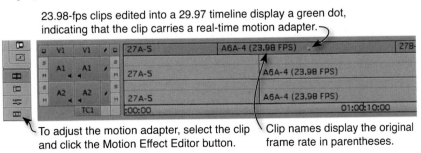

To adjust the motion adapter, select the clip and click the Motion Effect Editor button.

Clip names display the original frame rate in parentheses.

Play through the clips to examine the effect of the motion adapter. Pay particular attention to your video quality setting. Motion adapters look best when the video quality is set to green/green. If your hardware will not permit a green/green setting, then render the clip for the smoothest playback.

To make changes to the default motion adapter, select the clip and open the Motion Effect Editor, either from the Tools menu or by clicking its timeline button. Make adjustments using the Type pop-up menu. Note that the best quality setting for 23.98 material in a 29.97 project is Blended Interpolated. This applies a standard 2:3 cadence. You can also promote an adapter to a Timewarp. This applies an effect icon to your clip and allows you to make further adjustments. In this way you can convert a motion adapter to Fluidmotion, if needed. (See "Timewarp and Fluidmotion" on page 187.)

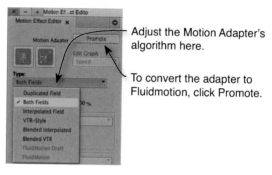

Adjust the Motion Adapter's algorithm here.

To convert the adapter to Fluidmotion, click Promote.

Changing Sequence Formats

It's now possible to change a sequence's frame rate and format after it's been created. This can be handy in special circumstances. To check your sequence's current format, display the Format column in your bin. To change the format, select your sequence and choose Clip > Modify. In the Modify dialog box, open the pop-up menu and choose Select Format. You'll see the same options you saw when you created your project.

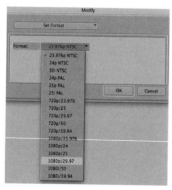

Choose a format and a copy of your sequence will be created at the new frame rate. Motion adapters will automatically adjust, as needed (promoted motion effects will be preserved).

Video Aspect Ratio

The Composer window can display video in 4:3 or 16:9 monitors. Standard definition is normally 4:3, but it can be stretched horizontally to create anamorphic, 16:9 video. (Dimensions of the underlying material don't change.) High definition is always 16:9. The source and record monitor aspect ratio is set in the Format tab of the Project window. When you switch from one project to another, windows and clipframes adjust.

Reformat Attribute

Using the Reformat bin column, you can alter the display of clips that don't match the image size or aspect ratio of your project, specifying the way you want the clip presented. If you load material into a 4:3, standard definition project, for example, and then open it in a high definition project, you can reformat it to display with a pillarbox, stretch it anamorphically, or crop it —all without adding an effect in the timeline. Keep in mind that this only applies to mismatched clips. It won't work with material that conforms to your project's aspect ratio and image size.

Display the Reformat column in the bin containing the clip. Then click (not right-click) the Reformat field to open a pop-up and make your adjustment. To change several clips at once, select them all and adjust any one of them. Multiple subclips made from the same master clip can each be formatted independently.

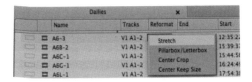

If you alter the reformat attribute after editing a clip into a sequence, the new setting will apply to future uses of the clip, but material already cut won't change. To have previously edited instances of a clip adopt a new setting, load the sequence in the record monitor and select Clip > Refresh Sequence > Reformatting Options.

A 4:3 source clip in a 16:9 project, with different reformat attributes applied.

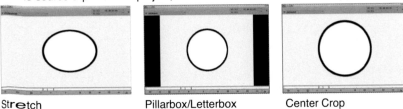

Stretch   Pillarbox/Letterbox   Center Crop

Copying Media For a Scene or Scenes

It's often useful to create a subset of your media for work on the road. You can use the Consolidate command for this, but it can be more straightforward to copy media using the OS. The problem is that you have to locate every relevant clip before copying. There's an easier way. It's hidden, but it can do what you want with less work.

Open the bin you're interested in and select your source clips: either master clips or sub-clips. (Group clips won't work. Only the media for the element showing in the bin will be copied.) Then select File > Export.

Start by creating an export setting. Select the Untitled setting and click the Options button to customize it. For Export As, select AAF. This makes an AAF for every clip. You won't need these files, but the system insists on creating them. To keep them organized, make a folder for them on your export drive. Choose Include All Video/Data Tracks in Sequence and All Audio Tracks in Sequence (even though you aren't exporting a sequence). The Audio and Video tabs will appear, and in each, select Export Method: Copy All Media. Then select a media destination. Choose Media Drive (not Folder) in both the Video and Audio tabs, and identify the drive.

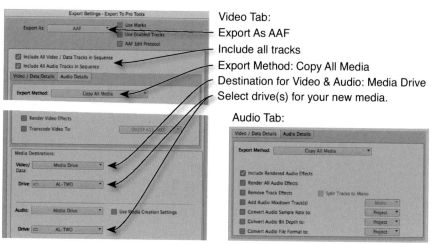

Video Tab:
Export As AAF
Include all tracks
Export Method: Copy All Media
Destination for Video & Audio: Media Drive
Select drive(s) for your new media.

Audio Tab:

When you've got your options set up correctly, save and name your setting so you can use it again later. You'll be returned to the Save dialog. Create a folder on your external drive to store your AAFs, and finally, hit Save.

Media Composer will churn for a while and you'll see a series of progress bars as the media is copied. If you don't have a MediaFiles folder on your target drive the system will create one. The folder you created will be populated with an AAF for every source clip. When the Export is finished you can delete them.

Finally, copy the bin or bins you need to your portable system and check to make sure everything works. The media will automatically link to the bins you copied—no relinking should be needed. (If not, try deleting your media databases on the portable drive.)

One nice feature of this technique is that in the future, if you add material to a bin and need to export media again, Media Composer will intelligently decide which files already exist on your external drive and copy only those that aren't already there. That's why it's helpful to delete your AAFs. If you leave them alone, MC will ask to overwrite them, one file at a time, and you'll have to confirm a separate dialog box for each clip. It's much easier to recreate them all.

Unlink

The Unlink command allows you to disconnect a master clip from its media. It can sometimes be useful if you want to redigitize audio or video or make other changes, but it can be tricky, so use it with caution.

Start by selecting a master clip. Then hold down the Command and Shift keys and pull down the Clip menu. The Relink command will change to Unlink. (You can also Command-Shift-right-click the clip to open a contextual menu that includes Unlink.)

If you've digitized a clip with incorrect settings, for example, (such as wrong tracks or wrong pullin) and you try to modify it, MC will tell you that it can't do this unless the clip is unlinked. But note that once clips are unlinked from their media, you can have problems relinking them to it. To be safe, start by either deleting the media or identifying it on disk so you can remove it later. Then unlink the clip, modify it and redigitize

17

Film and 24p Video

Film and digital workflows are changing so rapidly that it's hard for anyone to keep up. Every show presents new wrinkles, or often, an entirely new approach. For that reason, it's not possible to offer specific recommendations in a book like this. But it's important to understand the fundamental principles underlying 24-frame post-production. Armed with that knowledge, you should be able to tackle any kind of problem you're presented with.

A Multi-Frame-Rate World

Before television, editors didn't have to think much about frame rates. Film moved at 24 frames per second or 90 feet a minute. There were 16 frames in a foot of film. That was just about all you needed to know. But with the advent of video, the industry had to find ways of converting film-based materials to tape, which in the U.S. runs at 30 frames per second. The fact that video adds an extra 6 frames a second makes smooth conversions from one medium to the other difficult. It would have been easier, for example, if video ran at 48 fps, an even multiple of 24.

But the problem is much worse than this because color television doesn't run at 30 fps, but rather a tenth of a percent slower, at 29.97 fps. We say that the speed has been "pulled down" or slowed down. The combined effect of these two issues: adding frames to convert from 24 to 30 and changing the speed slightly to convert from 30 to 29.97 has come to be known colloquially as "3:2 pulldown."

A wide variety of digital formats can also run at 24 frames per second. And more often than not, you'll see them running pulled down, at 23.976 fps.

Telecine and Transfer Fundamentals

For now, let's simplify things and look at standard film telecine. (24p video works in exactly the same way—more on that later.) Assume for the moment that film travels at 24 frames per second and videotape at 30. Film is transferred to tape by creating duplicate frames, 6 per second. One second of the resulting videotape contains the original 24 film frames and 6 duplicate frames. In fact, we actually create 12 extra video *fields*. By using fields instead of frames we can distribute the extra images more evenly and produce smoother video.

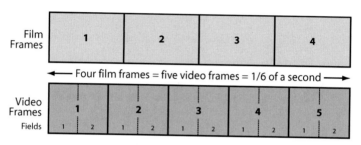

Film is converted to video according to the following diagram. The first film frame, labeled A, is converted to 2 video fields. The second, labeled B, is converted to three, the third to 2 and the fourth to 3 again. The conversion continues in this way, with the complete cycle beginning again every fourth film frame.

Film frames are converted into video fields in telecine.

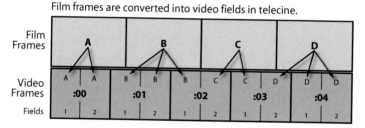

Each film frame in the four-frame cycle (or "cadence") is converted into a unique grouping of video fields. For example, a film frame that extends over two fields, both of which belong to the same video frame, can only be an A frame. Likewise, a film frame that extends over three fields and begins on a field 2 can only be a D frame. When we say that a frame is an A, B, C or D frame, we are describing the "pulldown phase," or the position that a frame takes in the four-frame sequence. Note that even though this is sometimes called 3:2 pulldown, if we start counting on an A frame, the cadence is really 2:3.

With old, tape-based editing systems, you worked with the video that was created in telecine, and only when the time came to conform film did you convert the 30-fps video edits into 24-fps film cuts. This involved many compromises. Media Composer and other modern editing systems do something different—they actually remove the pulldown sequence during capture, leaving only the original 24 frames. When you are working with such a system, you edit with exactly the same frames you'd see on film. This is what makes perfect conforms possible.

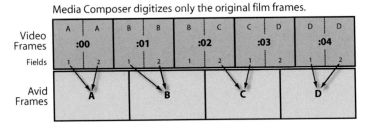

Media Composer digitizes only the original film frames.

As long as we work in the Media Composer environment, we use this 24-fps digital video. But the system must also make it possible for material to be output to 30-fps tape or DVD. To do this it converts the "virtual film" to video in exactly the same way that a telecine would, creating a new pulldown sequence and adding the specific 12 fields required.

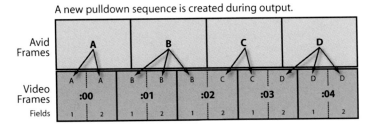

A new pulldown sequence is created during output.

24p Video

24-frame-per-second video works much like film. Source material is recorded as 24 discrete, progressive frames. It can then be converted to conventional 30-frame interlaced video for viewing in the same way film is—by duplicating fields in a standard 2:3 cadence.

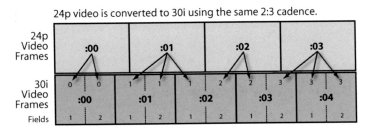

24p video is converted to 30i using the same 2:3 cadence.

24-fps Timecode

When you are working with 30-fps material that comes from a 24p source, you can calculate the original 24-frame timecode for any frame you're interested in. Hours, minutes and seconds are always identical. If you're looking at the first video field of any 30i frame, the 24p timecode associated with it is indicated in the following chart. Note that all 30i frames that are divisible by 5 are normally A frames.

Timecode Conversion — 30-fps to 24-fps

	30i = 24p		30i = 24p		30i = 24p		30i = 24p		30i = 24p		30i = 24p	
A Frames ➤	:00	:00	:05	:04	:10	:08	:15	:12	:20	:16	:25	:20
	:01	:01	:06	:05	:11	:09	:16	:13	:21	:17	:26	:21
	:02	:01	:07	:05	:12	:09	:17	:13	:22	:17	:27	:21
	:03	:02	:08	:06	:13	:10	:18	:14	:23	:18	:28	:22
	:04	:03	:09	:07	:14	:11	:19	:15	:24	:19	:29	:23

To convert timecode from 24-fps to 30-fps, use the following chart instead (again, it refers to the first field of each 30i frame). Hours, minutes and seconds don't change.

Timecode Conversion — 24-fps to 30-fps

	24p = 30i		24p = 30i		24p = 30i		24p = 30i		24p = 30i		24p = 30i	
A Frames ➤	:00	:00	:04	:05	:08	:10	:12	:15	:16	:20	:20	:25
	:01	:01	:05	:06	:09	:11	:13	:16	:17	:21	:21	:26
	:02	:03	:06	:08	:10	:13	:14	:18	:18	:23	:22	:28
	:03	:04	:07	:09	:11	:14	:15	:19	:19	:24	:23	:29

Advanced Pulldown

Standard pulldown repeats the sequence 2:3:2:3. But some cameras and decks offer an alternative cadence, sometimes called advanced pulldown. It uses the sequence 2:3:3:2, instead. It tends to produce more noticeable motion artifacts, but it's much easier to re-move in post-production. It works like this:

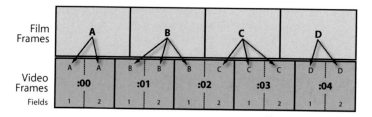

It takes less processing power to convert this kind of material back to the original 24 pro-gressive frames. All that's needed is to drop the third video frame.

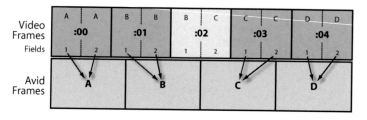

Use the Film and 24P settings panel to choose the type of pulldown employed in your source material. You can mix and match different types of pulldown in the same project, but be sure the pulldown cadence is set correctly when you digitize.

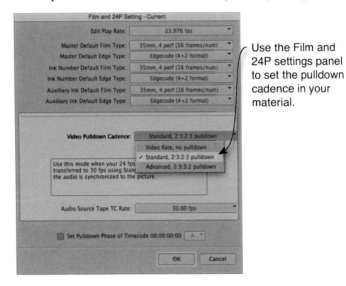

Use the Film and 24P settings panel to set the pulldown cadence in your material.

Pullin

In order for the Avid to perform its magic of removing false frames in telecined material, it has to know which pulldown frame each clip begins with—A, B, C or D. This is handled through a bin column called Pullin, which is an Avid-invented term for the pulldown phase (where you are in the pulldown sequence) at the first frame of the clip. The system needs to know the Pullin for every master clip in a 24-frame project. Pullin is automatically entered by the system as an A frame. If you have a non-standard tape, you may need to change it to B, C or D, prior to digitization, experimenting until video in the Avid plays smoothly.

Name	Tracks	Pullin	Start	End
84-1B	V1 A1 EC1	A	13:16:22:25	13:17:42:00
84-3A	V1 A1 EC1	A	13:01:57:20	13:03:26:00
84-3B	V1 A1 EC1	A	13:17:42:20	13:19:09:05
84A-1	V1 A1 EC1	A	13:03:26:20	13:04:47:15
84A-2	V1 A1 EC1	A	13:04:48:05	13:06:26:00
84B-1A	V1 A1 EC1	A	13:06:26:25	13:08:01:25
84B-1B	V1 A1 EC1	A	13:19:09:25	13:20:39:15
84B-2A	V1 A1 EC1	A	13:08:06:25	13:09:40:15
84B-2B	V1 A1 EC1	A	13:20:44:20	13:22:14:00
84C-1	V1 A1 EC1	A	13:09:41:10	13:11:12:20
84C-2	V1 A1 EC1	A	13:11:13:10	13:12:33:25
84C-3	V1 A1 EC1	A	13:12:34:15	13:13:48:15
84C-4	V1 A1 EC1	A	13:13:49:10	13:15:03:25
95-3	V1 A1 EC1	A	13:15:04:20	13:15:40:15
95-4	V1 A1 EC1	A	13:15:41:05	13:16:17:15

The Pullin column indicates whether each master clip begins with an A, B, C or D frame. A is standard.

Pulldown Problems

If there are problems in telecine or your editing system, the wrong pulldown sequence can be digitized. Instead of seeing smooth motion, some frames will be duplicated and some won't appear at all. The result will be noticeable, discontinuous motion in the resulting digital video and inaccurate lists.

After you digitize, play your clips and look for jerky movement (if there's no movement in the shot, jerkiness won't be apparent). If you have continuous burn-ins, examine the burned-in pulldown phase indicator. Each frame in the Avid should carry a different letter and should run in order: A, B, C, D, etc.

If the pulldown sequence contains repeating letters, for example, A, B, B, D, or A, B, D, D, or you see letters superimposed over each other, you have a pulldown problem. The following diagram shows how such problems can occur.

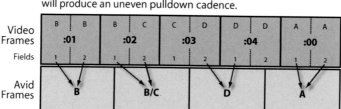

When you see jerky video in the Avid, you should start by trying to identify the source of the problem. There are several places to look: the Avid, the deck you used for capture (if you used one), telecine or transfer.

It's much easier to analyze this kind of problem if you have continuous burn-ins that indicate pulldown phase and video field. If your dailies don't have them, you may want to make copies of problem shots with the burn-ins added. First, determine whether the issue is continuous. Scan through problem clips from head to tail by holding down the Step Forward 8 Frames button. Watch the pulldown phase burn-in. It should not change at all. If it does, then something went wrong at the frame where it changes.

If the phase indicator doesn't change, then your problem is continuous. Check the burn-in on the first frame of the master clip against the pullin frame displayed in your source bin column. If they don't match you can try changing the pullin and re-digitizing. This can sometimes solve the problem—but it probably won't go to its source. You should to go back to the original material and trace forward through your workflow to determine where the error was introduced, and redo those steps, as needed.

You should avoid editing material that contains pulldown problems. There's a good chance it will have to be re-transferred. If so, you may have to re-cut, matching the old material to the new by eye.

30 vs. 29.97 fps

Black and white video originally ran at 30 frames per second. But when color technology arrived, adjustments had to be made so that the video signal could carry color information. One design goal was to avoid making black and white televisions obsolete. The engineers found that if they could slightly change the video frame rate, they could add color without much disruption. The frame rate chosen, one-tenth of one percent slower than normal, or 29.97 fps, was so close to the old speed that black-and-white sets could display the color signal without modification. Thus was NTSC color born—and we who deal with film and video have suffered ever since.

Transferring film to video suddenly became more complicated. If the film side of the te-lecine was running at 24 fps, how could the video side be running at 29.97? We can add 12 extra fields per second, but how do we add 11.97? The only possible answer was to run the film slower, to match the slowed-down video. All telecines now work this way: the film is actually moving at 23.976 frames per second, to match the video at 29.97.

In effect, what was created was a dual frame-rate world: the standard, full rate and the slower, pulled-down rate. Film could now travel at either of two speeds. As a result, every piece of material that could play in sync with picture came to have two available speeds or frame rates. Some common examples are shown in the following chart. To figure out the pulled-down rate, simply multiply the normal rate by .999.

	Full Rate	Pulled-Down Rate
30-fps Video	30 fps (theoretical—not used)	29.97 fps
Film & 24-fps Video	24 fps	23.976 fps
DAT	44,100 samples per second	44,056 samples per second.
DAT	48,000 samples per second	47,952 samples per second.
Audio TC	30 fps	29.97 fps
	24 fps	23.976 fps

The dual frame-rate world has been responsible for countless mistakes and lots of head scratching. A tenth of a percent is a very slight change and we usually can't see or hear the difference it makes. But we can see cumulative speed changes easily: when picture runs normally and sync sound runs slow, we'll see an error within a minute or two. Once we have a world with two speeds for everything, we have to be very careful about sync.

Digital Audio

Digital audio can be visualized as a series of numbers. Each number represents the volume or loudness of the sound being played for a tiny fraction of a second. Converting traditional analog sound into digital data means measuring the volume of that sound thousands of times a second and recording those measurements. We can visualize the sound being sliced like a salami into samples or volume measurements, each represented by a number.

The standard sample rates, or speeds, at which the audio is sliced up, are 44,100 (44.1k) or 48,000 (48k) times a second. When we play back digital audio we take these samples and play them at the proper rate, either 44,100 or 48,000 times a second.

Raw digital audio isn't divided into frames, but it can carry timecode, which is frame-based. And like all the other speeds we've been examining, timecode can be recorded or played back at several speeds: 24 fps, 30 fps, and the pulled-down rates of 23.976 and 29.97. When we work with digital audio we must be conscious not only of sample rate but of timecode rate, as well.

Drop-Frame vs. Non-Drop-Frame Timecode

Like keycode does in film, timecode identifies frames in videotape. But timecode attempts to do something else, namely measure the amount of time it will take for a tape to play. That doesn't seem difficult—the problem is that pesky pulled-down frame rate.

In a typical piece of videotape the seconds counter rolls over after 30 frames have elapsed: 00:00:01:00 is 30 frames away from 00:00:00:00. But since video isn't traveling at a full 30 frames per second, at the end of that 30th frame, a full second of time has *not* elapsed. Instead of being at the one-second point in our program, we're at the .999 second point. The error seems trivial, but the longer the program, the more significant it becomes. In a one-hour show, the difference amounts to about three seconds.

Drop-frame timecode was developed to compensate for this error. It makes some simple adjustments so that when the timecode displays one hour of elapsed time, one hour has really gone by. It does this not by a complex frame rate adjustment, but by simply skipping frame numbers. We indicate drop-frame timecode with semicolons (00;00;00;00) and non-drop-frame code with colons (00:00:00:00).

If we shuttle through a piece of tape that has been coded with drop-frame timecode we'll find that certain frame numbers are simply missing. Here's an example:

Non-Drop-Frame Timecode

| 00:00:59:28 | 00:00:59:29 | 00:01:00:00 | 00:01:00:01 | 00:01:00:02 | 00:01:00:03 |

Drop-Frame Timecode

| 00;00;59;28 | 00;00;59;29 | 00;01;00;02 | 00;01;00;03 | 00;01;00;04 | 00;01;00;05 |

We skip two numbers every minute, *except* every 10th minute. That produces 18 skipped frame numbers every 10 minutes or 108 skipped numbers every hour. This is exactly the difference between our elapsed clock time and our timecode, so that at the end of an hour, the timecode correctly reads 01;00;00;00.

Drop-frame code is simply a way of numbering frames; it doesn't change the frames and it doesn't change the speed at which they're played. The same piece of video can be coded with drop or with non-drop code—the video itself won't change.

Note that drop-frame code doesn't keep perfect clock time because it compensates only once per minute. At the start of every minute the code is pretty accurate, but as the minute elapses, the code becomes progressively less accurate. At the next minute mark, frame numbers are again skipped and the code jumps back in step with clock time.

Pulled down and normal frame rates are not synonymous with drop-frame and non-drop-frame timecode. They tend to go together—it would make no sense to put drop-frame code on full-rate material. But pulled-down material can carry either kind of code.

Sync Problems

What happens when you find drifting sync? First, you must determine whether the sync problem is the result of pulldown. Since pulldown problems represent a consistent one tenth of one percent sync drift, you'll need to measure the drift as accurately as possible. Start by putting picture and sound in sync, say, at the head of a take. Then find a spot several minutes later where you can accurately check sync. Determine how far you are out of sync at this point, in frames, and divide by the distance between the two points, also in frames. If your problem is the result of a pulldown error, then the result will be .001 or a tenth of a percent—one frame of drift for every 1000 frames of material.

Once you've determined whether your sync error is caused by pulldown, you can go through your workflow and figure out what went wrong. Audio or video has gotten longer or shorter at some point, and you'll have to go step-by-step through the chain and figure out where it occurred.

Hopefully, you'll be able to redo that step. But sometimes this isn't possible, especially if the problem occurred in production. In that case you'll have to deliberately make a copy or transfer that changes length again—this time in the opposite direction. This often means a sample-rate conversion to lengthen or shorten audio, in order to match whatever happened to video.

Avid Project Types for 24-fps Media

Avid now offers two project types for 24-fps media, the traditional "24p" project, and a variant, dubbed "23.976p." The difference between the two is subtle. In both, the system digitizes video running at 29.97 fps and removes pulldown (aka "reverse telecine"), so you end up with the original 24 film or progressive video frames. What makes the project types different is the audio sample rate that's synchronized with picture.

In a standard 24p project, pulled-down audio is synched with pulled-down video. That is, video running at 23.976 fps (or 29.97 fps) is synched with audio running at 47,952 samples per second. All the speeds are consistently a tenth of a percent slower than their "normal" rates.

That worked well for the film industry for a long time. But when this scheme was originally developed there was no such thing as digital videotape—and therein lies the rub.

Digital video works differently, synchronizing pulled-down video with *full-rate* audio. Video running at 29.97 or 23.976 is synchronized with audio running at 48K—not 47,952.

A 23.976 project works like digital videotape, synchronizing pulled-down video with full-rate audio. That makes it appropriate for video and file-based material shot at 23.976, and it can be useful for film-originated material, as well. Since the Avid's frame rates match those of digital videotape, you'll be able to load audio from tape digitally without sample-rate conversion. But sound editors will need to work differently. If you normally work in a 24p project, you'll want to check with them before making changes. For a complete end-to-end digital workflow, film-based productions may prefer to record audio at a different sample rate, as well.

Matchback

Matchback is a method for conforming frame-based material from one rate to another. Before there were true 24-fps editing systems, matchback was used to conform 24-fps film from edited, 30-fps videotape. Today, it's rarely used.

Matchback works, but it introduces two kinds of errors. First, while some video cuts are unambiguous—a video frame 00 would be conformed as a film A frame, for example—some aren't. Video frame 02 is composed of film frames B and C. How should it be conformed, as a B or C?

Another kind of error results from the fact that at any particular cut point, the ends of the video and film don't necessarily line up. In the figure below, we conform one cut. The outgoing side of the cut is a video frame 01 and is conformed as a film B frame. Notice that this shot is now slightly longer on film than it was on tape. The same is true of the incoming shot. The difference in frame rates means that most cuts are like this: they can't be conformed without a slight length change. These changes add up, resulting in a sync error.

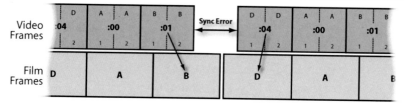

When 30-frame video is conformed to 24-frame film, most cuts produce a sync error. Here, a video frame 1 is cut to a video frame 4 and conformed as B to D.

Matchback solves these problems by cheating. As it conforms, it tallies the cumulative sync error, and when the error exceeds half a frame, it adds or deletes a frame of film to put the sequence back into the best sync possible.

Editors generally don't relish the idea that their work can be arbitrarily adjusted this way, and that's one reason why matchback has fallen out of favor. If you must use this technique, then you have to assume that any cut can be adjusted, and edit accordingly. If a gunshot occurs on a certain frame, for example, and you want to use all the material prior to the shot, give yourself a cushion to avoid the possibility that matchback will move your cut and reveal the muzzle flash.

18

Film
Lists

Avid's FilmScribe application generates lists designed to help editors conform and manage film and digital intermediate materials. It creates two classes of lists: cut lists, which contain information about individual sequences, and change lists, which compare sequences to each other. FilmScribe lists can provide data that can't be included in an EDL—just about anything in any bin column.

Assemble Lists

An assemble list is the most basic kind of cut list and is a fundamental tool in any conform. It describes each shot in your sequence, in sequence order, and looks something like the following. (Pull lists provide similar information but can be sorted by camera roll, source timecode, or other criteria.)

	Footage	Record TC	Duration	First/Last Key	Cam Roll	Clip Name
1.	0000+00	01:00:00:00	0005+11	FN 73 4981-7296+02	B179	84-1B
	0005+10	01:00:03:18		FN 73 4981-7301+12		
2.	0005+11	01:00:03:19	0003+06	FN 73 4956-4428+04	A203	84-3A
	0009+00	01:00:06:00		FN 73 4956-4431+09		
3.	0009+01	01:00:06:01	0004+08	FN 73 4956-4543+11	A203	84A-1
	0013+08	01:00:09:00		FN 73 4956-4548+02		
4.	0013+09	01:00:09:01	0004+06	FN 73 4981-6300+11	A204	84C-3
	0017+14	01:00:11:22		FN 73 4981-6305+00		

To make an assemble list, start by locating the sequence you're interested in and clearly identifying it in a bin. Then open FilmScribe by selecting it from the Output menu (you can also open it independently from the OS). It will display a single window: an empty Cut List Tool.

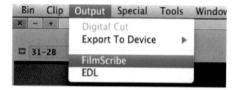

Then, from within FilmScribe, select File > Open and navigate to your project. Find the bin containing your sequence and select it. It will open in a FilmScribe window in text view. If necessary, click on a heading to sort the list. Locate your sequence and drag it to the Sequences well in the Cut List Tool. (If you make lists frequently, you may want to create a shortcut to your project. On the Mac you can do this from the Open dialog box. Just drag your project folder to an appropriate place in the sidebar.)

Now choose your settings. Click a list button to display its options in the panel on the right. Start with Global settings and begin by selecting a template. The old standby was Columnar, which produces a list that is displayed in a Filmscribe window. If you have problems, you may want to try WebLists. This creates a folder containing an HTML document and associated image files, which are displayed in a browser. You'll need to pick a location for the files.

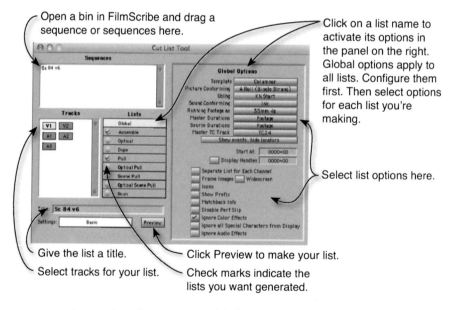

Open a bin in FilmScribe and drag a sequence or sequences here.

Click on a list name to activate its options in the panel on the right. Global options apply to all lists. Configure them first. Then select options for each list you're making.

Select list options here.

Give the list a title.

Select tracks for your list.

Click Preview to make your list.

Check marks indicate the lists you want generated.

Then move on to select options for your assemble list and for any other lists you need. Pay careful attention to the columns you want displayed. Unnecessary data makes a list harder to read and use. You'll probably want Name (clip name), KN Start, and either

StartTC or TC24. You can transfer these settings to all other lists by clicking the Set All Cut Lists button. To see a brief summary of the data you've selected, click the Summary button.

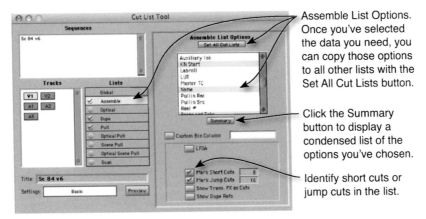

Assemble List Options. Once you've selected the data you need, you can copy those options to all other lists with the Set All Cut Lists button.

Click the Summary button to display a condensed list of the options you've chosen.

Identify short cuts or jump cuts in the list.

Once you've chosen your settings, save them by clicking the Settings pop-up. This makes it easier to experiment with different settings and create consistent lists.

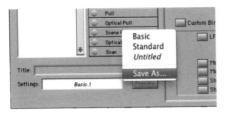

If you change your settings you can replace them the same way you can in the timeline or a bin—hold down the Option key when you open the pop-up.

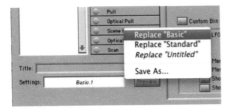

Select the tracks for which you want lists by clicking them in the Tracks pane. Again, avoid unnecessary information. Then click the Preview button to create your lists. They'll appear in a separate window. If you selected WebLists, they'll open in your web browser. Print and save, as needed.

Note that in FilmScribe lists, all numbers are inclusive (what editors used to call "inside/inside"). Tail numbers are not incremented by one as they would be in an EDL. (If the master timecode at the last frame of a shot is 00, a film list will display 00. An EDL will display 01.)

FilmScribe and Media Composer

It's important to understand that FilmScribe has no idea what you are doing in Media Composer. So if you open a bin in FilmScribe and then make changes to it in Media Composer, FilmScribe will not reflect those changes. You must save your bin in Media Composer and then close and re-open it in FilmScribe. If you loaded a sequence into the Cut List Tool, closing and re-opening the bin in FilmScribe won't clear it. You'll need to drag your sequence to the tool again, as well.

Change Lists

Change lists compare an old version and a new version of a sequence, and produce a list of instructions that represents the differences between them. The list works like a recipe that converts the old sequence into the new one, and it has to be executed in order. A typical list might look something like this:

	At This Footage	For This Length	Do This	First/Last Key	Clip Name	Total Change
1.	0005+11 0005+13	+0000+03	Lengthen Tail	FN 73 4981-7301+13 FN 73 4981-7301+15	84-1B	+00+03
2.	0013+12 0018+01	-0004+06	Delete 1 Shot	FN 73 4981-6300+11 FN 73 4981-6305+00	84C-3	-04+03
3.	0017+00 0018+00	+0001+01	Lengthen Head	FN 73 4956-4870+12 FN 73 4956-4871+12	84B-1A	-03+02
4.	0024+07 0025+01	-0000+11	Trim Head	FN 73 4956-4691+12 FN 73 4956-4692+06	84A-2	-03+13

To create a list, open FilmScribe and select File > New Change List. This opens the Change List Tool. Then drag your old sequence to the Old Sequences well and your new sequence to the New Sequences well. Click the Global button and begin selecting your options.

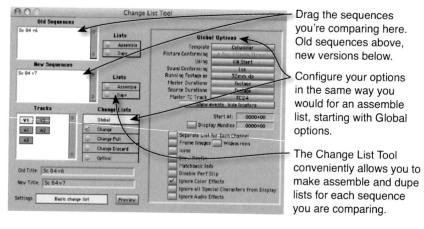

Drag the sequences you're comparing here. Old sequences above, new versions below.

Configure your options in the same way you would for an assemble list, starting with Global options.

The Change List Tool conveniently allows you to make assemble and dupe lists for each sequence you are comparing.

Then click the Change button and choose the data you want displayed in the list. As with assemble lists, it's best to keep it simple. Change lists tend to be fairly complicated and a more straightforward list will be easier to check. Select Show Only Changes to suppress events that describe sections where nothing has changed. Select Combine Deletions to collect adjacent deletions and present them as a single event.

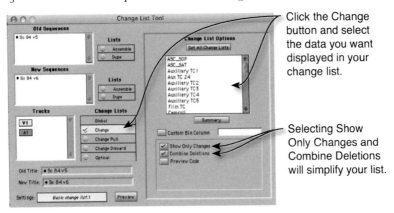

Click the Change button and select the data you want displayed in your change list.

Selecting Show Only Changes and Combine Deletions will simplify your list.

Even if you're not making an assemble list, you should configure assemble list options for both the old and new sequence. Click each Assemble button and then click Same as Change List. This often avoids consistency problems and potential crashes.

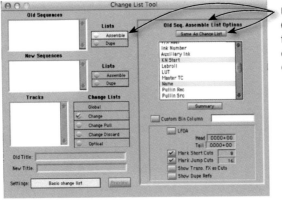

Use the Same as Change List buttons to quickly copy options from your change list.

Checking a Change List

Because a change list is a recipe, downstream numbers reflect the fact that upstream events have been conformed. That makes it difficult to check a list. If your list is simple, you can usually look it over, spot check event durations, and determine that the changes you expect to see are present. But with a complex list the only way to be sure is to create a copy of your old sequence and actually follow the list, conforming each change, in order, in Media Composer. If the list is correct, you'll transform your old sequence into your new one.

Timecodes in Cut and Change Lists

If you need lists based on time in addition to footage, select Master TC from the options dialog. Your list will indicate start and end timecodes for every event, and in change lists, durations will be listed in timecode as well as footage. (Change list options are illustrated below, but cut list options work the same way.)

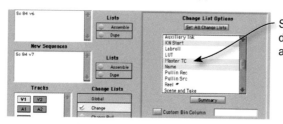

Select Master TC to display durations in time as well as footage.

You should also choose the timecode rate for Master TC in the Global settings pane. If your rate doesn't match your project's frame rate, Master TC values will be interpolated. For 24 and 23.976 projects choose TC24.

To show source timecodes for every change, select a source timecode column, typically either Start TC or TC24 depending on the frame rate of your material.

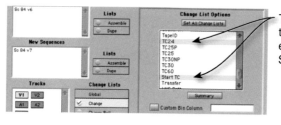

To display source timecodes for each event in your list, select Start TC or TC24.

Lock Tracks

If you make a cut or change list from a sequence, turn it over to sound or conform it, and then *change the sequence in Media Composer,* you'll break the essential connection between the Media Composer sequence and the conformed elements, and you won't be able to make further change lists for that sequence. You must retain a sequence in Media Composer that accurately represents the condition of the conformed material.

1. Select the sequence you want to conform, and duplicate it using Command-D.

2. Load the original sequence in the record monitor and select all tracks.

3. Select Clip > Lock Tracks. This will prevent further editorial changes. For additional safety, you may want to select the sequence in the bin and choose Clip > Lock Bin Selection. This will prevent it from being inadvertently deleted.

4. Now use it to make your lists. Use the duplicated sequence for further changes.

It's also helpful to add a conform date to the clip name of any sequence that you turn over.

Multi-Sequence Change Lists

Many people aren't aware of it, but FilmScribe will accurately track moves from one sequence to another. If you moved a shot from Reel 3 to Reel 4, for example, drag both old sequences to the Old Sequence pane of the Change List Tool and both new sequences to the New Sequence pane. Your list will be created with appropriate cross-sequence moves.

To make this feature work you must give the sequences reel numbers, so the software can figure out which is which. Put your sequence bin into text view in Media Composer, show the Reel # column and give each sequence a number. The software will use these numbers to track cross-sequence changes.

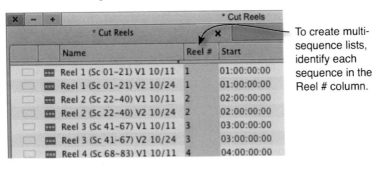

To create multi-sequence lists, identify each sequence in the Reel # column.

Note that when you drag material to a sequence well in FilmScribe, the sequence you drag replaces anything already there. If you want to add additional sequences to those already present, Option-drag them.

Rebalancing Reels

Using FilmScribe's multi-sequence capability, you can easily conform changes that rebalance reels: where material moves from the tail of one reel to the head of another or vice versa. It's best to make a list for the rebalance as a separate step. If you will be making changes in a scene and also moving it from one reel to another, try to do the two steps independently. Make your changes and create a change list for them. Then do the rebalance and make a change list for that. Then conform the lists separately, in the same order. If you try to conform internal changes and a move of an entire scene in one step, the change list will be much more complicated.

Same Number of Old and New Sequences

When making multi-sequence change lists, it's essential that you load the same number of old and new sequences into the Change List Tool. If you rebalance your show and *delete a reel*, for example, you'll have fewer new sequences than old ones and the change list will report an error. You'll need to make a dummy sequence and insert it into the New or Old Sequences pane to ensure that they both contain the same number of reels. You can't use an empty sequence for this—it must contain at least one frame of actual material.

If you build your reels in Media Composer with standard head and tail leaders, then when you rebalance, you'll delete all the material from a reel, leaving only the leaders. This empty reel (now consisting of only a head and tail leader) will be your dummy sequence. If you don't work with leaders, you'll need to create a new sequence and edit one frame of material into it. You'll get the lists you need as well as a change list for the dummy reel, which you can ignore.

Either way, be absolutely certain that all the reels, old and new, are labeled properly in the Reel # column. If you try to make lists where some sequences are identified with reel numbers and some aren't, the software may not report an error, but your list will be impossibly complicated.

Optical Lists

The Cut List Tool can't fully describe what's happening in a complex visual effect, but it can provide limited data for each layer, which may be helpful when communicating with visual effects artists. Click the Optical button to select your options. To show data for each keyframe, click the Key Frames check box, but note that FilmScribe won't provide information on advanced keyframes. In Global settings, experiment with different templates.

To generate data for a stack of effects, try selecting the topmost track. FilmScribe will include information for all the tracks underneath simultaneously.

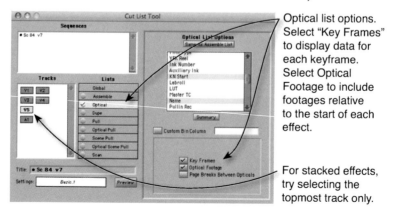

Optical list options. Select "Key Frames" to display data for each keyframe. Select Optical Footage to include footages relative to the start of each effect.

For stacked effects, try selecting the topmost track only.

Submaster Effects

FilmScribe can't parse sequences containing submaster effects. Not only will you be unable to make an optical list from such a effect, but you won't be able to make any lists at all from the sequence containing it. You'll have to eliminate the submaster editorially, prior to making your list (see "Collapse/Submaster" on page 173).

3-Perf & 4-Perf Film Originals

You can mix 3-perf and 4-perf 35 mm as well as 16 mm materials in the KN Start bin column. This is possible because the film type is indicated separately, in the KN Film column, with values that look like this: 35.3, 35.4. and 16.20. This way all gauges are under one column for a DI conform. You can then display the KN Film column in your lists so that the different sources can be identified.

FilmScribe Versions

Whenever you update Media Composer it's a good idea to update FilmScribe, as well. And if you're not using Avid's unified installer (page 14), FilmScribe should be installed after Media Composer. Changing the order of installation or using non-matching versions can create instability and list problems.

19 Settings

Terminology

Avid uses several terms to describe the different parts of the Media Composer's settings architecture. *Settings* are displayed as a list in the Settings tab of the Project window. Each one controls a specific part of the system. When you double-click a setting in the list it opens in its own window, where you can make adjustments.

Users and *User Profiles* are collections of settings, the sum total of all the settings in the Settings Tab. There isn't much difference between a User and a Profile. When you first start it up, the Media Composer creates a User named to match the currently logged-in user in the operating system. Each User can then have several User Profiles, and you can switch between them with the User Profile Selection menu, in the Settings tab.

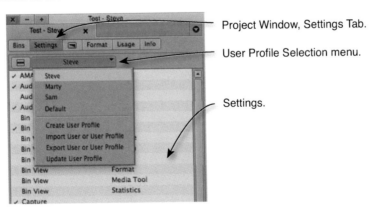

Project Window, Settings Tab.

User Profile Selection menu.

Settings.

Workspaces and *Bin Layouts* are window arrangements: which windows are open, how they're sized and configured, and where they're placed on the screen. They're accessed from the Windows menu and are also available as settings in the Project window.

Making New Settings

The system allows you to create multiple copies of a setting, each with different options enabled. You can then switch back and forth between them with a single click. To do this, go to the Project window, choose the Settings tab, and single-click the setting you want to change. Then select Duplicate from the Edit menu. This will create a new setting for the item selected. To identify your settings, click in the column indicated below, and give each one a name. Double-click the new setting to open and customize it. Finally, activate the setting by single-clicking to the left of the setting name. This will put a check mark there to indicate that the setting is active.

For example, you may like working with only one row of information in the Composer window, but for certain purposes you need two. Just create two settings and switch between them by activating the one you need.

Project Window, Settings Tab

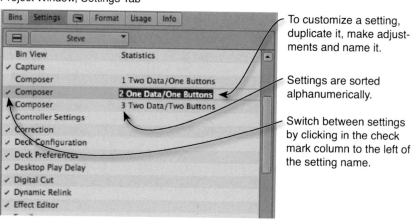

To customize a setting, duplicate it, make adjustments and name it.

Settings are sorted alphanumerically.

Switch between settings by clicking in the check mark column to the left of the setting name.

Restore Default Settings

You can restore any setting to its default values. Single-click the setting in the Project window to select it, and then either select Special > Restore to Default or right-click the setting and make the same selection from the contextual menu.

The system will ask you whether you want to make a new default setting and preserve the one you've been using, or restore the current setting to default values.

Users and User Profiles

Your settings are stored in the Avid Users folder. You'll typically find it here:

> Mac:
> Macintosh HD/Users/Shared/AvidMediaComposer/Avid Users

> Windows:
> C:/Users/Public/Public Documents/Avid Media Composer/Avid Users

Inside the Avid Users folder, Media Composer installs a User folder, named to match the current user account on your computer. Inside, you'll find three files, a settings file with the extension xml, another with the extention avs (for compatibility with older systems), and third file with the extension ave. You'll also find an MCState file, which saves the state of the system when you quit. With a typical, one-user setup that's all you need.

If your user name on your computer is Mike, your Avid Users folder will look like this:

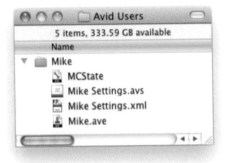

Working within that User, you can then create additional User Profiles. This lets several editors work on the same machine without having to log in and out of the OS, and it also lets a single editor set up separate user profiles for different tasks.

To create a User Profile, go to the Settings tab in the Project window, open the User Profile Selection menu and choose Create User Profile.

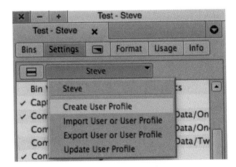

The file structure with multiple Users and User Profiles looks like this:

Avid Users folder.

User folders named to match the user account or accounts on the host computer.

Two User Profiles, located inside the User named Mike.

Each User or Profile contains these four files, named as indicated, to match the folder name.

When Mike logs in to the OS and starts Media Composer, he'll have a choice of three profiles: Mike, Sam and Tom. When Mike logs out and Charlie logs in, he'll have only one, named Charlie.

Taking Your Settings With You

To move a profile from one system to another, open the User Profile menu on the first machine and select Export User or User Profile. This will create a folder on disk. Move it to the second machine, select Import User or User Profile and point the system at the folder (not the files within it). Your settings will be imported with the same name they had on the first machine.

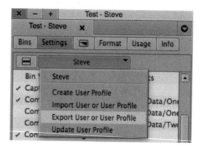

You can also move the appropriate files at the operating system level, but be sure you preserve the file structure from the illustrations in the previous section. The xml, ave and avs files must be named to match the folder that contains them.

If you are moving a profile to a machine with a newer version of Media Composer, you may want to select Update User Profile after importing. This will install any missing settings that are specific to the new version. But note that because the settings architecture has changed, you should create a new user when migrating from MC5 to MC6.

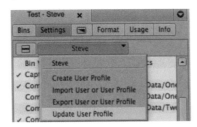

Moving Individual Settings

To transfer individual settings from one profile to another, click the Settings tab in the project window and select File > Open Setting File. Navigate to the xml file in the profile containing the setting you need. All the settings in that profile will open in a new window. Drag an item from the list to the settings tab of your project window. MC will ask if you want to overwrite the existing version of that setting or create a new one. You probably want to create a new one so you can go back to your old setting, if needed. Name the new setting, and activate it by clicking to the left of the name.

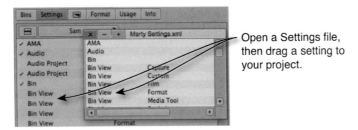

Open a Settings file, then drag a setting to your project.

You can also create new xml files to store or move individual settings. Click the Settings tab in the Project window and choose File > New Setting File. An Untitled window appears. Drag one or more settings from the Project window to the new settings window.

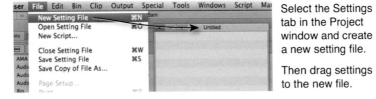

Select the Settings tab in the Project window and create a new setting file.

Then drag settings to the new file.

Select File > Close Setting File, indicate that you want to save it, and specify a file name and location. Note that if you select Save Setting File instead, you won't see a Save dialog. The file will be saved to your Avid Users folder with the name Untitled, and you'll have to navigate there to find it.

Move the xml file to another system, click on the Settings tab, select File > Open Setting File and drag settings to the Project window, as needed

Site Settings

With site settings you can create a group of settings that will be inherited by every new user on your machine. Select Special > Site Settings. Drag one or more settings from your Project window to the Site Settings window. Close the window and save settings by selecting the Project window and hitting Command-S. The settings you dragged will become part of every new user or user profile you subsequently create on that machine.

Workspaces and Bin Layouts

As the system becomes more complex and capable, editors tend to need specialized window layouts for different tasks. Avid allows you create and memorize such arrangements using Workspaces and Bin Layouts, and then recall them with a menu pick or button press. Workspaces control windows and tools (the composer, timeline, audio mixer, etc.); Bin Layouts control bins. (Older versions of the software offered both Toolsets and Workspaces. They were merged in Version 6.)

Workspaces

Default workspaces are provided for standard tasks such as Source/Record Editing, Audio Editing, Color Correction and the like. You can use them as is, customize them, or create workspaces of your own. Start by selecting a workspace from the Workspaces menu (Tools > Workspaces). Your screen will change to reflect Avid's default window positions for that space.

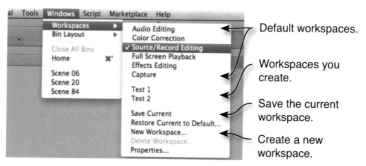

Move windows around, change their sizes, open tools such as the Audio Mixer or the Effect Editor, and display them any way you like (for example, you might want to show eight channels in the audio mixer). Select Save Current from the Workspace menu to memorize the view. Then move on and customize other workspaces. For Audio Editing you may want to hide video in the composer and expand the timeline (see "Hide Video" on page 61).

Alternatively, you can move your windows wherever you want and then select New Workspace. You'll be asked to give the workspace a name, which will then appear in the Workspace menu along with the default spaces. To activate a workspace, simply select it from the menu. Your screen instantly changes, with tools opening or closing, as needed.

In addition, you can associate any named setting with a workspace. When you select the workspace, the setting will be activated simultaneously. For the Audio Editing workspace, you might want to associate a timeline view with tall audio tracks and visible waveforms.

Select a workspace, and then choose Properties from the Workspace menu. In the dialog box that follows, select Link to Named Settings and enter the name of the timeline view or other setting to associate with that workspace.

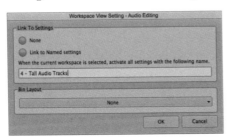

After that, with a single menu pick you can completely customize your work environment. And you can get back to where you were just as easily. If you want to make an adjustment to a workspace, select it, make your change, and choose Save Current.

To activate a workspace from the keyboard, use the Workspace tab in the Command Palette. Each default workspace is associated with a button, labeled with a text abbreviation. Additional buttons can be assigned to your custom workspaces with pop-up menus. Drag a button to your keyboard settings, or anywhere else on the interface.

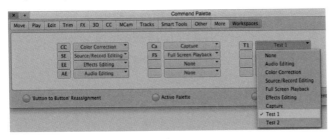

You can also associate a workspace with the Mode buttons at the bottom left of the timeline, allowing you to change modes and activate a workspace simultaneously. Open the Workspace Linking settings pane and choose the workspace to associate with each button, using the pop-up menus.

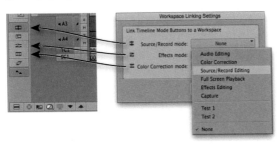

Bin Layouts

Workspaces allow you to memorize the positions of windows and tools, but they don't let you save bin positions. For that, you'll use Bin Layouts. They work in much the same way, saving all the bins you have open along with their positions on screen.

Open the bins whose positions you want to memorize. Move them around, choose text, frame or script view, and tab them together, as needed. Then select Windows > Bin Layouts, and create a new layout. Later, when you want to reopen those bins, simply choose the setting from the Bin Layout menu. They'll come back exactly as you had them, with tabs and positions restored. Any currently open bins that are not part of the layout will close.

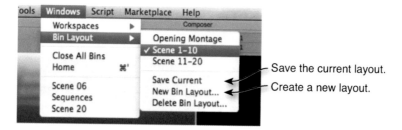

Finally, you can associate a bin layout with a workspace, so they open simultaneously. Select the workspace and then chose the layout to associate with it from the Properties window.

Workspaces and bin layouts are saved in the settings tab of the project window, allowing you to rename, copy or delete them. You can also switch between views by clicking in the check mark column.

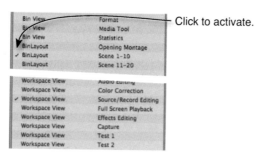

20 Suggested Settings

I use Media Composer in an unusual way, and many people have asked me to describe my approach. I'll lay out some of my preferred settings in the following pages. Needless to say, you should treat them as suggestions only. Part of the value of the system lies in how easily it can be customized. If you like the way your Media Composer is set up, there's no reason to change it.

Interface

Interface brightness is a matter of personal preference. Some people find the darker settings more attractive, but white text on a dark background can be harder to use for long periods. I prefer the default blue highlight color and set the ToolTip delay to one second.

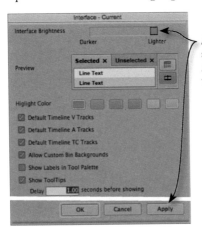

Adjust interface brightness and select a highlight color. Then click Apply to preview your change without closing the panel.

Keyboard

The most basic interface choice I've made lies in the way I use the keyboard. I had several goals in mind when setting this up. First, I wanted a simple layout. The more you can free yourself from thinking about the machine, the more your focus will be on the material you're editing. I also wanted to avoid the need to look at the keyboard. Every time you look down, you slow down. Most important, I wanted a layout focused on JKL play, which I use constantly. With the default Avid setup I had to move my hand from the mouse to the keyboard to use JKL, and all that switching slowed me down. I wanted the keyboard optimized for things that are rhythmic—marking, playing, stopping precisely—because those things are best done with the sense of touch.

The layout I settled on is simple enough to memorize, so I don't need to label the buttons. That means I can choose from a wide variety of keyboards and pick the one that feels best. Newer keyboards tend to have shorter key travel and are easier to use over long periods of time. And unlike some Avid keyboards, they usually have bumps on the F and J keys, which allows you position your hands by feel.

Without Shift

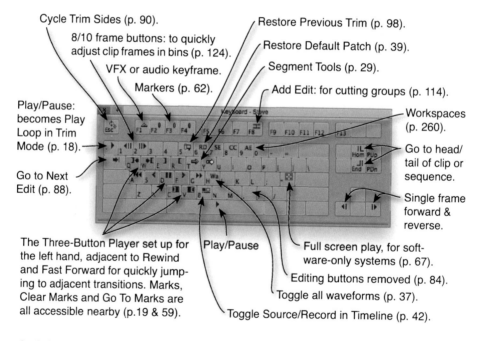

Cycle Trim Sides (p. 90).
8/10 frame buttons: to quickly adjust clip frames in bins (p. 124).
VFX or audio keyframe.
Markers (p. 62).
Restore Previous Trim (p. 98).
Restore Default Patch (p. 39).
Segment Tools (p. 29).
Add Edit: for cutting groups (p. 114).

Play/Pause: becomes Play Loop in Trim Mode (p. 18).
Go to Next Edit (p. 88).

Workspaces (p. 260).
Go to head/ tail of clip or sequence.
Single frame forward & reverse.

The Three-Button Player set up for the left hand, adjacent to Rewind and Fast Forward for quickly jumping to adjacent transitions. Marks, Clear Marks and Go To Marks are all accessible nearby (p.19 & 59).
Play/Pause
Full screen play, for software-only systems (p. 67).
Editing buttons removed (p. 84).
Toggle all waveforms (p. 37).
Toggle Source/Record in Timeline (p. 42).

Using the left hand for JKL play seemed awkward at first, but I'm right handed and incapable of using the mouse with my left. To have one hand on the keyboard and one on the mouse, I had to operate the keyboard with the left hand. The rest of the layout grew naturally from that basic decision and is explained in the screen shots. (Southpaws will want to switch things around a bit.) Some of the specifics, such as the use of the function keys, are necessarily arbitrary. But the basic idea was to put the three-button player on the S, D and F keys. Try it. If you're like me, after a little practice you'll wonder how you worked any other way.

With Shift

Go to Previous Edit (p. 88).   Audio Mark In and Out (p. 75).

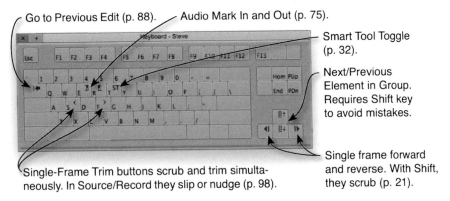

Smart Tool Toggle (p. 32).

Next/Previous Element in Group. Requires Shift key to avoid mistakes.

Single-Frame Trim buttons scrub and trim simultaneously. In Source/Record they slip or nudge (p. 98).

Single frame forward and reverse. With Shift, they scrub (p. 21).

With the single-frame trim buttons on the shifted keyboard, I can trim one frame at a time, with scrub audio, using Shift-S and Shift-F. For small adjustments, this is more precise than using the three-button player. In Source/Record Mode, the same buttons slip the clips you are parked over. With a clip selected and the Lift/Overwrite (red) Segment Tool active, they nudge the selected clip a frame at a time.

Settings

I put the Fast Forward and Rewind Buttons next to the three-button player. They're handy if you want to jump to the next cut, locator, or to the beginning or end of a clip. You can customize them via the FF/REW tab in Composer Settings.

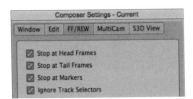

Audio Scrub

By default, audio scrub settings are set as 0/1 0/1, and you shouldn't need to change them. When you move one frame at a time, you will always hear the frame you land on, regardless of which direction you're moving (see page 21).

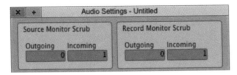

Mouse

I use a multi-button mouse with one button dedicated to a double-click. That makes loading shots into a monitor more positive and reduces repetitive strain to the forearm. Note that some mouse drivers don't allow you to assign a double-click to a button. But the flexible Microsoft mouse software, which only works with their mice, allows for this and many other options, as well. Scroll wheel settings were covered on page 10. You'll also want to experiment with different mouse pads. They can make a significant difference in the precision and smoothness of mouse tracking.

Trim Settings

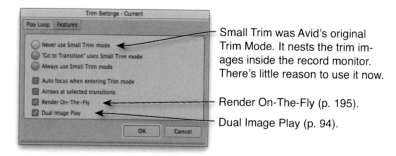

Small Trim was Avid's original Trim Mode. It nests the trim images inside the record monitor. There's little reason to use it now.

Render On-The-Fly (p. 195).

Dual Image Play (p. 94).

Composer Window

If you mark in and out from the keyboard, you can probably use one row of buttons in the Composer window. This simplifies the interface and gives you more room for the timeline. I prefer two rows of data above the monitors. This makes it easier to compare a pair of numbers to check sync and adds the Group Menu when a group is loaded.

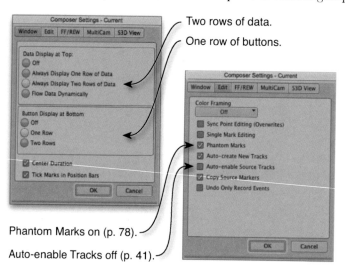

Two rows of data.

One row of buttons.

Phantom Marks on (p. 78).

Auto-enable Tracks off (p. 41).

Record Monitor

Center Duration

Two rows of data makes it easy to
check sync and adds the Group Menu.

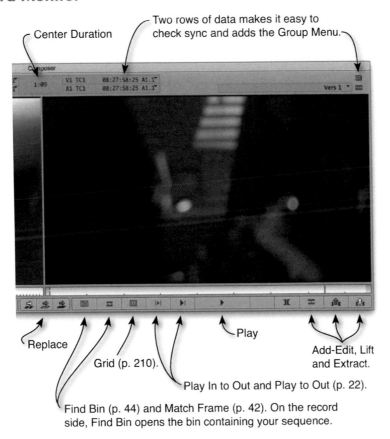

Replace

Grid (p. 210).

Play

Add-Edit, Lift
and Extract.

Play In to Out and Play to Out (p. 22).

Find Bin (p. 44) and Match Frame (p. 42). On the record
side, Find Bin opens the bin containing your sequence.

Source Monitor

Play In to Out and Play to Out: useful for
checking material prior to cutting it in (p. 22).

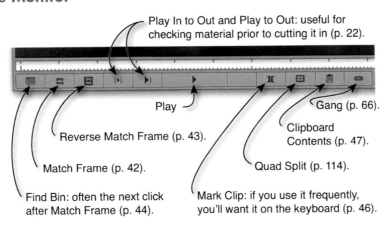

Play

Gang (p. 66).

Reverse Match Frame (p. 43).

Clipboard
Contents (p. 47).

Match Frame (p. 42).

Quad Split (p. 114).

Find Bin: often the next click
after Match Frame (p. 44).

Mark Clip: if you use it frequently,
you'll want it on the keyboard (p. 46).

Timeline

Smart Tool

I typically leave the Keyframe Tool on, activating the Segment Tools from the keyboard, as needed, and turning on Trim Mode by lassoing transitions. Linked Selection is usually off, and I add it when needed, using the Option key.

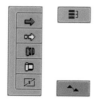

Button Bar

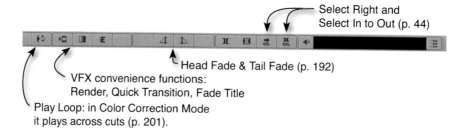

Select Right and
Select In to Out (p. 44)

Head Fade & Tail Fade (p. 192)

VFX convenience functions:
Render, Quick Transition, Fade Title

Play Loop: in Color Correction Mode
it plays across cuts (p. 201).

Fast Menu

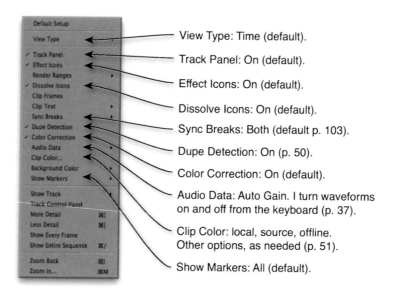

View Type: Time (default).

Track Panel: On (default).

Effect Icons: On (default).

Dissolve Icons: On (default).

Sync Breaks: Both (default p. 103).

Dupe Detection: On (p. 50).

Color Correction: On (default).

Audio Data: Auto Gain. I turn waveforms
on and off from the keyboard (p. 37).

Clip Color: local, source, offline.
Other options, as needed (p. 51).

Show Markers: All (default).

Settings

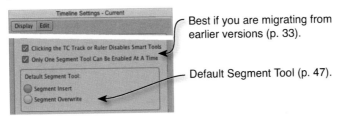

Best if you are migrating from earlier versions (p. 33).

Default Segment Tool (p. 47).

Bin Settings/Save and Auto-Save

Examine your Bin Settings carefully and set up the Auto-Save parameters to match your working style. The different time intervals should work together to protect your work and yet interrupt you as little as possible.

The system will attempt to save at the Auto-Save Interval, but it will wait until you've been inactive for the duration set in Inactivity Period before it saves. If you keep working continuously and don't pause long enough, the system will eventually save anyway, when you've worked for the time specified in Force Auto-Save.

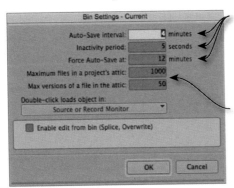

Set this way, the system will attempt to save every four minutes, but it will wait for you to pause for five seconds before interrupting you. If you don't stop, it will force a save after twelve minutes.

Maximum bins is the total number of files saved in a each project's attic. Maximum versions represents the number of saved versions for each individual bin.

Afterword

It's fitting that this volume should end with a discussion of the way Media Composer can be customized. There's no right or wrong in this, only what works for you. That's part of the elegance of the system: you can shape it to fit the way you work and the kind of material you're dealing with.

I've always been fascinated by tools for artists. It's no small thing to design a machine that facilitates the creative process. A device that feels organic, offers maximal control with minimal effort, and works so well that it magically seems to disappear in the artist's hands—that is beautiful, in and of itself.

A friend of mine watched an editor work recently and after a few minutes exclaimed, "Wow, it's like you're playing a musical instrument!" Digital professionals get to play that kind of music every day, and when we're lucky, we create something of lasting value in the process. The more the machine allows you, encourages you, frees you to do that, the better it is.

It's rare to see the tools of any trade go through the kind of transformation that we've seen recently in post-production. It has affected not just the machines we use; the social, physical and psychological changes have been, if anything, even more profound. And the pace of change, so far, only seems to accelerate. I feel privileged to have been, and to be, part of this revolution. It's been exciting and more than a little disruptive. But in the end, none of it means anything except that it enables us to create motion pictures that affect audiences. I hope this book has helped you find better ways of working with Media Composer. But above all, I hope it's helped you create work that you're proud of.

Acknowledgments

Like the Media Composer application itself, this book has evolved out of a collaborative process, and wouldn't exist without the help of many friends and colleagues. Loren Miller provided the initial spark, without which I wouldn't have started. Several people read early drafts and provided crucial feedback. Paul Rubell, cofounder of the Avid Editors Advisory Committee, has been a trusted adviser, and his meticulous analysis made the text far more useful. Stephanie Argy's astute insight revealed many areas in need of additional explanation and materially broadened the scope of the book. Robin Buday offered a multitude of thoughtful suggestions, helping me clarify key issues.

Norman Hollyn, Tom Ohanian, Steve Hullfish and Joe Torelli gave me important advice about the publication process, and my sister, Nora Cohen, guided me throughout. My brother-in-law, Steven Adler, and my sister, Amara Willey, were valuable advisers, as well. Mary Lee was there from the beginning and helped in countless ways, large and small.

I'm indebted to a host of people from Avid: my friends Bill Warner and Eric Peters, who started all this and still inspire me; Frank Capria, who as liaison to our committee has been an essential source of insight; Tim Claman, Dave Colantuoni, Matt Feury, Doug Hansel, Michael Krulik, Randy Martens, Michael Phillips, Greg Staten, Alan Swartz, Martin Vann and Linda White—all have helped me dig deeper into this very deep application. Avid's intrepid leaders, Gary Greenfield and Kirk Arnold, have galvanized the company and given impetus to this project.

I'm grateful also to many colleagues who have answered my questions and offered insight. The list is long, but it includes Steve Ansell, Darryl Bates, Phil Benson, Randy Blim, Alec Boehm, JC Bond, Charles Bornstein, Rik Breniser, Jay Cassidy, Terence Curren, David Gaines, Jordan Goldman, Larry Jordan, Phil Mendelson, Kåre Nejmann, Blaine Rawdon, Carl Sealove, Leslie Shatz, Leon Silverman, Howard Smith and Sidney Wolinsky, as well as all the dedicated members of the Avid Editors Advisory Committee.

My heartfelt thanks to each of you and to the many others who have helped bring this project to fruition.

Index